MARRIAGE —

Just a Piece of Paper?

RELIGION, MARRIAGE, AND FAMILY

Series Editors

Don S. Browning
John Wall

MARRIAGE —
Just a Piece of Paper?

Edited by

Katherine Anderson,
Don Browning,
and
Brian Boyer

William B. Eerdmans Publishing Company
Grand Rapids, Michigan / Cambridge, U.K.

Published 2002 by Wm. B. Eerdmans Publishing Co.
255 Jefferson Ave. S.E., Grand Rapids, Michigan 49503 /
P.O. Box 163, Cambridge CB3 9PU U.K.

Printed in the United States of America

07 06 05 04 03 02   7 6 5 4 3 2 1

ISBN 0-8028-3976-2

www.eerdmans.com

Contents

CONTENTS

Preface

Marriage — Just a Piece of Paper? is best read in connection with viewing the film documentary by the same name. The one-hour PBS version of this film was first aired nationally on Valentine's Day, 2002. It is narrated by Cokie Roberts and based on research done by the Religion, Culture, and Family Project located at the University of Chicago. The film and book are the culmination of this ten-year research and publication endeavor. After the project produced over a dozen books by scores of renowned authors on the topic of family, the issue of marriage itself became more and more central to our research. We began to ask, is it possible to have strong families if the institution of marriage is itself in trouble? Can children thrive if their parents divorce or never marry in the first place? How do women and mothers fare if marriage as an institution declines? And men and fathers: what will happen to them if marriage gradually disappears?

Many people think our society needs strong families, but they are not sure that marriage is essential for that goal. Most of us know that there are more divorces, more children born out of wedlock, more instances of cohabitation, fewer marriages, and more people living longer in the single state than was the case thirty or forty years ago. But what do these trends really mean? Are they actually hurting anyone? Is society suffering? Do these trends damage children? Do they have negative effects on women—at least on some of them? Can men really be responsible fathers outside the institution of marriage? And what about cohabitation? What does the new research say about it? Does it help or hinder good marriages? Finally, where do the religious ideas of covenant and sacrament fit into marriage today? How did the Western marriage tradition come into existence? Is it worth preserving?

The book *Marriage — Just a Piece of Paper?* addresses these questions. It includes fuller versions of the interviews than appear in the film documentary. It also includes a number of wonderful interviews that could not be used in the documentary. Shortly after completing the interviews, we realized that only small excerpts could be crowded into either our one- or two-hour versions of the film. We asked ourselves, why waste all these wonderful stories? Why not tell more of Sadie's story, Nissa's story, and the stories of many other "real people" who are struggling with marriage and sexuality issues in their everyday lives? Why not give fuller voice to such nationally respected experts as Judith Wallerstein, William Doherty, William Julius Wilson, Steven Ozment, John Witte, Diane Sollee, and many, many others?

So we set out to do just that. I want to thank Kathy Anderson for employing her unflagging energy and superb journalistic skills in editing this book; Brian Boyer of Boyer Productions for his brilliant direction of the documentary and for providing the interview transcripts; Barbara Dafoe Whitehead for the marvelous script of the documentary and hence the outline of this book; and David Clairmont and Kelly Brotzman of the Religion, Culture, and Family staff for their vital contributions to both the documentary and this book. I want to thank Jon Pott of Wm. B. Eerdmans, who not only encouraged this book but has supported the Religion, Marriage, and Family Series of which it is a part. I also want to thank Hannah Timmermans at Eerdmans for her splendid editorial work in collaborating with Kathy Anderson and the documentary team. And finally, I want to thank Craig Dykstra, Vice President of the Division of Religion of the Lilly Endowment, Inc., for his sage advice on this project and the generous support of the Lilly Endowment in making it possible.

Don Browning, Series Editor

Where Are We and How Did We Get Here?

What we've seen is a massive change in one generation, a change so great that the majority of parents of young children today were raised in a different type of family than they live in today.

TOM W. SMITH

But it's like why, why make this ridiculous commitment? What does marriage lead to? Worst-case scenario — a lawyer gets half or a bunch of your stuff.

JOHN H.

The result of all this is one simple, tragic fact — African Americans are the most unpartnered group of people in the nation.

ORLANDO PATTERSON

You've got the carpools. You've got work. You've got to make a career. The kids need to go to camp. Need, need, need. All of a sudden you blink your eyes and realize you haven't been with each other in a month.

JEFF

A *New York Times* reporter said he overheard at a wedding reception a relative of the groom say of the bride, "She'll make a nice first wife for Jason."

WILLIAM J. DOHERTY

Americans love weddings. The bigger, the better. The typical American wedding today has 185 guests and costs upwards of twenty thousand dollars. Couples today devote exquisite attention to every detail. The flowers. The caterer. The cake. And, of course, the wedding gown.

There is a good reason why we love weddings. The wedding is one of our most enduring social and religious rituals. The structure of a religious wedding itself is very old and includes elements from the Jewish as well as the Christian tradition. Both mirror practices of ancient Rome. In weddings today as in weddings in the past, the couple takes on the trappings of royalty and makes promises before God and before family and friends to love and honor each other forever.

The exchange of wedding vows only takes a few minutes. Yet these words change our lives forever. They create a new family from two separate families, a new legal and social identity, a common history.

The popularity of weddings tells us something about marriage. We prize marriage as a personal goal in life. Most Americans want to marry, and when they do they expect their marriages to be happy and to last a lifetime. But marriage today faces a historic crisis. Americans are less likely to marry today than in the past, and once married they are less likely to stay married to the same person for a lifetime. Perhaps the greatest change has to do with the way we think about marriage. Many young couples today aren't sure why we need marriage at all.

It was not that long ago that things were very different. By the early 1960s, marriage had reached a high point of stability. Thanks to medical advances, people lived longer and their marriages were less likely to be broken by the death of a spouse. Divorce, though not unheard of, was still rare. But marriage faced great changes ahead, as the turbulent decade of the sixties unleashed one revolution after another, each of which would have a profound impact on marriage. The feminist revolution opened doors to women in education and work, and with new and better opportunities for paid work, women became less economically dependent on marriage and a male breadwinner. With the sexual revolution, men and women gained greater freedom to have sex outside of marriage. One result was a surge in unwed pregnancies and births. None of these upheavals in the social landscape had a more profound impact on marriage than the psychological revolution. It emphasized individual self-fulfillment and happiness over family obligation and responsibility. By the time the revolutions had slowed, and the dust settled in the early '90s, marriage had changed. It had become, many would say, no longer an institution with broad public, social, and religious influence but a private contract, and little more.

Nissa's first marriage didn't involve church or family or the larger community or even love. It was a business deal, plain and simple. . . .

Nissa

Nissa is a photographer and has been married twice.
She is twenty-five years old.

My Parents: Married and Divorced Four Times

My parents met when they were eighteen, and they married and divorced four times between the ages of eighteen and forty-seven. I honestly can't remember the first divorce, which was when I was four. The last divorce was when I was twenty-two.

How long did they stay divorced? I don't even know. I think once they stayed divorced, like, maybe eight years. There was a lot of manipulation going on, because they had a company together. Now that I'm older, I see that a lot of it was Uncle Sam and stuff like that. When I was a kid, I thought it was love.

When I was twelve, we were living in Texas. There was a lot of yelling and running away — my mom and I jumping in her convertible and just kept going, because I think there was so much water under the bridge. There was no communication left at this point. There hadn't been for years. So, it was a lot of running away. There was yelling, but it was more just running away. Eventually we just packed up and ran for good. A lot of U-Hauls.

The Yelling

I just wanted to be alone. That's what I remember most. I wanted to be away, and I wanted my mom to be away. I talked to my brothers about it. A lot of people that have been through a divorce and the yelling and everything say they wanted their parents to just get along and work it out. But I didn't. I wanted my mom to be happy. I was an extension of her; like, I felt her pain and I wanted her to get away, as well as I wanted to get away myself.

I used to be alone a lot. Pissed off. It made me angry and tough. I don't remember feeling sad about it. I definitely bottled the sadness and let the anger live. I didn't want anyone to know that I was sad.

The Divorce I Remember the Most

We had a big house on a hill, Mercedes, motorcycles, a lake, twenty acres. You name it, we had it. They had a real successful company. When the divorce happened we hit the road. My mom and I packed up and moved to Florida, which was the family vacation spot for years. Both of us kind of went crazy. Neither one of us had any rules or that controlling man around anymore.

My mom started dating. She was never easy like that. She was just free. She never got to date, because at eighteen years old she got married and had kids. So, here she is in her late thirties and I'm twelve. We're like two sixteen-year-old girls together. She was dating and we had a nice condo. It was probably the best year of my life. It was the first time I really saw my mom happy.

I remember my dad would call just to torture her. He never really called to check on me. He never called on my birthday or anything like that, or to see how I was in my new school. I would be on the phone and he would be manipulating me, trying to see what my mom was doing. My mom would say, "Don't answer the phone, it's your dad." That was the divorce I remember the most.

Just out of Control

We lived in Florida about a year and a half. It was definitely the best year of my life. I remember outfits that I had. I remember the blue jeans I owned that year. I remember the way my room looked, the hairspray I used.

Then I got really wild, sneaking out every night and sticking trash bags under my covers to make it look like I was there. I was boy crazy

— not sexually, just boy crazy. Looking back, I was starved for a man. Just, I didn't know, you know? Any attention from a boy was like a drug. So I always had boys throwing rocks at my windows and I was sneaking out.

My mom couldn't stop it. I had an uncontrollable mouth. At school I was like Satan, I guess, to the teachers. I was a good kid, but I was just out of control. So my mom broke down, went back to my dad. I said, "I'm not going. I'll kill myself. I will not go back with you to him. I won't go back to Texas; I love Florida. I love my friends, I love my life."

So she asked one of my best friends' mothers to raise me. They left me there. I don't know what the agreement was. I guess they were going to send her so much money a month to take care of me. I was going to the same school, same grade as this friend. About a month and half later, my friend's mother shipped me home. She said, "I can't control her either. She's making my kid wild. She's just disrupting our house." So they sent me back to Texas. And I got even wilder. If Mom said, "Don't cut your hair, I'll take you to the salon," then I would want to shave my head. I never shaved my head, but you see what I'm saying. Just an uncontrollable mouth. You know, "Nissa, you have to go to school today." "I don't want to go to school today." "You're going. I'm your parent. You're going to school." So, I would go to school and show my face, and then I'd leave. Just do whatever. Go shoplifting. I was a terrible kleptomaniac. That was my drug.

A Song about Ripping His Head Off

I don't know who I was mad at. I still haven't discovered that. I don't know if I was mad at God or my dad. It probably points a little more to my dad, because of the poetry I write. In my midterm project in my photo class we were supposed to take three rolls of film and put either a poem or a song to it and then present it to the class. The pictures were supposed to tell the story. Mine was a bunch of self-portraits, really disturbing self-portraits. I don't even know why I took them. They're just really dark and morbid, and the song is by Jewel. It's about her dad and how she wants to rip his head off. It just happened. It wasn't something I thought out. So, yeah, maybe it was my dad. It definitely wasn't my mom, though. She tried so hard.

Hell Broke Loose

After Florida, when she went back to him and I got shipped back to Texas, it was the whole family again. I was thirteen. Hell broke loose. I don't know if it was a divorce or a separation, but we packed up a U-Haul and we moved to Atlanta, Georgia. My mom got a job as a nurse and that didn't work out. So we went back to Texas when I was fifteen. Then, at sixteen, we moved to another part of Florida, St. Petersburg.

No, I didn't finish high school. I dropped out when I was sixteen. That was the last move. Moved a lot. At that point I was just like a six-teen-year-old kid going on forty-five. That's what I felt like. The kids at school talked about who's kissing who, and this teacher sucks, and would say, "Oh, my God, my mom wouldn't buy me this outfit for the dance." And I'm dealing with much bigger issues. I really couldn't deal with them. I had a thing with older men, too. Not *older*, but at thirteen, they were eighteen, and at sixteen, they were twenty-five. So, I couldn't really tolerate kids my age.

Was I confused? Oh yeah! What did I think about marriage at that point? I'm never getting married. That was my thought. My strongest feeling was being a freak. I always thought I was a freak. I was the new kid in school, and I didn't understand always being in a new place and having to prove myself. It's hard as a kid. Kids are mean in school. So it was really tough. That was the hardest thing for me, making new friends.

I didn't have the family and the mom and dad and the dinners at 6 P.M. So, I had all the kids and me at lunch having food fights, or whatever. That was my family time, that time with my friends. So every time I had to move and make new friends, it ripped my heart out. Leaving my friends was so hard, because it was like leaving family, like leaving a nest.

Knowing what I had to look forward to, going to a school where everyone looked . . . You know, the cheerleaders, and the little cliques. I was so outgoing and so friendly. I had to be. I had no choice. My tool was comedy. I realized that making someone laugh was the key into any place, any clique, or into anyone's heart. So I was the class clown. That's how I got in.

So I Married Him

When I moved to St. Petersburg at sixteen, I went to school one day and I said, "I don't have to prove myself anymore. I can make it in this world." So I dropped out. I was going to get my GED within a week or two. Of course, it was a lot more fun at the beach getting a tan than taking a GED test. I put it off until I was eighteen. I got my GED and went to junior college for a week. Hated that. I said, "I'm going to go to Hollywood. I'm going to go to New York. I'm going to take care of myself."

Of course, at eighteen I lived in a fantasy world already. Instead of getting an agent and some work, I just ate acid and drank tequila and shaved my head and started dating a guy in a punk rock band. My parents hated him. So I married him a couple months later. Lost my virginity to him. He supposedly was a virgin. After we got married I found out he'd been with, like, 130 women. It all went downhill from there.

He was in love with me, supposedly. I don't know if you can be in love at eighteen. He wanted to own me, basically. I was like his little jewel. He said he was a virgin just because he was always trying to get in my pants. And I'm like, "No. I'm a virgin, you know. I'm waiting until I get married." He's like, "Yeah, but you said you were never getting married, so that would make you a nun." I'm like, "Well, that just makes me confused. I don't really know yet." But he's like, "Well, if you're never going to get married, then what are you waiting for?" Sex was a big issue at eighteen with this guy. I'm like, "Well, I'm a virgin. I'm clean and I'm just not ready." He was like, "Well, I'm a virgin, too. It'd be perfect." This was like a gift to me. So I married this guy and we had sex.

"You Think Your Husband Was a Virgin?"

His band was basically like my three other husbands, because they were always around. They ended up moving in with us. A bunch of little punk rockers, you know, they can't make it. These guys couldn't. We all lived together and shared a big four-bedroom house. But one night I was sitting around with one of the guys in the band, and I made a comment about how neat it was to be with someone for the first time. And he started laughing. I'm like, "What's so funny?" It came out. He's like, "You think your husband was a virgin when you got married?" He's like, "Are you kidding me? I know of at least fifty girls he's been with."

How did that strike me? It struck me so bad that I don't even remember how I felt. It goes back to all the stuff I went through before, and being able to turn a switch on and off in your heart, where something's so painful you just block it. I just blocked it. But it definitely surfaced later. Putting up with all the stuff I put up with.

I didn't know what to expect from a man because my mom tolerated so much. She tolerated everything. So I was very tolerant. When I found this out, I just tolerated it until it eventually surfaced. I would be drinking, and I would say something, and then he'd admit. Then I would be like, "Is there any more? You can't lie to me. I'm not going to leave you, just tell me." And he kept naming them and naming them. He didn't realize how many there were. I was writing them down. I became obsessed, psychotic and jealous. That's, so, not, not like me. If he was talking to a girl, I was like, "You slept with her, didn't you? No! I can tell." He was like the guy in high school who slept with everyone and their sister.

That Wasn't My First Marriage

Yeah, my first marriage occurred when I was living on my own. As I told you, I dropped out of high school at sixteen. For the next couple of years I was trying to be an adult, but I was still a kid. Still partying. There was a guy who was a friend of mine. He became my first husband. He had lived in Florida but moved off to California to be in the Air Force.

I'm assuming if you're not married you don't live as well as a married person, because he called me and said, "It's going to be more like a business deal. They're going to give me an extra grand a month. They'll give me extra grocery money. They'll give you medical and dental insurance. You don't have a car, I can help you get a car. All these benefits, you know? You don't want to get married anyway, so now you have the privileges that married people have, but you're not married. You don't have to wear a ring." I was like, "Oh my God, this is perfect!" I, of course, I want to be taken care of like a married woman, but I just don't want to be married.

So we went to the courthouse. I was real unsure about it. He said, "What do you want? Anything you want, I'll do it." He was just looking at this money and all these conveniences he was going to have. I said, "I want a ferret and a fish tank." So, real easy to please. He took me to a pet store and I got a little albino ferret and a fish tank and loaded it up with fish and threw it in his back seat.

We went to the courthouse in Clearwater, Florida, and got married. We're in this little room, and the woman said, "You can kiss your bride." I was like, "Oh, I have mono. I should probably just shake his hand." So we shook hands and he went back to California a week later. A month later it was, "Where's my five hundred dollars?" It wasn't there. He said it'd be here next month. The checks didn't kick in. Two months later, "Where's my five hundred dollars?"

Yeah, I was going to get five hundred dollars a month and he was going to keep the other five hundred. I needed the dental and medical benefits. I had cavities by this point. I hadn't been at home. I needed my cavities filled. You know, all the basic stuff. I tried to go to the dentist and they said, "What are you talking about? You're not on this insurance plan." It was a lot of embarrassment. A lot of disappointed walks to my mailbox.

I was working as a cocktail waitress at night until 2 A.M. I was working at a beach hut in the day. I used to sleep in the hut. The manager would walk by and I'd be asleep because I was exhausted. I was a kid. I was going to do that until the money started coming. I was going live off the five hundred and play. About eight months later I'm like, "Uh, you owe me some money. You need to pay up." I was so naive, so patient. My friends and my older brother said, "This guy is just flat-out jerking you around. He's not going to send you any money." I was like, "Well, he sent me an answering machine and a windbreaker. He bought me a fish tank and a ferret." I was so easy to please. I thought eventually the money was going to come, and it didn't.

I Was Young and Dumb

I don't remember who I talked to that woke me up. Maybe it was myself. I realized that this was a joke. This guy was taking me for a ride, and he was getting all the money, and it really pissed me off. So I called him and I said, "we have to get a divorce." He, of course, didn't want to. He'd gone from a bunk to an apartment, extra grocery money, an extra one thousand dollars a month. I didn't threaten him. I just begged him for a divorce. I didn't want anything to do with him. He was bringing bitterness and depression into my life.

I said, "Why am I doing this? Why am I letting you be married to me so you can get all this stuff?" He wouldn't give me the divorce. I was young and dumb. I didn't know what a commanding officer was. He had told them that I was a model and an actress and that's why no one ever saw me. I eventually spoke with the person I needed to. My ex-husband went into some kind of lockup for two weeks, and he said, "I'm going to give you the divorce. Just, don't torture me." He strung me along for another two months and it dragged on for a year. He was a procrastinator, just like my dad.

John H.

John works in a sandwich shop and is a student in Madison, Wisconsin. He wonders why anyone would sign an agreement for life.

Looking for . . .

I am not looking for marriage at all. Just dating. Why? Well, the difference is that marriage is a lifelong commitment, and I am not ready for that. It just seems like a ridiculous thing. It's a lifelong contract, it's legally binding, and there is no other lifelong contract that people sign into so readily as marriage and break so easily.

I've been to two weddings in my life. My brother got married but he's getting divorced already. That's kind of disappointing but, I don't know, to each their own. If people want to get married, great. Maybe someday I will, but for now I really don't want to get married.

What I look for when I'm dating a person is good hair, nice body, and a good personality. They have to be funny and smart, too. I like smarter people. So intelligence, looks, humor, I guess, are the three basic elements of a potential mate.

I've lived with women in the past, and I'm all for it. I think love is cool. I think marriage works for a lot of people, and for a lot of people it doesn't. But it's like, why, why make this ridiculous commitment? What does marriage lead to? Worst-case scenario, a lawyer gets half or a bunch of your stuff, and you just split up what you have. I have nothing, but if I had a lot of money I certainly wouldn't want to enter into marriage, because the potential of losing half of what you already have is pretty likely.

I think I'm a pretty hard person to live with because I'm kind of a strange mix of an introvert and an extrovert. I live a very private life, and it's hard for me to share my innermost feelings with someone, but I'm also fun.

The Last Time I Lived with Someone

We're both students, and it was just kind of an odd thing to be living with each other at that point in our lives. I felt like we were tied down, not even in the good sense of being tied down. It seemed like the thing to do. I mean, we were very much in love and we spent all our free time with each other anyway. It was cheaper and more convenient and, yes, that definitely played into the choice.

Twenty Years down the Line

I think the reason a lot of people get divorced is because people change over time. A lot of times you don't know what you're going to be in two years or two months, let alone twenty years down the line. My parents were married, I think, twenty-five years, or almost twenty-five years, when they got divorced. I think they both realized they wanted different things, and the best decision they could make for themselves was to do it apart from each other.

I think that marriage is basically just in place to keep lawyers in business. If there wasn't marriage, there wouldn't be divorce, and then lawyers really wouldn't have much work to do. They'd just have to chase ambulances up and down the street instead of taking big chunks of people's hard-earned money by wrecking their lives. But I'm really not against lawyers.

Kids and Marriage

I think I would like to have kids, because it would be a shame to deprive the world of more people like myself. But that's just me. Maybe other people don't feel that way. Yeah, I think it would be cool to have a "mini me" running around out there. But not right now, that's for sure.

If I wanted a child but didn't want to get married, what would I do? Well, I guess in that case I would have to find a woman willing to sleep with me, which for me right now is the major problem. But I would hope to think that I could somehow. Yeah, if I wanted a child. No, it wouldn't be a problem. I'm not very committed to marriage. I would be if I got married, but I think it's a silly institution.

It's every girl's dream to get married. It's the big day. You have a huge party and all your friends come there and ooh and ahh over you. But I don't know why a guy gets married. I guess it is sex, you know. Nah, I don't know why. I don't know why anyone gets married. It's ridiculous.

Do I think it's important for the father to be in the picture? Yes, I do. If a girlfriend became pregnant, at this point I think I would probably be in favor of an abortion. But then again, I think that the male should have a say in an abortion. Otherwise he shouldn't have to pay child support, because, like, if he wants to keep the baby and the woman decides to abort it, then he's screwed over. But if she wants to keep it and he doesn't want it, then he's screwed over, too. So the guy is kind of in a tough situation. But I'm actually all for father support. It's his responsibility under the law. I believe in that too. I would be as supportive as I could. I would like to think that if I were to have a child it would be with someone who I could get along with. I don't foresee having a child with a person and not being a part of raising the child.

My Dating Strategy

I meet women by throwing myself at them, flattering them with compliments, and showering them with alcoholic beverages. Nah, I just try and talk to them. I just try to be myself around them. Maybe that's why it has gotten me nowhere so far. I meet a lot of women, but, I don't know, I don't seem to date a lot. Unfortunately.

Marline Pearson

Marline Pearson is a social science instructor at Madison Area Technical College in Madison, Wisconsin. She describes herself as a feminist and progressive liberal who learned the importance of family structure from her students.

A Poverty of Human Connections

I really got into teaching about relationships through the back door. My academic training is in history and sociology, and I'm a feminist and a progressive liberal. I really came to it through my interest in criminology. I'm very interested in juveniles and juvenile delinquency and the kinds of environments that put kids at risk. My focus has been on prevention, the kinds of interventions that can help high-risk kids and families.

One day I came across an article in *The Atlantic Monthly* summarizing the effects of family disruption and divorce on children. I was quite intrigued, because up until that time I had never stressed family structure very much. I paid lip service to family breakdown in understanding crime and delinquency, but I really thought it was the material resources that made the biggest difference.

I gave this article to my students without any comment and asked them to write their responses. The responses literally blew me away. Many of them strongly identified with the article and wrote about the turmoil in their families. They wrote about father loss, about mother loss, about feeling caught between parents, about feeling that they came second to their parents' love lives. A number of them said, "You're the first person who has asked us about this." It turned me on to a reality that I hadn't looked at. I knew I had tapped into something pretty important.

The way I look at it today, we not only have material impoverishment, we have another kind of poverty; I call it the poverty of connections, the poverty of human connections.

Kids Become the Shock Absorbers

Before this time, I really focused on concrete impoverishment. We don't have enough school programs. We don't have enough early-childhood education or child care or resources in the communities to help families. I still have a very, very strong belief in all of those things, and I would never want to be interpreted in any way, shape, or form as downplaying the need for those things. But my students taught me about this other kind of poverty. It's not only material poverty, it's this impoverishment, this poverty of human connections.

For so many of my students, their solid base, their family foundation, is eroding. They have fewer adults in their lives that they can depend upon. While I'm totally committed, as strong as ever, about dealing with the material conditions of people's lives, this poverty of connections is something that has its own dynamics, and we must focus on it. I don't think that educational reform, school reform, job programs, and community resources will necessarily translate automatically into more stable family structures and better marriages.

The college I teach at serves mostly working-class students. Many of them are the first people in their families to have ever gone to college. I started teaching here twenty-three years ago, and my students have always carried extra economic burdens. Many of them work full-time and go to school full-time. But what I've been seeing over the years is this extra layer, this layer of burdens from the erosion of their immediate families.

My students tell me their life stories or write about them, but the sad thing is that they often don't make the connection between their own problems and the fact that their basic family or community support system has eroded. I think one of the biggest crimes here is that you have a generation of young people who have clearly been the shock absorbers for a massive breakdown in parental partnerships. Nowhere are we helping them understand their own personal issues and personal problems or the problems of their generation. They just got the rug pulled out. I'm not surprised anymore when I find out how many of my students are on antidepressants or are in therapy.

What really upsets me the most is seeing so many students in emotional pain and problems thinking that there's something wrong with them. Kids need a stable cast of adults in their family and in their communities to do well. Increasingly, young people don't have that stable cast. They have adults that move in and out of their lives, and they just simply have fewer adults in their lives.

That's why I feel that it's not enough just to look at education and jobs. There's this other area about relationships and helping young people form more stable relationships that may lead to more stable marriage or family systems. I've just seen too many students derailed and disadvantaged by the troubles in their personal lives.

Kids Fending for Themselves

I think that there is starting to be a general lowering of expectations about what you can expect from parents. I remember a young woman, maybe twenty-one; I can't remember exactly. She had told me earlier in the semester that she suffers with depression. After the Christmas holidays, I saw her in the hallway and she said, "Oh I went to New York to find my father. I haven't seen him in many years and I just wanted to make contact with him. My father wasn't at all happy to see me. His new wife and family, they weren't happy either. But I really reassured him that I could understand his discomfort and he didn't need to worry, I wasn't gonna expect anything from him. I just wanted to see him." Here is this young woman trying to tell me that she should understand his discomfort and why he doesn't want to see her. She's not expecting anything. My students really are educating me about the heart and soul of what all of this family disruption and instability has meant.

Again, it's this lowering of expectations. Parents have to follow their own needs and do their own thing, and the kids can't really expect much. So they'll fend for themselves. That's it. I see my students having to fend for themselves.

Lowering Expectations for Partners, Too

I see this lowering of expectations with my young female students, who may get pregnant and decide they're going to have the child but don't expect the man to marry them and don't expect that he needs to be committed in a very formal way to the child. It's such a lowering of expectations about what you would expect from the father of your child.

I also think a lot of young men may be getting the message that they really aren't central to raising children. We have this idea that if you're a father you need to support this child and need to be a good father. But what are we doing to help young men understand why it is so difficult to be a good father if you don't live with your child? You're not there. You're not hooked in to their daily rhythms, their ups and downs. It is damn hard to be a good father when you don't live in the same house. It's hard to be a father when you're not married to the mother.

I feel like there's almost a disconnect that exists among young people. They say, "Well, I'll have this baby and, yes, he'll be there to help, but, no, we're not going to get married and, no, we're not going live in the same house, even sometimes." Then a few years down the line we'll be complaining that these guys are deadbeat dads. Yet nobody helped these young men understand why it is so difficult to support two households, and why it's so difficult to be connected fathers when you don't live with the child.

William J. Doherty

William J. Doherty is a professor of family social science and director of the Marriage and Family Therapy Program at the University of Minnesota. He says people have begun to view marriage as a consumer product.

If It's Not Working for You

For the last thirty years of the twentieth century, we were liberating people from marriages that did not work for them. The increase in the divorce rate started in 1970 with the no-fault divorce movement in California, skyrocketing through about 1980. It then leveled off, and it has gone down a little bit.

We really were focused on helping people feel they didn't have to get married if they didn't really want to. They have the right to be a parent without necessarily being married. If you're unhappy in your marriage, the social trends indicated you should really get out. Two-thirds or more of people in the 1960s said that if people were not happy in the marriage they should probably stay together for the children. Now less than one-third would say that. So we've had a big change in social values about marriage, and we've created laws and popular support saying, "If it's not working for you, get on with your life. Try again if you want."

I think what started to happen, say, in the early 1990s was some re-visiting of the downside of the social revolution that brought us optional marriage and easier divorce. I don't think many people, certainly I, don't want to go back to a century ago or even fifty years ago, when many felt trapped in destructive marriages. But we've really put most of our energy during the time frame of the '60s through the '90s in helping to free people to be able to get out. Now I think there is some sense that marriage is pretty fragile, and we need to not only be helping people get out, but we need to help people make a success when they're in a marriage.

Children of the Divorce Revolution

One factor is that the children of the divorce revolution are now coming to a marriage age. They are like my children (although I've never been divorced). My children are twenty-six and twenty-four. Their generation's parents have had high levels of divorce and they're nervous.

My generation, whose parents stayed together, felt like we could experiment with getting out of marriages more easily. We sort of took for granted the stable families we came from, and we wanted to liberate ourselves.

Now we have a generation coming along that is no longer taking stable marriage for granted. In fact, they've experienced the other side and they are sobered by it. They're nervous. That's what the research indicates. They're nervous. I think that contributes to something of a movement to try to revitalize marriage, to try to help people succeed in something that 90 percent or more of Americans rank as a high personal goal.

High Expectations, Easy Exits

What we had in the late '60s into the '70s was the sexual revolution and the feminist movement. We had the anti-authority movements against the Vietnam War. We had a much stronger kind of rhetoric of individualism. That was my era in college. Society was a bad thing. Rules were oppressive. What happened inside marriage and for people considering marriage was a historically high emphasis on individual happiness and satisfaction out of marriage.

Throughout history, marriage had always been more about duty, more about family, more about property, more about raising children. And to be happy? — if that was possible. What we had in the late '60s into the '70s was a real reversal of that. Marriage was about personal happiness and fulfillment more than anything else. Obviously, these trends didn't just start there — these trends have gone back for 150 years or more — but a spiking of it occurred in the late '6os and the '7os with all those social movements.

What we had was a tremendous increase in expectations of marriage. This person is supposed to be your soul mate, your confidant, your best friend, and your sexually fulfilling partner. I got married in 1971, and, like my generation, I had far higher expectations for what the relationship was to be than my parents who got married in 1941. Over those thirty years, you had a very different culture of marriage. The high expectations coupled with the notion that if those expectations were not met you should be able to exit without too much difficulty combined to bring about a very dramatic change in the way we looked at marriage.

The Kids Will Be Fine If You're Fine

When I started out as a marriage therapist in the late 1970s, I took the attitude that if somebody was thinking of getting out of a marriage it was my job was to help them figure out what was best for them as an individual. When they said things like, "Well, I'm not sure I'm being fair to the kids," I, and a lot of my colleagues, said, "Well, the kids will be fine if you're fine. Do what you need to do for you. Are you going to be happy? Where are you going to be happiest?" That was pretty much the prevailing attitude among many therapists of all stripes.

If somebody says that to me now, I'm much more likely to honor that concern of how the kids are going to do, including how their extended family will feel about it. That's an example of a change in my attitude that is reflected in some other people in this marriage movement.

Marriage, once you're in it, is not just a private lifestyle. There are a lot of stakeholders in it. Obviously, your spouse is a stakeholder. Your children, but not just your dependent children, because even when kids grow up they are dependent in some way. They relate to their parents' marriage, and it changes their life a lot if their parents break up. There's also your extended family, common friends, and a faith community, if you're in one.

I see marriage now much more as something embedded in a community of people, all of whom have an interest or stake in the marriage. That does not mean you have to stay married for them if you're abused or your spouse is a chronic adulterer or anything like that. I'm not talking about turning the clock back to an era when there was no escape. I am talking about turning the clock back from the beginning of my career, when many of us approached somebody thinking of getting out of a marriage more like somebody thinking about getting out of a job that they didn't like. We just helped them do a cost-benefit analysis. There really were no other stakeholders in it.

I Used to Be Neutral

If you go back to the 1950s, my observation is that counselors and therapists were saying you should almost always stay married and if you got divorced it was probably something wrong with you.

Counselors and therapists changed with the '60s and the '70s and moved toward a position where I was at the beginning of my career in the '70s. It was a position of neutrality about whether you stay married or get divorced. "I'm not here to save marriages. I'm here to help people. Whatever you need to do to be happy as an individual, that's what I'm here to help you do." On the face of it, it sounded terribly reasonable.

What's wrong with neutrality? The problem with it is that if people have a lifelong commitment to each other, even if they don't have children, and the counselor/therapist is neutral about whether they can find a way to fulfill the commitment, it's undermining.

Let me give you an analogy that I think will make this clear. Suppose somebody comes to you and says, "Look, this parenting thing is not working out. I'm not getting along with my kid. Parenting is not what I wanted. In fact, it's a pain and I'm thinking of getting out." Most of us would say, "Slow down. You've got a kid. You're a parent. You've got responsibilities, and I'm not neutral about whether you fulfill those responsibilities."

As a counselor, I would be supportive of your concern, I'd be empathic, but I would not be neutral. I wouldn't give you a lecture, but I would be assuming that my job is to help you be a parent and raise your kid. I understand there could be exceptions, such as if your kid turns into an ax murderer and is trying to kill you. But mainly I would not be neutral.

A Nice First Wife for Jason

I believe that the consumer culture has invaded the family. What I mean by that is the attitude that we go through life primarily in the role of a customer or a consumer of what the world offers. I think we're entering what I call the consumer culture of marriage.

People in my field are starting to talk about starter marriages. Okay? With the expectation that your first marriage won't last, that this is like a starter home. A California futurist is talking about icebreaker marriages to kind of get used to it. A *New York Times* reporter said he overheard at a wedding reception a relative of the groom say of the bride, "She'll make a nice first wife for Jason."

There is this notion that marriage is a consumer lifestyle. "It's got to work for me. If it doesn't work for me, I can move on." There's a self-fulfillment if marriage is just another consumer lifestyle. "It may work for me, and it must be shed if it's not working for me." I'm afraid we are starting to view marriage like my car. I don't necessarily gut it out with my car. I get a new model.

I'm afraid, if we're not careful, the consumer ethic that really dominates our society now can enter marriage. We have to name that as a problem. That's why we need to be talking about a higher commitment rather than just how is it working for me now.

Tom W. Smith

Tom W. Smith is director of the General Social Survey of the National Opinion Research Center at the University of Chicago. He has studied the dramatic social changes that have occurred over the last forty years.

What's Going On with Us?

I wrote the report entitled "The Emerging 21st Century American Family," but I would actually change the title now and call it the "Emerging 21st Century American Families." As late as the 1970s, 75 percent of all children were being raised in traditional families with a full-time employed father, a full-time caregiving mother, and then the children. What we have now is no dominant family type, nor are we likely to have one in the near future. What we have instead are several different family types that have emerged to replace the traditional family. One of these is the dual-earner family, in which the mother and the father both work. The second is the single-parent family, in which there is only one adult in the household raising the children. And the third major type is the blended, reconstituted, or mixed family, in which you have children being raised by stepparents or with stepbrothers and stepsisters.

We talk a lot about how America has become a more diverse society. When we say that we usually mean racially and ethnically diverse. But we also have become much more diverse in terms of family structure. The two biggest changes are the increase in dual-earner families, which have gone from about 33 percent of families in the early 1970s to 66 percent today, and the number of children being raised in single-parent families. In 1960, 5 percent of children were born to unmarried women. Now one-third of children are born to unmarried women. Among the African-American community, it's nearly two-thirds. So we've had this huge increase in children being born to women who are either entirely on their own or do not have a stable marriage backing up or assisting with the raising of that child. That level has now held steady for about the last three years. It has leveled off, but it has leveled off at a very high rate. All the empirical research shows that while, of course, single-parent families can be successful, it's much harder in terms of children succeeding in school and children staying out of trouble.

About half of children will spend some part of their formative years with a single parent, either at the beginning, if there's no marriage, or after a divorce. So now it's just as common to be raised at least partly by a single parent as it is to be raised by two parents. The proportion of children currently, at any one given point in time, living with a single parent has increased from 5 percent in the early '70s to nearly 20 percent today.

Are We Coping?

What we've seen is a massive change in one generation, a change that is so great that the majority of parents of young children today were raised in a different type of family than they live in today. They were raised in traditional families. The importance of this change is not only in terms of the shifting share of the population but in terms of how we learn to be parents.

We learn to be parents by being children first. We don't learn in school how to be a good parent. We don't learn from our neighbors how to be a good parent. We learn by being raised by good parents.

Now the difficulty is that parents today are raising their children in family types that are fundamentally different than the family type they themselves were raised in. So they don't have the experience of how to take care of and raise children in the type of family they are themselves living in.

Whenever you have massive change, you have a lot of stress. Even though the change may be just as good, just as positive, just as able to produce happy, productive children, there is a definite stress as you make the transition. It's a steep learning curve to shift from the practices and the behaviors you know under traditional families to adopting ways to make modern families work just as well.

Take the example of what was a very bad solution to some of the needs of dual-earner families: latchkey kids. Everyone agrees that the latchkey kid is a very bad way to take care of children. But that was a solution that a number of families felt that they were forced to adopt. Now, increasingly, schools are adopting after-school care programs, where the child remains often with the same teachers and teachers' aides until one of the parents can take the child home. That is obviously a much better solution. We're finding out how to better service the needs of the modern family. But, as I say, any period of transition creates a lot of stress.

It's Not Simple Anymore

We have to see the family as representing many different ways of raising children, many different ways of people living together. We can't just think of one simple family type anymore. The important thing is that each family type has different positives and negatives associated with it.

Let's look at the traditional family first. Here we have the advantage of a full-time caregiver who can concentrate on raising the children and taking care of the other domestic needs of the family. That allows the other partner to devote the classic 110 percent of efforts toward the job. So you have a simple, sharp division of labor. But you sacrifice the possibility of having two earners. That family type on average has lower income than the dual-earner family.

The dual-earner families — both the mom and the dad working — can bring in more income, which can clearly help the family with a larger house, the possibility of getting into a better college, all the ways in which better finances can help a family. But that family has much greater difficulty in taking care of its domestic needs in general and child care in particular. It may involve day care. It may involve one of the parents trading off workdays, so they work on complementary shifts to take care of the children. It may involve a nanny. There's lots of different ways. But the point is the resources aren't just within the family itself.

A third type, of course, is the single-parent family. The demands on single parents are even greater and the ability of a single parent to cope with the raising of the children is much more difficult. If the parent's marriage was very unstable, if it was an abusive relationship, then the single-parent arrangement would be better than a dysfunctional family might be. But it is very difficult for single-parent families to supply the stable economic condition needed to raise children. And with only one parent trying to be both the caregiver and the breadwinner, the stress on that parent and the resulting tensions and difficulties passed on to the children are on average greater. It does not mean that single-parent families can't be successful, but it is much more difficult.

Are Married Parents Happier Than Single Parents?

Well, the first thing to consider about happiness is the following: If there was a product that you could offer to the marketplace that would let you live longer, be twice as happy, and have better and more frequent sex, you'd probably earn billions of dollars and end up as rich as Bill Gates. And there is such a product. That product is marriage.

Married people live longer than unmarried people do. They also report twice the level of personal happiness — not happiness in their marriage, but response in just the general question about how happy is your life. About 40 percent of married people say they are very happy. About 20 percent of never-married, widowed, divorced, and separated people say they are very happy. In addition to that, married couples have sex more frequently and report a greater level of emotional as well as physical pleasure from their sex lives compared to unmarried people.

Why So Much Change in Family Structure?

The structural changes in the family have been so massive, and so fundamentally important, that these changes would not come about out of whim. These are driven by a series of quite distinct important changes. One of the most important things to understand about the changes in family structure is that they have been accompanied by and facilitated by a change in family values. We've talked about how the dual-earner families have increased from one-third of children to two-thirds. Accompanying that change has been a great increase in society's approval of women in general and mothers in particular having careers. Because people have become more approving, this, of course, has facilitated the increase in the actual practice. And because the actual practice has increased, this has helped to increase the approval. So the shift in the attitudes and the shift in the structures have fed off of one another.

We also see what happens when the changes in values stop. If we look at the doubling in the divorce rate from the 1960s to the early 1980s, that was accompanied by increasing public support for the idea that people should be able to get divorces. However, then there became a resistance to the idea of easy divorce in the 1980s. Attitudes today are no longer more supportive of easy or permissive divorce laws. What has been the result in terms of the divorce rate? Well, it stopped going up after the early 1980s. It is a little bit lower today than it was in the 1980s — not fallen back to the levels of the 1960s, but it *has* fallen because values and public support for easy divorce stopped going up. The divorce rate at least leveled off and actually fell slightly.

Let's Talk about Sex

Since the early 1970s, we've monitored the attitudes on three types of sexual behavior: having sex before marriage, having sex outside your marriage, and homosexual relationships.

Starting in the 1960s there was great increase in approval, or at least acceptance, of premarital sex. The plurality of people now considers premarital sex not wrong at all, and that number has increased appreciably during the last generation.

However, if you look at extramarital relationships, you get just the opposite pattern. You get a high level of disapproval throughout the period, and actually an increase in disapproval. From about 70 percent saying extramarital relationships were always wrong in the early 1970s to 80 percent saying that adultery is always wrong today. So you can't talk in very sweeping terms about the growth of sexual permissiveness or even about a sexual revolution. While there have been massive changes in some areas like attitudes toward cohabitation and premarital sex, in other areas like attitudes toward extramarital sex, the change has been in the opposite direction. We are less approving of it today.

We get an intermediate pattern if we look at homosexual relationships. There was little change from the 1970s to the late 1980s. There was a very high level of disapproval of homosexual relationships — basically, about 75 percent of the public saying such relationships were always wrong. But then after 1992 we had a shift toward more acceptance. The majority, 58 percent, still says that such relationships are always wrong, but that's fallen from nearly 80 percent in the early 1990s. So here we have a permissive change, but one that did not occur earlier, did not occur in the 1970s and early 1980s when attitudes toward premarital sex became more permissive. This change only occurred in the 1990s.

A Fifty-Fifty Chance

It's not true that half of all marriages have ended in divorce. But the projections are that half of all recent marriages — and by recent I really mean over a fairly long period, the last ten to twenty years — that half of all marriages formed in the last twenty years or so will eventually end in a divorce. The current figures are, of all married people, about a third of them have gone through a divorce — either currently being divorced or having been through a divorce at one time. The projection is that enough of those who have not gone through a divorce will eventually divorce so that at least half of all marriages will end in divorce.

Marriage remains an extremely important institution in society. It is the institution under which all other aspects of life are organized. But marriage is declining in terms of its centrality.

First of all, the average age of those getting married has increased about four to five years in the last generation. In 1960, the average age of marriage for a man was twenty, and the single most common age for a woman to marry was age eighteen, right out of high school, basically. Now the average age of marriage for a woman has moved up to twenty-five. It's even a couple of years older for men. So now you spend, on average, the first seven to ten years of your adult life not being married, as opposed to getting married practically as soon as you became an adult.

Second of all, the divorce rate more than doubled from the 1960s to the 1980s. It has leveled off a little bit and it hasn't gone up since the early 1980s, but hasn't gone down much either. It is still over twice as high as it was in the 1960s.

And third, while most people who divorce eventually remarry, there's a growing gap of years between a marriage and a second marriage.

Now, when you take the delayed marriage, the higher divorce, and the delay in remarrying, what you get is that people are spending a smaller and smaller share of their adult life within a marriage. Matter of fact, the figures might indicate very soon that people would on average spend a majority of their adult life outside of a marriage.

A Slowdown, but Change Isn't Stopping

In terms of family change, I think we are getting a bit of slowdown. Change is not stopping, and certainly change isn't reversing. There is little or no sign that society will in the foreseeable future move back toward traditional families. But a number of the changes have leveled off or their rate of change has slowed down.

In some cases it's because the rate of change has been so massive it doesn't have a lot further to go. We've already got to a situation in which both parents are working in 66 percent of intact marriages. That may well go up to as high as 75 percent. But you're going to hit a ceiling effect much beyond that. So that trend will probably level off early in this first decade of the new millennium. Some trends have already leveled off. The proportion of children born to unmarried women rose from 5 percent to 33 percent, but has held at 33 percent for the last two to three years. So, I think the rate of family change will continue, but will be at a slower pace, and there may be more stability over the next decade than we've seen over the last twenty years.

Another sign of improvement is that the other institutions in society, as well as the family itself, are learning now how to adapt to the needs of the modern family. Families are learning how they can best deal with the needs of children, especially in a dual-earner family or a single-parent family. Schools are offering more and more after-school care programs. More and more employers are offering flextime and parental leave. And of course you have the federal government having passed the Parental Leave Act in the early '90s. The point is that all institutions in society are paying more attention to the needs of the modern family types and are making changes in their policies to better meet those needs. This will make it easier for those families to be successful.

Judith Stacey

Judith Stacey is Senior Scholar at the Council on Contemporary Families, as well as a professor of sociology and the Streisand Professor of Contemporary Gender Studies at the University of Southern California. She believes that marriage has always been changing and there isn't a simple truth.

The Decline in Marriage Isn't the Entire Story

Generally there are big differences and disagreements among social scientists about what social science can and can't tell us about the causes of family changes and their consequences. We can certainly map some of those changes. There are social science methods you could use to get to the meanings and causes, but people are very complicated and relationships are very complicated. So there are always going to be enormous debates about what any association or correlation means.

The Council on Contemporary Families is a group of scholars, clinical professors, and faculty who focus on family formation. We did this because many of us found ourselves in the situation of being interviewed in the media or participating in debates around these issues. We were very disturbed by the overly simplified use of social science in the public arena and what we thought were major distortions of the research and the overheated nature of the debate. We wanted to have a much more responsible conversation and to do public education for ourselves and for others. We wanted to really look at the nuances of the issues.

The arguments of the people who claim that marriage is in decline say this is disastrous and the decline is the central cause in a whole set of social problems leading to almost every imaginable social ill: crime, welfare dependency, sexual disease, domestic abuse, and children dropping out of school. You name it. So that's their basic argument, and put on that level, I would say that's just simply wrong. There is nothing in social science that is ever explainable in that way. Other issues that are far more complicated and nuanced never make it into the public. There are very complicated things to say about the vast ways in which marriage is changing, the enormous ways in which families are changing, and the great changes in the ways people are choosing to lead their lives together.

Families: Ever Changing

If you go back to the nineteenth century, African Americans weren't allowed to marry until the end of the Civil War. Slaves were forbidden marriage. The institution of marriage is always changing. Even when we talk about traditional marriage, we're really talking about what historians call "modern marriage" — *modern* in the historical sense of modern European history, history since the Industrial Revolution.

What we think of now as the traditional family is the male breadwinner, the female homemaker, and their children. That was actually a modern development that came in with the Industrial Revolution. It came in with the industrial society as productive work was sent outside the home. First young women, and later mainly men, were the ones who went outside the home to do work for pay instead of working at home, which is what everyone tended to do in pre-modern society.

So marriage has always been changing. What we think of as traditional marriage in fact wasn't traditional. As we know, the Bible has polygamy as a norm. There are many different kinds of marriage systems around the world today and historically. It's ever changing.

What we have today are debates about whether marriage is the best form of relationship. Should it receive privilege by society? Who should be allowed to participate in it? Think back to 1967, when the U.S. Supreme Court ruled in *Loving vs. Virginia* that it was unconstitutional to forbid interracial marriage. At the time the Supreme Court rendered that decision, there were still 48 percent of people who thought that interracial marriage should be a crime. That's a much higher percent than are now opposed to gay marriage. So marriage is always in the process of change. It's a historical thing.

While marriage has always been changing, it changed far more rapidly and dramatically, along with lots of other family changes, in the period since 1965. Today far more white women are single heads of households than African-American women were in 1965. We now have family change on a vast level not just in the United States, but around the world.

There Isn't a Simple Truth

There certainly are women who believe that the decline of marriage has been really harmful to women and it has let men off the hook. They believe that men, who have problems with commitment anyway, are less committed, are less responsible as fathers, etc.; and therefore, they want a marriage system that would give them more security. I certainly understand and have sympathy for that perspective. However, I think that approach won't work. It assumes that it is just a matter of will or something the state can impose.

I believe women who look to marriage as their primary form of security need to be very careful about how vulnerable they're making themselves. I believe that women want to have a secure relationship that is not based on inequality and dependence. I would be for making and honoring commitments based on equality and a fair situation. You cannot legislate that.

There isn't a simple truth. But the underlying truth, in my view, is that all of those things happened in response to the massive economic shifts and technological shifts that made possible female survival outside of marriage. We have to ask ourselves two things: Why is it that the children of the people who celebrate the '50s as the high tide of good families, traditional values, and stable marriages rebelled against that marriage system? Now, that's an interesting question. Why did that happen? It really was, exactly, the children of that postwar marriage system that were in the forefront of all of the experiments, or digressions, or diversification. The second thing is that those children were also the generation, the Baby Boomers, that came of age exactly when you had the shift from an industrial to a postindustrial economy, in which white collar labor and service labor came to replace the working-class male breadwinner's job. Those things were interacting at the same time, and that's really why the commitments declined. Women could get out of marriages they didn't want, and men could escape marriages that they didn't want.

Living the Complexities

There are people who are uninterested in marriage. But the vast majority of Americans are very interested in marriage. Sometimes too interested; they do it too often. They marry again and again — much more so than Europeans, as a matter of fact. I think that the question is what promotes marriage and what promotes *good* marriage as opposed to just marriages that are still on the books.

What often gets left out of the conversation is what is a good marriage and what are the social conditions? What can we do as a society to make good marriages more likely? What can we do to make marriage more available to those who want it and to make successful relationships more likely for everybody, especially for children, in whatever kind of family they find themselves?

I could boil the argument down to those who believe that one family pattern is best for everyone, that society should promote it, that legal marriage should be between heterosexuals only, and that divorce should be made more difficult. On the other side of the argument are those of us who believe there is no single model of family or relationship that is best for everybody, that all children and all families need a lot of social support, and that good relationships are better for everybody.

I'm on the second side. Most people are living my side. People say different things when you ask them in surveys than they do when you look at what they're doing in their own lives. For example, if you ask people what's the state of marriage, the overwhelming majority of people will say it's worse, it's declining, it's going to hell in a handbasket. But if you ask people about their own relationships, their own marriages, their own families, by vast majorities they will tell you that they're better off than they used to be and that their particular families are fine.

I think it has a lot to do with people making choices themselves and understanding the complexities of their own lives. There are real reasons to be concerned about family change. But there are probably more reasons to be concerned about lots of other changes, including less of a sense of safety in our schools, on our streets, on the road, in our lives.

We are concerned about relationships breaking up. We all know stories that are very sad. We tend to mythologize what things were like or imagine that there is some simple solution, like everyone joining a pep squad for marriage will somehow cure all of our social ills. I believe that's just vastly wrong.

Men and Women — It's Never Easy

There certainly is a problem for a lot of men in this society. There is a crisis in masculinity for a lot of men in this society and it's more serious than the crisis for women, although women often pay the price for the crisis. Our definitions of what it is to be a man have certainly changed in the period in which women's workforce participation came to be expected as normal. There have been a lot of changes for men who lack a great deal of higher education; the decline of the working-class breadwinner, the blue-collar job that was secure for life, the home of your own, and a full-time wife at home. It's become a very competitive work situation.

It's a mean economic system that has winners and losers. Yes, there are problems between men and women. Men and women need to learn new ways of getting along. It doesn't work the way they used to get along or not get along. But the power dimension was very, very clear. Women were economically dependent. They didn't have the option of being able to leave marriages. You had a different system. Now we really do need to find ways to get along.

I can say something that I think is pretty provocative. When we say the divorce rate is high, approximately half of all marriages will end in divorce in the U.S., and increasingly in most Western societies, I say, that's actually not very high. That's kind of an amazing achievement. We have moved to a system in which marriage is for the sake of the relationship, for the most part, that people have very high expectations of what a relationship should be. They want an egalitarian relationship by and large, and they want one that is good for all of the parties. That half of all people think they've more or less approximated that is really quite remarkable. Historically we never came anywhere near there.

It's Not about Kids in General — It's about Your Kids

The question of what is best for children is a complicated one. Certainly having successful parents who are happy with each other, who are economically successful, who care about their children, who want their children, is a very good thing. We should do everything to support that. But that can come in a variety of packages and historically has come in a variety of packages.

The big debate is whether people who are really wretched together should stay together for the sake of the children. That's really what it boils down to. There is no simple answer to that. There's a lot of research to demonstrate that hostile, conflicted marriages are worse for children than successful divorce. There are those who say that even an unhappy marriage is better for a child than a divorce. But there is no correct answer to that question.

What an actual parent needs to know is not whether marriage in general would be better for children in general, whether divorce in general would be harmful to children in general. They need to know, in their particular bad marriage, whether staying together in that bad marriage would be better or worse for their particular children. No sociologist can answer that question for them. There are so many factors that will affect that. By and large, we can say that high levels of conflict in the house are bad for children. They're not bad for all children (there are some children who do just fine despite that), but generally speaking, that's not a good thing. We know that economic resources absolutely are good for children. There is very little dispute about that. Nonetheless, there are people from unbelievably destitute situations who achieve phenomenal things and are maybe even stronger for it. So when you're making your individual decision, you have to know the particulars of your situation.

One of the big disagreements I have with those who argue that the decline of marriage is terrible is the image they portray as though people just somehow change their minds and decide they're only going to be selfish, that they are going to do whatever is best for them and they don't care at all about their children. I'm sure there are people like this, but they really are a minority. Most sociology can demonstrate that people do not wake up and say, "This marriage is kind of boring. I think I'll go look for another one." Or, "I'll go do something else. I'll get a sports car or — forget the kids." Least of all do women do that. By and large people agonize over the decision to divorce when they have children. I'm sure there are people who do not, but they don't show up very much in very many of our studies. It does not help them at all to add to the guilt and anxiety that they're going to feel.

There are things we can do to make divorce much less harmful to children. There also are things we can do to make marriages more likely to succeed. Those are the things I think we should be doing. We should be providing support for children in all kinds of families rather than singling out one as the preferred model for all.

We know that safe neighborhoods are good for children. We know that when a man loses his job, he is more likely to become abusive. People who really wanted to promote marriage would be much more effective if they were working for an above-poverty guaranteed income level for all people. If they were providing educational incentives, programs, and supports, you would do more to promote good marriages than by moralizing about it.

Jeff

Jeff is an attorney. He and his wife recently separated after ten years of marriage and he expects a divorce.

The Last Straw

What brought it about was, I think, that my wife believed that I could no longer love her in a way that was meaningful to her. In a nutshell, there were events that were supposedly the straw that broke the camel's back, and I think it was a very emotional event for her. I could go on for hours.

I lost my job. My last day of work was the fifteenth of March and the nineteenth of March is when my wife told me she wanted a divorce. On the seventeenth I was very depressed, because when you are thirteen years out in the legal profession without a book of business you are a dime a dozen. I was extremely depressed. It was my first or second day alone in the house. I got some bad information about where my wife was, and I completely lost it. I said things to her I should not have said and acted in a manner that was deplorable. I did not hit her or anything like that. Jewish boys don't hit. But I accused her of something that I thought she did, and I turned out to be dead wrong. I felt terrible. It was done in front of my daughter. I apologized. Two days later, I was told she wants a divorce. That was it. She never went back. There's no excuse for what I did. Truthfully there is no excuse for it, and I am responsible for that. She felt that something died in her as a result of that.

I'm not proud of my behavior, but I was really in a bad place at that time. I always had what I would call a volatility problem. But this was nothing qualitatively or quantitatively like anything I had experienced, perhaps in our entire marriage. I had been working mightily on improving it. But, ultimately, it's a much deeper fundamental difference that led to this divorce, I think.

The Road

We noticed our fundamental differences from the inception of the marriage. Even before the marriage, I felt we were having difficulty communicating. By difficulty, I mean I was very leery that she could not really articulate her feelings. She could not sit down and say, "I'm angry, I'm hurt," in a direct, meaningful way to give you a sense of what was going on with her. That was very, very disconcerting to me.

It is so ironic. I knew this before the marriage. Just like she knew I was volatile before the marriage. She asks herself now, "Why would I marry you?" She said to me once in a fit, "I should have known when you yelled about burning the toast that I shouldn't marry you."

A more profound question is, Why did she marry me? From an object relation standpoint, because she had someone who could express the anger that she couldn't express. And I had someone who created a sense of nurturing and dependency and some lack of volatility. Not that this really amounts to a hill of shit, quite frankly, in trying to go forward in your life. But if you are asking me, we knew from the very beginning that there were these differences.

The Frying Pan

It's really quite extraordinary. One of the reasons my wife wanted to leave me is because she felt I was very self-absorbed and disengaged. She is not incorrect to this extent: I was under tremendous stress for five years because I was involved in a lawsuit in which I was the defendant. I was completely preoccupied about it. I felt I was under siege. I did not cope with it well, and I think it took a tremendous amount of psychic energy.

Unfortunately, during the course of our marriage there was a very, very unhealthy, almost childlike dependency that was created by our relationship. On one hand, she would rail against it, and on the other hand it's what happened. She went from being wife to being mother.

At first, being alone in the house was incredibly daunting. I literally said, "How am I going to prepare a meal, and how am I going to clean?" The things I did when I was a bachelor without any problem suddenly became incredibly fearful tasks. What I'm doing now may not be Julia Child, but I'm doing it. And I'm cleaning.

Initially, I was in the midst of tremendous despair about the loss of her and the ruthlessness of the divorce. There was no ambiguity. There was no, "We'll go to marital therapy." We were not people who were knocking each other's brains out for nine months and finally someone threw in the towel and gave up. This was, "You did this. You did this five years ago." Frying pan on the side of the head. "I've made my decision. I've never doubted it." I begged, I pleaded, and I urged marital therapy.

Unfortunately, we seek the advice of those that confirm our prejudices. I think certain people were telling her that this is the right thing to do. "He's a bad guy. He's psychotic. He's a lunatic." All this based upon very nonexistent knowledge of me as a human being except through her. So, she would come back fortified. You'd hear these quotes that she never said in fourteen years of our relationship. "We have a toxic relationship," as she put it. There were voices that were not her own, which doesn't mean the feelings and the pain, which initially expressed itself in tremendous anger and tremendous cruelty toward me, weren't there. That pain was very real. It was caused by me. Do you understand?

We may not have understood each other. But the pain she was feeling that caused that kind of rage was very authentic and extraordinarily painful for me. I bring this up because in some sense that aloneness was a relief. At least, it was a distance from that assault. It was a relief to get her the hell out of the house, because I couldn't stand it. I mean, some of the things she was doing and some of the things she was saying were just very painful. She did not have the psychological capacity to say to herself that she was trying to bring this man to his knees or to a psychological point where he just wants out of the relationship. She would push buttons that she knew would drive me mad. And they did. She succeeded. It was extraordinarily painful, and I was extraordinarily angry and extraordinarily hurt and extraordinarily trying to figure it out. You can't figure it out by yourself. I mean, you can figure it out, but you can't salvage it by yourself.

If the person says, "I have no doubts. This is what I want. You cannot love me the way I need to be loved, no matter what you do or say, no matter how you change or are committed to change," eventually, what do you do? You have a choice. You can sit there and kill yourself. Literally just say I can't live without this woman and my life is an empty void without her, and I am going to go throw myself in front of a bus. Or you sit there and say you're better than that. You cannot let this woman define your self-respect.

Who Are We?

It was a side of her I had never seen. It was like there was a different person there. It wasn't so much the side of the arguments as much as a burst of assaults. There was just a tremendous amount of things that she is going to have to live with. I told her that I might have failed in our marriage. I may not have been the man she wanted. But I never did anything to hurt her deliberately — except for one time three weeks ago when I just wanted to elicit some kind of response because the indifference on her face was so stunningly hurtful to me. I may have been callous. I may have been uncaring. But I never tried to hurt her. But the things she did and said can only be construed as intentional. She will have to live with them. Right now they don't bother her.

This process brings out the absolute most inhumane aspects. I am as responsible or as guilty. But, truly, I cannot think of anything, perhaps other than a gulag or a concentration camp, where the dynamism between two people is both to survive and destroy at the same time. It brings out the horrific, the horrific. It's just an incredible thing.

I Was Preoccupied

She was in such tremendous pain, so unhappy. I didn't know because I was preoccupied and stressed. But I also didn't know because she didn't sit down and say to me, "I'm in agony here. I have one step out the door. There are portions of myself that are not being expressed in this marriage."

She says, "I should have gotten rid of you five years ago." Maybe she's right. Maybe she's right. It would have made more sense to me five years ago. I wouldn't have had a chance to reconcile myself to her as a human being and realize what a wonderful person she was and how fortunate I was to have married her, despite my own misgivings in the inception of the relationship. Maybe it would have been easier. But that didn't happen that way.

The plus side is that despite the dependency, despite the sickness in the relationship, despite the toxicity, I know I loved her. I know I still love her. I know I can live with the knowledge that it is okay to still love her and still move very productively forward in life — not to be fearful of that love and not to allow her to kill that love. If you let her, she will.

Oh, to Turn Back That Clock

What's up is that I think that you have a culture and society that makes tremendous demands on us, especially in American culture. It is just easy, too easy, to allow marriages to wither on the vine without knowing. You've got the carpools. You've got this. You've got work. You've got to make a career. You need a new car. The kids need to go to camp. Need, need, need. All of a sudden you blink your eyes and you realize that you haven't been with each other in a month. Or you haven't gone on a vacation together in three years. Or you haven't spent a weekend away together, or even taken your wife out to dinner. I mean, to a romantic place. Or you haven't taken a bottle of wine — it doesn't have to be an expensive one — and sneak down to Lake Michigan, crack it open, and look at the moonlight. Romance dies. Not providing enough opportunity to make a woman feel like there is passion and there is value in her through those little things. You blink your eyes and it's like Thornton Wilder in *Our Town*.

You look back and it's over. That's the hardest thing. One of the hardest things for me is that I think of all the time I squandered. I could have devoted it to her. How much time I spent on the golf course. I was under such stress. Knocking a golf ball was the only thing that could take my mind off my stress. So I used to go bang balls. How much I disengaged. That precious time with both my children and my wife is the great regret.

Attention Must Be Paid

I think there is an epidemic. I don't think I'm unusual. You think it is more important to watch Michael Jordan? You think it's more important to watch the World Series? Attention must be paid. You have to bear in mind that that person has to be the most important thing in your life.

We certainly can look at the warning signs in the beginning of our marriage — the tumultuous courtship, which was a paradigm for disaster. But that being said, there may have been a chance for survival had we learned to nurture the similarities. There was passion there. I never tired of kissing her. I never tired of hugging her. I never tired of making love to her. The first time, and the last time. I only wish I could remember the last time as the last time. That was always there.

I think if people really pay attention, if there is some little thing and suddenly you start feeling distance . . . For example, you suddenly feel the need to always be with other people when you go out, as opposed to just being with each other, because you really have nothing to say to each other. If you can't sit there and nonjudgmentally listen to somebody instead of jumping to conclusions. If you blink your eyes and you haven't made love to each other in a month, or two months. It's those little things. If you develop that awareness, and that acuity, you'll be fine. But if you don't, you're doomed.

Believe me, you don't want to go through this. This is not something that I would wish on my worst enemy, what I've been through for the last twelve weeks, and what I *will* go through. I feel good right now. I feel functional right now. But I know — I *know* — there will be times when I'm looking out that window on a cold November night or December night around the holidays, and I will have to live with it. And I will never know, ever, what it is like to walk through that door with them here again. That's hard. That I can't get back. I can reclaim myself, but I can't reclaim those moments.

The Song

My wife filed her divorce papers three days after our anniversary, and I bought this Keith Jarrett CD. Jarett plays this absolutely beautiful version of *Someone to Watch Over Me*, which was always our song. After all the cruelty and all the terrible things, I asked her for one last dance.

I held her. She really didn't want to do it, because she didn't want any ambiguity. But she did it, and I whispered in her ear, "I am so sorry, I failed you." She cried. That will always be the last moment of my marriage. If it had to end, that's the way it should end. And that was it. That was the end. At least I'll have that. That's it.

Judith

Judith, who is the mother of two sons, divorced her husband after twenty-five years of marriage. She feels that her husband didn't respect her contributions to their partnership.

Life before Divorce

I was a "corporate wife," and I referred to myself as June Cleaver. I did all of the typical mother/son things in life. I helped support my husband in his career and drove my children to and from school, participated in all their school activities, and did all of the things within the school. They went to small Catholic schools, so there was a lot of parental participation in those schools and I was very involved in that. I was a stay-at-home mother. I mean, your typical stay-at-home mother, if there is such a thing.

The perfect marriage to me was where both of the partners respected each other. I feel that you cannot have love if you don't have respect. It was sort of the June and Ward Cleaver thing, where the husband went off to work and the wife supported him in his career. He came home and there was a wonderful dinner. The children were ideal, good students. You know, a couple of vacations per year, lovely home, that was it. However, that was based on not so much the model that I lived, but it was more the model that I had created in my mind. Actually I lived the opposite of that.

I Never Raised My Voice

As a child both of my parents worked outside of the home, and it was very typical in that we were left alone for very long hours. My mother was a very demanding and critical mother. She had four daughters and did not get along with any of us, so I think I decided early on that I was going to be the exact opposite of my mother.

When I had children, I never raised my voice. I was very stoic. I was a borderline Stepford Wife. I hate to admit, but, I think maybe I was. That was a pattern that I developed in my own mind.

My husband was a professional. He was very successful. He was extremely confident, extremely confident. I was very supportive in his career when we first married at the age of twenty-six; he was, of course, just starting out in the business world. But after the twenty-five-year marriage, he had reached a tremendous degree of success. We, of course, had all of what I now refer to as trappings of success. At the time I wouldn't have referred to them as trappings, but now I look back on it and I think it was the trappings of success.

I think based on my background I entered the marriage not feeling particularly good about myself. I certainly felt that I had characteristics and gifts that were given to me, and talents, but I married someone who, in my mind, was very similar to my mother. He was extremely confident — I would say arrogant. We kind of played into each other in that I held him in such high esteem, much higher than I held myself.

So I behaved toward him exactly the way I did with my mother. After five years of seeing a psychotherapist, I realized that I had developed a pattern and that I married someone that was very much like my mother. When I was a young woman, the men that I dated or came in contact with who were very nice to me, it did not feel right. It just didn't feel right. I needed to be in a relationship with someone where I was always on edge. I was always trying to prove that I was lovable.

When people are conditional in their love, they can kind of turn on you whenever and I never knew. So I really walked on eggshells around him. I had actually developed two personalities, one that I had with him and one that I had with everybody else.

Do you know how exhausting that is? It is exhausting. I think part of it was that I was incredibly fatigued, emotionally fatigued, and trying to get somebody to think that you are lovable and have value. . . . You can teach somebody certain things if they are not a reluctant student.

But if they are a reluctant student, you're never going to reach them. That's the kind of person that I married. It's not that I blame him. He came a certain way. I came a certain way. As I got older and matured and got out into the world, I no longer wanted to tolerate that kind of a relationship. When I addressed this with him, I got nowhere. So, I decided to end the relationship.

My Children Were Going Off

One of the similarities between my mother and my husband that I think had the greatest impact on me, and certainly on our marriage, was that my mother was a conditional lover as was my husband. As I matured, I was always on the fence with my husband. It was never 100 percent that he was a nasty man or anything, but there was a good 90 percent or 10 percent. I never knew where I stood with him. I never felt that I was loved by him through a great deal of the marriage.

One of the terrible things that I did is because I had sons, I think that I developed the relationship with my sons that I really should have had with my husband. I think that was one of the things that served as the impetus for me to end the marriage. As my children got older and they were going off on their own and being with their friends, I realized, my God, all these years have gone by and I don't have a relationship with this man that's healthy, emotionally healthy.

I would address this with my husband, realizing my children were going off, but he couldn't see it. I think his needs — an overused word — but his needs in the marriage were met and mine were not. I think he felt that I should have been grateful for all of the fancy home, the fancy cars, the fancy vacations, educating my children. But he did not have the emotional need for the relationship that I needed. Because he came as a more confident person and he was very successful in his career, he was getting all of the strokes that he needed and I was not.

I went to work when my oldest son was in college and my youngest one was in high school. When I returned to the workplace and when I got out there and I saw the impact that I had on other people, that's when I really questioned my relationship with my husband. It just became very difficult for me. I had recommended that he and I seek marital counseling.

Unraveled

Marital counseling is extremely painful. Before they can fix a marriage they have to address the individuals. It's not an easy process. My husband had a great deal of difficulty with it. The way that we approached marriage counseling was that the counselor would first see one of us, then she would see us together, then she would see the other of us, and then together, because she was trying to simultaneously work on the individual and the marriage.

My husband went only about six times. He didn't believe in it, but I did. When I saw that he wasn't going to put forth any effort into this, I just knew that our marriage had unraveled. If he wasn't going to address what he was bringing to it both negative and positive, it couldn't be repaired.

There was just no communication whatsoever, none. My husband didn't want to go anywhere with me. For years, he didn't want to go anywhere with me — unless it was something dealing with business, then he would go. I made those attempts to try to rebuild the marriage. But I would say the biggest thing was no communication.

I think the person is not a priority in the other person's life, and I think that's what happened to me. I knew I was not a priority in his life and emotionally I couldn't reach him. He was a very, I think, shut-down emotional person. Some of that might be the generation. I don't think young men today are like that.

I finally did the postmortem on everything and I realized that there were a lot of signs that I just didn't pick up on. I think that's where going to see a counselor is extremely helpful to me. I really worked out a lot of different issues and what I had done to bring about the demise of this marriage. Prior to that, if you had told me that I had been any part of the failure, I wouldn't have believed it. But I realize now what it was that made it or helped to bring the end to it.

The Divorce

I don't recommend it. It was excruciating. It was excruciating. It was extremely painful for me. First of all, I didn't want to be divorced. I would go to see my attorney and he would be telling me things, and I would sit there and say to him, "I don't want to be divorced, I don't want to be divorced." His question to me was always, "Do you think there's a chance of reconciliation?" And I said, "No."

I knew that there wasn't. I knew that I couldn't make my husband love me no matter what I did. It just wasn't there. He just didn't love me. I think that he just was used to living with me and that was it. I found it very difficult. First of all, I was very much by myself. I had no family here. My children were off in school. So I was by myself. I moved from a suburban community where I had some friends to the city. I really struggled. It was really a low time in my life.

My husband did not want to share. I think that he looked back on all of the years that we were together and he was the wage earner and I stayed at home and raised the children, and he didn't put any value in what it was that I did. So, he was not really generous. He fought for two years. There were certain things that I wanted in the divorce that he fought. Finally he did relent.

I had lived in a home for twenty-five years, so the minute that the divorce was final I started to find a home. I love to do rehabbing, so I found a small house in a regentrification area. I bought it and I rehabbed it and moved into it on May tenth. On May twentieth, exactly ten days later, my husband was dismissed from his employer and he filed papers to no longer give me any maintenance — because maintenance is based on income, and if someone does not have income (though he had investments and money) he did not have to pay me anything. So, for over four years, during this period of time when he was unemployed, I did not get any maintenance from him. I scraped by.

It Comes Down to Respect

Oh, I think there are some wonderful marriages. I think it just comes down to respect. If you don't respect someone, I think it would be hard to love them, or almost impossible. But I think that there are some of the old-fashioned values in marriage that exist today, even in the young marriages that I see.

I work with a lot of young people that are married, and when I see them together the respect that they have for each other is almost tangible, and you can just tell. I don't think that existed in my marriage. It did from my side to my husband. I had a great deal of respect for him, for his intellect, for what he more or less brought to our party. But I don't think that he did. I don't think he really respected me. I think I was undereducated for him, and I think that what I brought to the marriage, he didn't think that it had value.

Time is a healer. Our son got married last July, so I did see my ex-husband then and it was a little strained but I wish him well. I really do wish him well. I can't say that I always felt that way. I think I always felt that I wished him well, except I never could really get to the point where I wished him love. But now, I'm even beyond that. I think that he had his value system, I had my value system. They didn't gel and I can forgive him for what I thought at the time were transgressions against me but I'm perfectly okay now.

David Blankenhorn

David Blankenhorn is president of the Institute for American Values, a think tank on family issues that involves more than one hundred scholars. He discusses the Moynihan Report and the White House Conference on Families as important turning points in the discussion about family structure.

It Really Blew Up in Their Face

If you wanted to look at important turning points, I think you would have to look to the famous Moynihan Report of 1965. Daniel Patrick Moynihan was an Assistant Secretary of Labor and he issued his famous, and what would soon be infamous, report on the black family. He talked about the tangle of pathology (and those were his words) that emerges when you have the widespread growth of single-parent, father-absent homes in urban black communities. He said this is the barrier that will prevent black Americans from taking advantage of the new opportunities that they have won through the civil rights movement. He said a lot of black Americans won't be able to take advantage of this because of this family crisis, and, therefore, we should mobilize the resources of government to provide job opportunities, anti-poverty, and so on.

A huge controversy erupted. Moynihan was widely vilified as a racist and the worst kind of person for speaking this way, using words like *pathology*. President Johnson immediately stopped talking about it, and the whole thing just went underground for about twenty-five years. You could not talk about this issue in the black community without being labeled a terrible person giving aid and comfort to racism. So nobody talked about it. Then the family trend in white America began to look more and more in conformity with the trend that was present in black America.

The Moynihan Report and then President Johnson in his 1965 Howard University speech did mention solutions. The most important were jobs and employment. Don't forget Moynihan was an Assistant Secretary of Labor, so he was looking for a full employment policy. He really in part grabbed upon the issue of the deterioration of family structure in black America as a way to make his case for federal spending on a full employment strategy. There were also little things like the war on poverty, which in part originated from this analysis of the black family. So these were people in the liberal tradition.

Moynihan was drawing upon leading black scholars who, since the 1930s, had made this argument about the weakening of marriage among African Americans and the need to have an economic strategy in order to have black men be breadwinners that could support a family. This was the argument but it really blew up in their face. They got caught up in a lot of cultural and political currents in the mid to late 1960s. It just became a code word for blaming the victim. Anybody who said anything about the deterioration of the family structure was blaming the victim. So nobody wanted to be blaming the victim, and so nobody said a word about it until the late 1980s, when William Julius Wilson of Harvard and other black scholars picked it up again.

Meanwhile, white family structure was following the same pattern. By 1995, white family structure was exactly where black family structure was in 1965. President Johnson declared a crisis of family structure in black America in 1965. If you look at the rates of divorce and unwed childbearing and single-parent homes, white America reached that exact point in 1995. By that time, of course, in some African-American communities, 80 percent of children were being born to unmarried mothers. So by the 1990s, it certainly was no longer a minority problem, it was a societal problem.

The Word Revolution *Is Overworked, But . . .*

This thesis, which connected the problems of black Americans to the problem with the black family, presupposed the view that marriage is a desirable and important institution, that children ought to grow up in a two parent home — that was best for children and that was morally good. This idea would not have been contested by anyone before about 1965, but about that time it began to be seriously contested.

The word *revolution* is an overworked word, but a demographic or moral revolution cut through the society beginning in the mid to late 1960s and escalating phenomenally during the entire course of the 1970s. American society just changed. By the end of that period we as a society had changed our minds in really important ways on that question. The whole issue of making a moral claim about the importance of marriage and the monopoly that marriage should have on procreation and childbearing was over. Elite people in universities, TV shows, and so on, they just stopped believing that, and a lot of the public stopped believing it and voted with their feet, with very rapidly escalating rates of divorce and out-of-wedlock childbearing.

A Clash of Cultures

The second really important historical marker for the modern family debate was the White House Conference on Families in 1980. When President Carter ran for office in 1976, he said that if you will elect me, I'm going to do what I can to restore and strengthen the family. It was the first time that a president had ever talked about this in a presidential campaign. This was 1976, at the very height of the breathtaking cultural, social changes that were going on with regard to marriage.

Obviously, there was some anxiety in the country about all of this. This was the very height of the shifting of marriage law toward a no-fault divorce, and there was an enormous concern. Are we doing the right thing? What's this going to mean? Carter, although a Democrat, essentially campaigned as something of a social conservative and said, "I'm going to have a conference on the family. We're going to try to get on top of this." He won and he did.

But a couple of interesting things happened as a result of this conference. One was that the conference itself, in a kind of the eerie echo of the Moynihan controversy, self-immolated. They couldn't figure out whether to call it the White House Conference on the Family or the White House Conference on Families, suggesting pluralism, diversity, and that all family forms are fine. They couldn't decide who would be in charge of it. So finally there was a single mother who was the chairwoman of it, and it was the White House Conference on Families, plural. A lot of the establishment types pushed the whole thing in that direction.

Well, there was a difference between the spirit of the campaign promise, which was "let's shore up this weakening institution of marriage in the family," and then in the actual event. It got taken over by the professionals and the academics, all of which wanted to emphasize pluralism, respect for diverse family forms.

Meanwhile, unbeknownst to them there was an unknown fellow named Jerry Falwell and there was a little-known woman named Phyllis Schlafly, and friends of theirs, who were more than a little outraged about the whole matter, more than a little upset about the current family trends. They began to organize what they would call in 1978 and 1979 the Pro-Family Movement, which was a grassroots, largely church-based organization of mostly evangelical Protestants and other people of faith. In 1980, politically it began to be called the New Right, but it was organized as the Pro-Family Movement.

Dr. Robert Rice, who at the time was a high official at the Family Service of America and on the committee to organize this White House Conference on Families, was telling me that the committee was all academics, social workers, service providers, and government agencies. They were all kind of like-minded. He said in one of the early meetings, they looked out and a bunch of buses were pulling up, and people started getting off the buses carrying signs with angry slogans like, "They're Our Children."

This was a clash of cultures when these very angry grassroots people came to the meeting. It was a public meeting and they were furious. They kept shouting, "They're our children, they're our children." The whole thing just kind of blew up in an angry conflagration.

On the one hand, the managers clearly wanted to tilt the tone and tenure of the thing toward an idea that different family forms are good, we don't want to become overly moralistic, and we don't want to point our fingers, and we don't want to blame the victim. We want to voice a measured amount of concern for the well-being of children, and we want essentially to encourage the rest of the society to do helpful things to accommodate the changing family structure. On the other hand, the people from the pro-family movement, who are coming from the grassroots and coming from the churches, wanted none of that talk at all. They wanted to say that this trend was wrong, morally wrong. Americans needed to wake up to the fact that they were messing up their basic institution, they needed to stop having illegitimate babies, they needed to stop getting divorced so frequently, they needed to go to church and remember the Ten Commandments and do what's right. They should not let this institution sink into the sewer. They didn't want to hear a bunch of professors and other people talk softly on this point. So they didn't mind being a little moralistic about it. It suited them just fine. They had a kind of a moral vocabulary on the whole subject. They did not want their children to be sucked up into these trends. There was anger and a bitterness that even extended to using the word *family* or *families.* Much of it centered on the issue of marriage. Is having a child outside of marriage morally wrong? They were very clear that it was. The other people were very clear that they weren't so sure. It all depended; who's to say. That was a huge thing, and I think that contributed, in a way, to the more years of silence on the issue, because it was widely viewed as a failure.

Politically Loaded Words

Did this draw the issue of the family further to the right? Yes. Politically, the result of this experience was the emergence of what was then called the Pro-Family Movement. It was a socially conservative, church-based, largely evangelical grassroots movement associated with Jerry Falwell and Phyllis Schlafly and many hundreds of pastors in these churches around the country.

The other thing it did was that *the family* and *marriage* became politically loaded words. It had a political charge to it. If you used those words, you were conservative or you were religious extremists. If you didn't use those words and if you used other words, you were progressive, you were liberal, you were approved by *The New York Times* editorial board. So it became a kind of politically divisive issue.

One of the things that we tried to do in The Institute for American Values is to try to take that whole debate out of this highly charged political way of thinking and acting. But the politicization occurred for very understandable reasons. I mean, these were genuinely different ways of thinking about the issue.

The Body Count

To me, the next phase is what I think of as the shift in elite opinion about the issue of marriage. I think it began in the late 1980s and really began to take shape in the early 1990s. Opinion leaders of the society, such as university researchers and the people doing the television shows and magazines, changed the subject from a sense that the trend is okay, that we can accommodate the trend and say good things about the trend and bad things about the traditional family. The evidence began to come in. People who were left of center politically, mostly Democrats, began publishing books and studies saying, "You know, there's a problem here. The promises and premises of the divorce revolution are not being borne out. There's a body count here, particularly a body count with regard to children and child well-being."

Politically, Democrats began talking about the issue, especially President Clinton in 1992, and it became a bipartisan political issue. It wasn't just predicting what was going to happen anymore. It was seeing real results, children that had grown up with 30, 40, 50 percent of a generation having their parents gotten divorced. Thirty percent of the children are now born to never-married mothers.

The scholars could tell us what was going on with those kids, and the sociologists and the magazine writers could tell us how the grown-ups were feeling. What about the person who is mid-forties, single, bitter that the marriage had ended, trying to get married again at midlife? How great was this, when it was happening on such a scale? What about the loneliness? What about the issue of so many fathers not seeing their kids?

It's gone too far. The divorce rate's too high, the out-of-wedlock childbearing rate is too high, marriage is too weak. We're not passing on any of these values to current young people. Young people today don't have a real sense that they can make a marriage that works. This is a big problem. We wish it was different, but we don't quite know what if anything we can do about it, except wring our hands a bit.

We don't quite know if we're really willing to change anything fundamental. We certainly aren't willing to change the divorce laws, for example, to move away from no-fault divorce. So, it's this period of recognition of the problem, but not quite sure if we're able or willing to do anything about it. I think that's really where we are now.

William Julius Wilson

William Julius Wilson is the Lewis P. and Linda L. Geyser University Professor at Harvard University. He studies the African-American community and says it is the lack of jobs that makes it difficult to create sustainable relationships between men and women.

The Vilification and the Void

If you're going to study the field of urban poverty, obviously you have to address the issue of family structure, because there is a strong relationship. In my work, I was trying to provide a historical backdrop for the contemporary scene. I focused on the impact of the Moynihan Report, because this report discouraged research on the inner city.

Daniel Patrick Moynihan was vilified in 1965 after he wrote his report on the black family, and it just scared a lot of researchers, particularly white researchers. They didn't want to address issues of the inner city or ghetto poverty because a lot of people felt these problems were too controversial, so why expose yourself to ideological attacks or criticisms of the kind that Moynihan received?

One of the reasons that Moynihan was so severely attacked was not because of what he said in his report. It was the interpretation of what he said; and a lot of what he said was distorted by others. People reacted to the distortions rather than to the report itself. In the distortions you would get the impression that Moynihan blamed the black family for the plight of so many black Americans, rather than looking at the broader structure of inequality and racism and so on. But if you read the report very carefully, what he was trying to say is that changes in the economy have created difficult conditions for some segments of the black family, particularly the poorer black families, who are falling further and further behind the rest of society. The impact of these changes is showing up in family relations and families are struggling more. Because of that you have a higher percentage of broken families in the African-American community than in the white community.

He obviously could have been a little more careful in some of the language he used; he was talking about the social pathology of the family breakdown, that kind of thing. But, basically, I think that his argument is fairly consistent with what later scholars have found in their research.

For many years after the Moynihan Report, researchers just shied away from studying the inner city, so a void was created. The researchers, the intellectuals or scholars, who did talk about inner-city problems for a period of time after the Moynihan Report were conservatives. They gave their own innate interpretation, which highlighted cultural values and the effect of the welfare state on the inner-city poor. They seldom paid attention to the larger structure of opportunity and the extent to which changes in the economy, something that Moynihan was concerned about, impacted adversely the African-American community.

It's about Work

Basically, I argued that neighborhoods have a profound influence on the social outcomes of families and individuals. It is one thing to be poor and live in a middle-class or stable working-class neighborhood. It's an entirely different thing to be poor and live in a neighborhood in which most of the people are poor.

I talk about concentration effects, the effects of living in an environment that's overwhelmingly impoverished. I talk about social isolation and the extent to which people are isolated from mainstream society because of limited opportunities and social constraints. I talk about this in connection with the out-migration of higher-income families from the inner city, leaving behind a more concentrated population suffering from joblessness and poverty.

I draw sharp contrast between contemporary scenes, particularly the first half of the 1990s, and some of the earlier periods. For example, I focused on the city of Chicago and I looked at three neighborhoods that represent the historic black belt in Chicago. Grand Boulevard,

Washington Park, and Douglas. In 1950, the majority of the adults in those city neighborhoods were working. These were neighborhoods that were 95 percent black. But by 1990, only one in four in the Grand Boulevard neighborhood was working, one in three were working in Washington Park, and only 40 percent in Douglas. I am talking about adults who are ages sixteen and over.

When we think about the inner city, we think about the problems of black males. In 1950, close to 70 percent of all black males ages fifteen and over in these three neighborhoods held a job in a typical week. By 1990, that figure had plummeted to 37 percent. So it went from close to 70 percent in 1950 to 37 percent in 1990.

Work not only provides a means to make a living, but it's also important because it organizes your life. It determines where you're going to be and when you're going to be there. Kids who grow up in a work environment are at a distinct advantage over kids who grow up in a nonwork environment, because work imposes discipline and regularity. Kids who grow up in a work environment — where they have parents who are working, where there is a steady breadwinner in the household — automatically develop the skills and the habits and the orientations that are associated with steady work.

It's Jobs

One of the things I argue is that the increasing problems in the African-American family, particularly the poor African-American family, are associated with the growing joblessness. So I developed this Male Marriageable Poor Index. It's the proportion of men per 100 women who are working. This index list has been dropping each year, so I associated the rise of single-parent families with joblessness. There are other factors involved, but joblessness is one of the significant factors.

We didn't find a relationship between joblessness and out-of-wedlock births. But we did find a strong relationship between joblessness and the rate in which these out-of-wedlock births were followed up by marriage. The rate of legitimization was strongly associated with joblessness. For example, we found that males ages eighteen to thirty-one who are employed and had their baby out of wedlock were eight times more likely to marry the mother of that child than those who were jobless.

The Significant Thing Is This

Here is the point. Joblessness, first of all, discourages marriage. And those who *are* married experience marital discord because of financial strain associated with joblessness. You eventually have a lot of marriages dissolving. You have a combination of women who have never been married and women who are experiencing separation or divorce.

The significant thing is this. The rise in joblessness over time in the inner city is associated primarily with the decreased relative demand for low-skilled labor due to the computer revolution and the growing internationalization of economic activity. The increased joblessness in the black community over time creates modes of adaptation. If increased joblessness is leading to friction or problems between men and women, the scene plays out over time. It's reflected in the kinds of attitudes that men and women develop toward one another. It's growing out of this increasing financial strain. After a while, because of repeated problems or failures, expectations change and women no longer are as comfortable or as optimistic about their marital chances. So, orientation changes and attitudes toward marriage and courtship change.

One thing that we've noticed is that the antagonisms between man and woman increase over time. You take a young man, for example; his prospects for employment are bleak. He knows that he can't live up to the societal expectations toward fatherhood. That is, he doesn't really believe that he can become a good father or a responsible father, because he doesn't have employment. He feels that this is due either to his own shortcomings or to the greater problems in society. Oftentimes this young man will rationalize his lack of involvement in the family in ways that will enhance his own self-esteem, instead of just facing up to the real problem. This changing attitude toward fatherhood creates frictions and problems with his mate. Then she reacts over time by giving up the idea that she can depend on her mate or these guys in the neighborhood. She just assumes that the chances of a stable marriage, something that they very much want, are just not really that great. So what has bothered me over time is that we haven't looked at the extent to which these changes and the opportunity structure interact with changes in the cultural traits of individuals as they try to adjust.

Race, Class, Tension, Frustration, and Strain

I would say that there are probably greater frictions between males and females in the African-American communities than in some of the other communities, except for the Native American community. I think to some extent that these tensions and problems and antagonisms between males and females in the lower-class black community have spilled over into working, middle-class communities.

It is true that middle-class blacks have a higher divorce and separation rate than comparable middle-class whites and Latinos. If there is a very strong antagonistic relationship among lower-class blacks, it eventually influences other segments of the African-American community because the African-American community is a highly segregated community. Middle-class blacks are much more likely to be in interaction with lower-working-class blacks than they are in other areas. Segregation reduces the class isolation that you see in some of these other communities. It doesn't surprise me that there may be some spill-over effect.

It's one thing to suffer from problems of low wages and income and trying to deal with all the problems associated with that. It's quite another thing to have those problems aggravated by problems of race. The combination of racial restrictions and class subordination create more tensions and frustrations and strains, which are reflected in personal relations including dating patterns and marital relations and so on.

Orlando Patterson

Orlando Patterson is the John Cowles Professor of Sociology at Harvard University. He says that it's often easier to change cultural factors than economic factors.

The Most Unpartnered Group in the Nation

The family today generally is in trouble, if one means that there are fundamental changes taking place and novel problems to resolve. African-American families, however, it seems to me, have a special set of problems amounting to what may be called a crisis.

In many ways, this crisis is not new. It's taking different forms. The 250 years of slavery constituted one long, externally imposed familial crisis. If one were to pinpoint the single most devastating effect of slavery, I'd say it's the impact on the roles of father and mother and husband. There was no room for the role of husband and father, as we normally understand the terms. There was no room for progenitor or male progenitor father. This continued afterward in different forms, although many of my historian friends don't seem to think so.

Today it has a new face, but the crisis is still very much there. It's reflected in many ways. To just cite figures, African Americans have the lowest rate of marriage of all groups. They're just not getting married in the first place. This is true, too, if we broaden the concept of marriage to include cohabitation — not necessarily legalized and ceremonially legalized marriages. We have the lowest rate of cohabitation.

When African Americans do get married or cohabit, they have the highest rate of marital or cohabitation disruption. When they divorce or their unions break up, they have the lowest rate of remarriage or getting back into unions. The result of all this is one simple, tragic fact —

African Americans are the most unpartnered group of people in the nation.

They have the highest rate of people who are single, who spend most of their lives being single. We African Americans are social animals, whatever else one may say, and that's a terrible situation for any group of people. It's also my view that this is the source of many other problems.

Who Owned the Children?

Slavery involved, first and foremost, having complete control over another person's labor power as well as the progeny, what they produce. Not just in the fields, but what they produced biologically. You own the children of your slaves. What is meant therefore is that you had to abolish the notion of somebody else having any custodial claims to the children of your slaves, the most obvious person being the father and also the mother.

The mother presented special problems. The legal rights of a child came from the fact that you owned the mother, so in a way you had to give some legal sanction to mothers having their children. But fathers had no claims over their children. Very often there was disruption of a family. But even if there wasn't an actual disruption, the threat of that and the possibility of that had devastating effects on the relationships between men and women.

One of the important things to remember when one speaks about family is to get away from the tendency to see it as a unit. Instead see it as a set of relationships. You can have two seemingly stable families: one is working harmoniously, but all hell is breaking loose in the other because of the underlying relationships that make up a family, those between the man and woman, the father and his children, the mother and her children, or the siblings. Those are the things one should look at. I think this point is important — slavery really devastated these relationships.

Just the General Turn-Off

The problem of the so-called African-American family involves several acute subproblems. One has to do with the relationship between parents and children. That's best reflected in the high rate of paternal abandonment. Sixty percent of African-American children are being brought up without the economic or emotional support of their fathers. This tendency toward paternal abandonment is also increasing in other communities, including the Euro-American community, but we're talking about a degree that is so much greater in the African-American community. The family involves the relationship between men and women.

Another major problem which I've explored and which many other people have explored, especially Afro-American feminist writers, has to do with the very fragile and tense nature of the relationship between men and women as lovers, as husbands and wives, as ex-lovers. That is again reflected partly in the figure I cited earlier of the low propensity to marry. People are just not getting married and that tells you something. It's the natural tendency of human beings to want to get married and establish relationships. That's not happening. The disillusionment with marriage among those who do get married is reflected in the very low rate of remarriage. When you ask people what they think about relationships, there is a high level of distrust reflected from both men and women. You get a cynicism among men and a sense of despair from women that, "I thought I was not getting into this kind of relationship again."

In certain quarters, there has been a focus and controversy on the level of misogyny that you get in the popular culture. That perhaps has gotten too much of the attention. The point is that there is a more profound problem which doesn't make the headlines. It is just the general turn-off of African-American men and women from long-term relationships.

So, Why?

If you survey African Americans, they all still idealize marriage. They'll tell you they want to get married. But, in practice, it doesn't work out. What is defined in terms of behavior is this very high rate of single living. Surveys indicate that women in particular still value and cherish the role of mother and would prefer to have that role within the framework of a marriage. But it doesn't work out, so they nonetheless recognize their desire to have children outside the context of marriage.

One common explanation for the low rate of marriage is jobless-ness, but I have a problem with that. I think employment rates are one factor, but a minor factor. The sociological evidence goes against that in that the rate of marriage does not correlate well with the rate of em-ployment. The problems of low propensity to marry and high divorce rates are as true for African Americans with jobs and with relatively high incomes as for low-income people. As a matter of fact, the rate of marriage is somewhat higher among lower-income African Americans than higher-income African Americans.

If joblessness is what accounts for low rates of marriage, high di-vorce rates, and paternal abandonment, then one would expect to see massive familial problems in other populations like India and Asia, where there are high rates of unemployment and poverty. You don't get that. As far as poverty goes, the Latino population is actually poorer in average terms than the Afro-American population. They do not reflect this. It just doesn't add up.

So, what explains this? You have to explain it interactively. It's partly a tragic consequence of adaptations to the past exigencies and the demands and the exigencies of slavery and the sharecropping era and what that did to attitudes toward childbearing. That in combina-tion with modern circumstances accounts for the present problems. A simple economic explanation or a simple explanation in terms of ghet-tos simply won't work. It just flies in the face of the facts.

Hogwash

It's more tangible to believe the problem comes from joblessness. This is the reason why there is a tendency to be very hostile to what we may call "cultural explanations" and prefer economic explanations. It is the mistaken belief that cultural explanations condemn you to view it as not much you can do, or worse, that it amounts to blaming the victim. I think that's hogwash.

If I were to say to someone who behaves in a self-destructive way, because they were abused as a child, "Look, you've got problems. You've got to see a therapist or get your act together because you're be-ing self-destructive," I'm not blaming the victim. I'm simply saying that in responding to that previous abuse, you've developed strategies of be-havior, patterns of behavior, that now results in you victimizing yourself. The analogy is direct. African Americans, I am saying, in adapting to an abusive past, developed patterns of behavior which become self-destructive and amount to self-victimization.

This is a standard explanation in other countries among radicals, for example. No one questions the concept of self-victimization as a result of adaptation to one's previous brutalization. British socialists speak of the self-victimization of the British working class as the result of their class exploitation. It's only in America that you get this nonsense about blaming the victim as soon as you mention the fact that you may have developed certain predispositions which are self-destructive.

Secondly, the view that culture cannot be changed is hogwash. In fact, it's easier to change culture, very often, than to change economic factors. Class, for example. What's class? Class, essentially, is economic inequality. Not only have we had economic inequality in this country, it's getting worse. I don't see much change there.

I've seen a lot of change in people's attitudes toward racism and attitudes toward gender. Gender was built up culturally over millennia of human history. Look what happened over the past few decades in terms of changes in gender attitudes. So it's stupid. It's simply wrong that you can't change cultures. It's easier to do that. The question is, how do you do this? How do you change attitudes? How do you change previous positions? And so on.

Are We Bringing Up Our Kids the Right Way?

Another important point: emphasizing culture does not mean washing your hands of the problem. That's how the conservatives interpret it. When a Dan Quayle says, "It's their values, their family values that are wrong," implicit in that claim is that we should wash our hands of that because there's nothing government can do about values. It's their problem. Now that kind of cultural explanation is indeed reactionary and should be condemned. When I say it has to do with predispositions, practices which are adaptations to an abusive past and which is now being self-perpetuated, I don't say wash your hands of it. I say, how are we going to change that? How we change that is by focusing on ways in which we can get to individuals when they're kids. Number one, you're now asking questions such as, "Do mothers and fathers have the opportunity and the resources to properly bring up their children? Are they bringing them up the right way?" Now, this sounds very reactionary, but I'm afraid liberals also have got to stop getting uptight about such questions, such as, "Are we bringing up our kids the right way?" We've got to start asking that kind of question.

This is the question that we not only need to ask of the poor, but also of the middle classes. When one thinks of the shootings at Columbine High School in Colorado and so on, there clearly are problems among middle-class people in the way they're bringing up their kids.

Leslie and Rich

Leslie and Rich are happily married and have three children. Leslie will soon start graduate school. Rich is finishing graduate school and works as a consultant.

We Got Pregnant

Rich: We actually met in our high school. Everybody stood outside the gym after school and just talked and all that kind of stuff. For whatever reason, Leslie didn't have practice and I didn't have practice that day, and we sat in the gym and just started talking. We probably talked for two hours. We had the same friends, we were at the same parties, we were pretty much following each other around, but we never actually ran into each other. So we started out just kind of talking and became friends. Then we started talking during school and just became closer and closer.

Leslie: We dated while we were still in school. I was dating somebody else, actually. We eventually got together and started dating and did a lot with friends. We had a great time, actually, that first summer. He was leaving for Carnegie Mellon in Pittsburgh in August. We weren't sure what was going to happen. But it worked out really well. He was great. He came home a lot and I went up a lot to visit him.

Rich: So that was two years until she finished high school, and we were on-again, off-again a little bit during that period — more on than off. Basically, then she started looking for colleges. It kind of came down to a couple of schools and Slippery Rock was one of them, and it was only an hour away from Pittsburgh.

Leslie: That was the main thing. Of course, I could say it wasn't, but it was an hour from him. It's hard to be in a long-distance relationship when you're in high school. He was five hours away. I mean, it's like almost impossible. It was really difficult. So I was ready to be with him.

Rich: When did we decide to get married? Well, I graduated in 1993 and the job market wasn't quite as sweet as it was now, at least for a chemical engineer. So I went back to the University of Pittsburgh to fill in some courses for medical school. Basically, I just kind of hung out and had fun.

Leslie: Had a good time.

Rich: And partied. And, needless to say, that leads to some consequences that are not always the greatest. In retrospect they are, but at the time it was tough. We ended up getting pregnant in February.

Leslie: I was a junior in college.

Rich: We sort of dealt with that issue from February until June and decided to get married in June. It was one of those things that was two years early. She had two more years of school. We were going to get married after that. It's not like we were planning on separating or breaking up; we were as strong as ever when that happened. So it just kind of moved up the timetable.

Leslie: We actually were talking about getting engaged. We had totally talked about it. By that point, we had been together five years and we knew. But it was really, really difficult in the transition. It's like a huge, a *huge*, life change. But we were lucky in that we knew we wanted to be together. I mean, that held us strong through the decisions that we had to make and our change in lifestyle.

In October, our son was born. Three and a half years later our second son was born. That was also the time we decided to go to graduate school. We like to do things all at once. Everyone says there's stress in life and you should do things one at a time. Well, we're the kind of people who like to have babies and go to graduate school and move all at the same time.

Rich: Just pile it all on. Get it done with and then you know it's smooth sailing from there on out.

Leslie: We don't mind it, but our parents definitely do.

I think we're just the types of people that make the best of whatever the situation is. We really make it so that it's a good situation for us. I think school was a good situation. He gave up a lot. He sacrificed a lot as far as maybe not being involved in everything that he wanted to be involved in so he could be home with the kids. But that's the choice he made as a father and as a husband. I think it really is all about the choices you make in that way. That's the way it is. Everybody interprets things in a different way, I guess. For us, we don't let the little stuff get to us, because there's a lot of little stuff. I mean, that would be insane. We really just kind of roll with it.

Really Hard to Trust

Leslie: I came from a background where my parents got divorced when I was three and I saw them both. It was a very rocky childhood overall, I would say. My mom got remarried and then got divorced again three years later. It was a very abusive relationship. Then over the next ten years she went in and out of relationships, and then finally met the man she is with now, who is wonderful and a great guy.

But I learned a lot from those experiences with her for sure because I was pretty much with her through the whole thing. Actually, I learned two things. First of all, the people that I'm attracted to are really, really nice guys for sure. I mean that's just the way it is. I'm not really attracted to the kind of people that she dated. That was a big thing.

I think the other thing that affected me the most from that situation was that it was really hard to trust, even though we met and we went through high school and college. It was really hard for me to totally commit for a long time, and to trust him enough to know that he wasn't going to leave, that I didn't need to have somebody else that was interested in me at the same time kind of thing, and to really, I guess, trust him. That's the big thing.

I think that has a lasting impact on your life and that is a big issue, because once you have kids you really have to take them into consideration as far as divorce goes. I think out of everybody in the situation, the kids get hurt the most. Both parents go either way and make their new life together, but those kids — their life is with their parents. I mean, that's their whole world and you're splitting that in half. I think that can be very difficult. But, at the same time, like I said, I've seen my mom in an abusive relationship and she really didn't have a choice as far as staying in the relationship or getting out. So I think it can go either way.

Rich: That's a good contrast because my parents have always been married; for the most part, always a stable relationship. My mom pretty much gave up everything for her kids and it was upper-middle class. So, I mean, my life was great. I guess growing up I was sort of the exact opposite. My parents have always been married and everything has always been, for the most part, happy and healthy. We kind of always had, for the most part, everything I wanted, and always had loving parents. So for me coming into a relationship, I didn't know that there was a dark side, I guess.

Leslie: I showed him the dark side. He needed some excitement!

Rich: I needed some excitement.

Leslie: That's true. I mean, we've had issues. It's funny, because he came from the upper-middle class, and I definitely came from lower economic level. My mom and I didn't have much money at all. So that was interesting as we got together. I lived on the other side of the tracks, literally.

It was like that cliché kind of thing, but it has been interesting how that's affected our relationship as far as money goes. Never having money and then having it, I'm definitely a little less likely to spend it. He's a little more likely to spend it. We kind of have to compromise. We were so different growing up; maybe that's why it works for us.

Rich: I was very sheltered. She brought me out of the shade and into the sunlight.

Blow Up and Lose It Completely

Leslie: How did we learn to handle differences? Actually, it's been an evolution for us, I think. We've been together so long; we've grown up together, basically. We've learned from each other what works and what doesn't work.

In the beginning of our relationship, when I'd get angry, I would blow up. I'm the type of person that would let it grow and grow and grow, and then I lose it completely. I would start screaming, and he'd completely tune me out. Then I'd get even madder, because he's not communicating with me, and I'd have a burning need to communicate at that moment and he won't. So then I learned through time and arguments — which, really, we don't fight very often — but I learned the best approach is to, you know, sit down and talk to him when I'm not angry, which is hard. It's hard to bury that long enough to get calmed down, and to say, "this is really hurting me."

Rich: I've learned the power of the statement, "Yeah, sure, whatever." That drives her up the wall. That's sort of what came out in the beginning of our relationship, when she would just blow up and I would just sit there. That's kind of what drove her, I guess, to change the way she argues. For me, I probably still go about it wrong.

Erin

Erin is a single mother. She says you shouldn't get married just because you have a child.

I'm eighteen years old, and I am a single mom of a two-and-a-half-year-old son. The father and I are no longer together, but we're still close, and he still keeps in contact with him. I've been on and off dating other people for about two years now.

I had never thought you should get married because you have a child. You should get married because you're happy. And, I was fifteen when I got pregnant, so then I wasn't ready to get married. And, I don't know if in the future, or what will happen, but as of right now I'm not, like, looking forward to a marriage commitment.

Larry Bumpass

*Larry Bumpass is a professor of sociology at the University of
Wisconsin in Madison, Wisconsin. He says the trends regarding
divorce, unwed pregnancy, and nonmarriage go as far back as the
1800s and are rooted in individualism.*

What's Going On?

I think it's widely recognized that there's an enormous amount of
change going on in just about every domain of family life. I think it's
useful to try to understand how the various changes are occurring
rather than to focus just on one in particular.

The story that ought to be told and understood is that these
changes are part of a long-term evolution of our economy, our culture,
and our society. They are not the result of some recent policy change,
welfare, divorce law, or what have you, as we often hear in the press and
from various interest groups. There's a lot of public discussion about
what it means for family values, the stability of the family, and the lives
of children. I think it's extremely important to put them in the context,
both historical and international context.

What's going on in the United States is not at all unique to this
country. The basic trends in cohabitation, unmarried childbearing, and
divorce are shared by virtually every Western industrial society. These
are changes whose roots reach well back into our history. They're part
of the evolution of our society and our economy. They're tied very
much to the growing individualism that is linked with a modern industrial market economy.

The Most Critical Underlying Dynamic

I think it's useful to start with divorce, simply as an example of a couple of major issues that are a part of this long-term evolution. The first, quite simply, is that our current high levels of divorce — which are on the order of one of every two marriages end in divorce — these current high levels of divorce are part of a long-term trend that reaches well back into the 1800s. There are fluctuations around those trends, periods of relative quiet and plateaus; then there are rapid increases and sometimes decreases.

It's clear that where we are now is part of this long-term trend. This is important for illustrating the most critical underlying dynamic. That is tied with the individualism, and it becomes increasingly legitimate for individuals in our society to make decisions based on what they judge to be their own self-interest.

Divorce is a critical test case in that regard, because without being involved in judgmental decisions, it's clearly a case where parents are deciding that because of their own happiness or unhappiness with their marriage that they're willing to break it up and create a single-parent family for their children. Indeed, one of the things that will weave this story together is that divorce itself and the high levels that we've experienced involves the creation of single-parent families *by choice.* That sets an enormity of context, if you will, that becomes important when we look at things like unmarried childbearing, which is also the establishment of single-parent families by choice. So as the stigma with respect to divorce has declined that begins to have an effect on these other parts of family life.

In earlier times, for whatever reasons, there was much more a sense of an obligation to a collectivity. The decisions one makes have to be made in terms of implications and the expectations of the larger society, and progressively narrowing down to one's individual family. Now it's increasingly to one's own individual perceived needs. We believe that people have a right to make decisions that are in their best interest, and this is not necessarily selfishness or such things but represents other concepts that we value.

The underlying themes of moving away from social expectations about how one ought to behave with respect to family patterns is really a part of the basic dynamic. Many people have talked about that in terms of a decreasing willingness to make long-term commitments and a decreasing willingness to hold to them once they're made. Of course, both of those patterns are illustrated in cohabitation.

Emphasis on Individualism

The important components of this are a decreased willingness to make long-term commitments and/or to hold to them once they're made. This is part of the emphasis on individualism that's tied to our economy, but it's also tied to particular traditions, cultural traditions emphasizing individualism that themselves reach well back into the 1800s.

You read commentators in the late 1800s who complain about how people were becoming increasingly individualistic and no longer honoring their obligations. You think of Confucian Japan as such a collective society, but when I'm at meetings with my Japanese colleagues I hear them complaining about the increasing individualism of young people.

So I really think it's built into the structure of a market economy that puts people in social environments that are not defined in terms of families. In competitive environments they are defined in terms of individual abilities and individual achievements. Industries or workplaces are not attuned to family needs, but rather to the production of the individual. All of this, I think, ties together in this increasing emphasis on individualism. It's not easy or even possible to put your finger on a single cause.

I, again, would emphasize that this is experienced in virtually every Western industrial society. The increased unmarried childbearing, increased cohabitation, increased divorce, span all of Europe from not only Sweden, where you might expect it, but to Italy and Spain in the south with every country in between. It's also happening in Canada, New Zealand, and Australia.

We're Not Alone

We've talked about divorce as illustrative of this process, but I would step back now and think through a series of other changes. A very important perspective on family change is to realize that this is not something that is limited to one area of family life. There are changes occurring in a wide number of domains of family life, and each of these have implications for and have effects on the changes occurring elsewhere.

One of the most productive places to start is simply to recognize that there have been very dramatic changes in the sexual experience of young people in this society. Moving away from old normative expectations, at least, if not always honored in fact, that sex was to be confined to marriage, we now live in a society where virtually all teenagers leave their teenage years having experienced sexual intercourse. Marriage is being delayed. Now we live in a society where a high proportion of young adults in their twenties are acknowledged to be sexually active and unmarried. I think that has a pretty dramatic effect on our culture and society as we see it even in the mass media.

An extremely important part of understanding these trends as being driven by similar forces is to recognize that there's no reason to expect the changes to be the same everywhere, either in their timing or in the levels they reach. It's long been understood that Scandinavia was way ahead of the United States, if that's the right word, with respect to high levels of cohabitation, high levels of unmarried childbearing. But even in Scandinavia there's been a sharp trend increasing in those respects. If you look at changes in the U.S., we are now at levels of cohabitation that were once the case in Scandinavia, let's say, three decades ago. So it remains the case that Scandinavia is the leader with respect to these trends. More or less as you move south across Europe, both the timing and the levels decrease.

We don't expect the same results in every country, but there is this pattern across Europe where the rates of unmarried childbearing and cohabitation tend to be highest in Scandinavia and lowest in southern Europe. There's a distribution across Europe, where they're in middle levels in, say, Germany and France, and the U.S. is pretty much in that group in the middle. We would have levels of cohabitation similar to Great Britain, very similar to France. But the important point is that we're not unique.

The other thing I would emphasize is that every country in Europe has experienced increases. That is to say, the direction of change is the same. This is particularly remarkable in some of the southern European countries. We've not talked about levels of childbearing themselves, but fertility has dropped very dramatically. People thought it simply would not occur. But in Catholic Spain and Italy, all of a sudden fertility began to drop and is exceedingly low. Surely in those countries one would not expect increases in divorce or increases in couples living together outside of marriage. But that's exactly what we're seeing now. They're at their lowest levels in Europe, but nonetheless they too are increasing.

So, when we come back to "Why is this happening?" there's no simple story. But there's a story that can be woven together that I think makes some sense.

What about the Children?

Some people say children may be upset for a little while, but they get over it. That would be very nice, but it's not true. Divorce is something that stays in one way or another with somebody through their entire life.

DAVID ROYKO

I was also thinking . . . "Oh, I hate you Mom. Dad, why are you doing this to me?"

ABE

Sometimes I tell parents, "Well, when your daughter gets married, where do you think you're going to sit at the church?"

JUDGE HELEN E. BROWN

People would say, "You should stay together for your kids." That used to make me so angry. Stay in a marriage where I'm not happy, for my child — then what am I teaching her?

CHRISTINA

Both my parents remarried and they both married people that I like a lot. My mom and stepdad had a baby, so now I have another little brother that I love a lot. Those are really good things.

ABBIE

We had children who had never been hungry in their lives who were suddenly frightened that they would starve to death, that they would wake up in the morning and there would be nobody to take care of them.

JUDITH WALLERSTEIN

Sometimes divorce is the best solution to a broken marriage, but it is never easy. Still, as time goes on, most adults build new lives and look ahead to happier times. It doesn't work that way for children. Their families are their lives and their happiness.

In 1969, the state of California kicked off the divorce revolution with the passage of the nation's first no-fault divorce law. This law eliminated the old requirement that a divorcing couple had to identify one or the other spouse as responsible, or at fault, for the divorce. By the end of the 1970s, virtually all fifty states had adopted laws that watered down or did away with fault provisions. At the time, reformers thought they were making life better by making it easier to get out of a bad marriage. Nobody was thinking about how tough life could be for kids when their parents divorced.

But even in the best cases, for children divorce means the loss of the family. And in many cases, as Judge Helen E. Brown knows all too well, it is a stranger in a black robe who begins to make decisions about the children's daily lives — where they will live, who they will see on holidays, and who will pay for their support.

For most children of divorce, the hurt, anger, and fear subside over time. Many go on to lead happy and successful lives. But the memory of divorce lingers. It is hard for adult children of divorce to shake the feeling that just when they least expect it, their lives could suddenly come apart again.

Blake

Blake is a graduate student at the University of Chicago. He broke up with his girlfriend eight months ago after dating her for two and a half years and says that his parents' divorce has made it harder to think of marriage as something worth taking a chance on.

What Happened?

Probably eight months ago, she wanted more of a commitment from me. In my mind, I was committed. We were together, we were dating, we lived together, I was very happy, and she was very happy. But she wanted a verbal commitment from me that I wanted to spend the rest of my life with her. In my point of view, if I were going to say that, then I would buy a ring and get engaged. But from her point of view, just hearing those words and knowing that in a few years, three years maybe, we'd get engaged and then married, that would be fine for her. But I wasn't ready to say that and I graduate in two months. So it started to get to a timeline where when Blake graduates, is he going to go to California to work? Is he going to go to Texas to work? Stay in Chicago? There were just a lot of questions there, and she wanted an answer, which I totally understand her point of view. But I wasn't ready to say those words or to get engaged. So she decided to go back home to Florida where her family and friends are.

My Family

My family has been very supportive. I am the youngest of four children and my oldest brother is thirty-seven. He's been good to talk to and he has two children of his own. My parents, who are in their mid-sixties now, are divorced. They were married for thirty years. Getting advice from my parents has been great. It's actually opened up my relationship with my mother and my father as well. Not so much telling me to do this or do that, but just give me a different perspective. Hearing it from their voice, from a parent, more so than, say, a book or a show that I watch.

My parents were married early, age eighteen and nineteen. They're both from small towns in Ohio. They had their four children. When I was growing up, there were a lot of arguments. In the early 1980s when they were divorced, it wasn't as common. I don't know the facts. But I know a lot of people maybe would stay together for the children. I know my parents definitely did, but then it got to a point where they couldn't any more. Initially and for about five years there was a lot of bitterness between my parents. Now they're friends, and they have the grandchildren. My sister was married five years ago, and they were there and friendly. So it's definitely healthy for the grandchildren. You're right, thirty years is a big section of their lives.

I didn't like the arguing that I would always hear as a child. I didn't like that. It was hard, because we had a nice home in the country in Michigan and then when my parents divorced we couldn't afford to have the house. My father went to an apartment and my mother and my brother and I went to a neighbor's house. We could see our old house across the street. It was just hard. It was hard for me, my brother, and for my mother. Then my father moved to Washington, D.C., where he took a job. Then the distance wasn't easy.

Has my parents' divorce made it hard to think of marriage as something worth taking a chance on? Definitely. I think there's two ways to think about it. I say to myself, "my parents are divorced, so maybe I know things not to do." But then again, being in a family where parents are together and very happy, I think it's very good to see that. But my parents, as far as raising us children, that was their number one priority. I think their relationship suffered because of that. I definitely am maybe a bit more cautious than most people in the fact that my parents were divorced.

Abe

Abe is a high school student whose parents recently divorced. He was relieved that the bickering might stop but felt that his family was "dead."

Remember the Day Your Parents Told You about the Divorce?

It was a few days before Christmas 1999. I'd sort of known. There were stirrings. A few months before, my Mom was really, really upset this one day. I didn't even ask her. She just sort of told me. She just said, "You know, I think Dad wants a divorce or wants to be separated." I didn't really, for some reason, take it that seriously. I don't know whether I was denying it or I couldn't believe it, but it didn't really register for me. I thought, well, you know, they'll work it out. They always have.

But then, when they actually told my sister and I, I didn't know how to respond. I felt really stupid. I just sort of sat there. I didn't say anything. It didn't seem like a response that was totally true. I wasn't completely dumbfounded by it. I just didn't really feel like saying anything about it.

Even then, it didn't seem to totally register, because they were still together. I mean, for like two months after that we were still technically a family. When they immediately told me, I just didn't really do anything about it. I don't know. I was being really reflexive. I wasn't being proactive about it, like making my opinions known, because I didn't really have any.

There was so much going on inside of me. There were feelings of, "Well, I'm glad this has happened," like a relief, because my parents had never really been totally, you know, I never really perceived them as a really great couple. Looking back, I was relieved that maybe now the constant bickering and yelling would stop.

I was also thinking sort of the automatic response I guess like everyone's supposed to have: "Oh, no, this is horrible. My family is dead." Thinking, "Oh, I hate you Mom. Dad, why are you doing this to me?" I don't know. It seemed like I couldn't really discern what I was really feeling and what I was supposed to feel. It just seemed so, like, empty. It seemed like just something that was happening, and I came to the emotional response. I can't even remember how I felt. I felt upset, but relieved, but angry, and I don't know. It was just so much that I can't really boil it all down.

If Everyone Could Redo That Conversation

I think they handled it the best they could. I was sort of irritated with my mom for a good long period, because she was always saying how we're going to survive this: "We're strong. We're survivors, and I'm a survivor. It'll be horrible, but it'll be okay in the end." I felt like I wasn't thinking it was going to be that horrible, and saying it was going to be horrible didn't really help a whole lot.

My dad seemed sort of hard to communicate about it. I didn't really get why it was all happening. My mom had sort of told me a lot of times about why things were going wrong, but my dad just seemed really distant about it. I remember having lunch with him one time before they told us that they were going to be separated, and he asked me what I thought he could be doing better, or what was wrong with the way he was handling his role in the family. I told him a lot of things, but I felt I wasn't getting a lot back from him. Even now, I'm sort of just confused about that.

I don't know. I think that maybe they could have told me, given me at least some idea of why it was happening. Also, try and at least to give an objective response, not sort of the subjective response of, "I'm really upset, and so you're all going to be upset too." But really, I don't think I can complain too much. I mean, there are much worse ways to do it. I think they handled it pretty well. You know, I'm fine with it.

Surprised?

I remember having a lot of memories of my parents yelling at each other. I'm thinking, "Why don't they just get divorced?" It just seemed like — I know it sounds bad, but it just seemed like, why the heck are they even bothering? I mean, from my perspective, it seemed like they just didn't like each other that much. It seemed like they were pretty good friends, but it seemed like they bickered and yelled at each other so much and hated so many elements of each other's personalities. I just never really understood how they were ever really a good match. So when it happened, I was not that surprised. I mean, like I said, in a lot of ways I was relieved.

I think that was one of the main things I was feeling and feeling right now: "it seems fine." Obviously, they yell at each other a good bit, because they have to be dealing with each other so much and it's such a difficult thing for them. I know it's immensely more difficult for them than it is for me and my sister, but it really doesn't seem like a whole lot has changed, and the things that have changed have changed for the better. At least for me personally. I don't know about my parents.

One thing about all of this is that there really hasn't been a huge gigantic adjustment. I really don't have that many memories of them really being together. It just seems like I was always with one of them. The other was working, or I was involved in doing something, like a project or some issue with one of them, and the other was sort of a nonplayer. It seems that that's the way it is now. I don't think my sister changed that much either, and it's not like we had to completely adjust to something totally new. I mean, it wasn't anything that new.

Advice for Other Kids?

I'm not a psychologist. I don't know this stuff. It's not like I've researched this. I only know from my personal experience. I'd just say don't submit to sort of the television sitcom response, which is being really mad or sad. Just go with what you feel and don't be afraid to communicate that to your parents, or to somebody. If you just keep it all bottled up inside, then nothing's going to get better at all.

I think the most important thing you can do if you're a parent and you're telling your children that you're going to be separating is just listen. I can't stress enough just how important being a parent and listening is, at least in my opinion. Just communicate and listen to them. Never just dismiss what they say. Understand that they are feeling a certain way. If they feel bad about something, communicate with them and then try and help them work through it by listening.

Anything Good about the Divorce?

I think there really is. There's a lot that's good about it. I just think they're two amazingly good people. I really think they're awesome. I mean, they're just spectacular members of the human race in so many respects. I just don't think they were a good couple, at least in my experience with them.

It was like they just really never seemed to show any real love toward each other. I just don't have any memories of them going up and saying, "I really love you," or being really intimately close at any time. It just seems that they were just sort of there because they had to be, at least by the time I was there. So I think there's this release now. They don't have to be totally committed to each other. They're still amazing human beings, they're just not being dampened by having to argue with each other about, "Why weren't you here at six o'clock last night when we were eating dinner?" It seems like petty things that were just not necessary in any of our lives.

Also, I don't have to deal with the stress as much anymore. I mean, oh, great, my parents are fighting again. I've got to go up in my room and just sit there; I can't come downstairs 'cause then I'll have to get involved. They'll be asking me, "Oh, well, don't you think he's an idiot?" or, "Well, don't you think she's being irrational?" I don't want to be in the middle of any of that. I think that's benefited me a whole lot.

It's really taught me a lot of things about the world and about love and marriage that I didn't know before that are really helpful for me to know — like, if you really love somebody you have to communicate with them a lot. You really need to decide whether you really belong together as a couple and that not everything is going happen the way it seems. I seem to have learned so much. Things are just so much easier now for me, at least at this point. I don't know. I could be repressing a lot of things, but I don't know.

What Does It Take to Have a Successful Marriage?

Jeez. Right when they told me that is all I could think about. How did my parents' marriage fail? I talked to my parents about that somewhat and they were not very helpful because they really did not understand either. Even before they got married, they'd been living together for a good long while and it's not like this was something they were rushing into — they went to counseling to make sure it would be a good marriage. But it seemed like none of that really mattered in the end.

That just really frightens me. I don't think there is any way to know that you have a good marriage. I mean, there are ways to know if you have a bad marriage. I mean, if you never talk to each other, or if it's an abusive relationship, then you know something's wrong. But if everything seems fine, that doesn't necessarily mean that everything is fine. If you get into these low undercurrents, where you don't even notice them until they've built up to the point where you can't go back and fix them anymore, you just have to end it. I don't want to go to that point, and I'm afraid that I will. So, I'm afraid for everybody that that might happen. I mean, there seems like there's no way to know. There are no guarantees at all.

It seems that there's no way at all to know what the future is going to bring in a marriage. My parents are perfect examples that it really doesn't mean anything in the end if you can't stand being together anymore. You just have to separate. There are just no guarantees at all. It's a total gamble. It all seems arbitrary. It's just like a flip of the coin. Or at least it seems that way from my parents. That may just be me with my emotional baggage, but it just seems that that's the way it is with marriage.

Sandy

Sandy is the mother of four children and is seeking a divorce after fifteen years of marriage. She sees troubling changes in all four of her children.

What Happened?

I was married at nineteen. He was thirty-six. I don't know; I suppose that he's content with his life as it is and feels that there's nothing wrong with his behavior. There just came a day when I looked in the mirror and could not, in good conscience, call myself any kind of good parent or good person to allow my children to continue to be exposed to the kind of behavior that he continues to try to justify.

Now?

I feel as if the weight of the world has been lifted off my shoulders. All I have now is the wreckage left for our kids. Since the separation, I've cried more for the children. The tears I've shed for the relationship, I've shed already. When it comes to the tears I shed, most were tears of frustration, wanting something that he was unwilling to give, wasn't able to give. I don't know. I don't really have tears left anymore. I'm done with those tears. Now the tears are for the kids.

They are breaking down under the pressure. My oldest son is very, very angry. I can see him exhibiting a lot of the same controlling behavior and a lot of the same anger as my husband. My oldest daughter is in enormous trouble at school and legally. She is just acting out in every which way, everything that she can do at this point. Running away, substance abuse, and who knows? She's making some real dangerous choices right now. My other daughter, who is eleven and was always my sunshine girl — sweet, loving — is hateful and spiteful and has turned into really a completely different personality. My youngest, who is seven and obviously still very young, has become very unmanageable — just will not comply. Simple things like, "Please pick up your toy" — he kicks, he spits, he bites. It's real scary. It's real scary.

I've got them in counseling, although, when one doesn't have money, one's counseling options become very limited. I'm trying to work because there isn't any other way to really get the things that the kids need other than for me to be working. So it's quite a challenge right now, although I am nothing if not persistent and tenacious. I will get them the help they need.

We'll do whatever it takes. On a daily basis, I just remind myself that it's not personal, that these kids don't hate me, although every outward appearance would certainly reinforce that. But they're kids. They don't have the capacity.

I'm a grown-up. My marriage didn't work out. Bummer, big deal. But the kids have a whole lot more issues because it is not something in their mind that they can separate. They're part of their mom, and they're part of their dad. When Mom and Dad split, I think even in the best of cases, it creates a tremendous conflict for a kid.

When one parent berates and downgrades another, what you're doing is you're actually downgrading that child. You're insulting that child, you're insulting who they are. Because they are as much a part of me as they are him. You can't denigrate one parent without causing very serious harm to that child.

Judith Wallerstein

Judith Wallerstein is a family researcher and founder of the Judith Wallerstein Center for the Family in Transition in Corte Madera, California. She has studied six thousand children of divorce over the last thirty years and says that divorce is entirely different in the life of a child than in the life of an adult.

The Great Celebration

In 1969, California, which is a flagship state in family law, passed the first no-fault divorce law. It was developed out of a consortium of the right and the left. The law was written as a result of several task forces, the last one headed by a woman who was a leading feminist and law professor, and it was signed by Ronald Reagan. It was a day of great celebration in California because it would end trouble in marriage: People who had made a mistake could leave the marriage. They would obviously agree quietly and happily. Remarkably, there was no consideration, despite all the task forces, about how this major piece of family legislation would impact on children. You know, I can't believe it. It's a major part of history that shows how little we consider the impact of so much of legislation and so much of social change on the family and especially on children, who unfortunately don't vote.

There was a general feeling that people shouldn't be yoked together for life in a miserable marriage and they shouldn't have to lie their way into court — hire a blonde so they could take pictures of adultery, hire somebody else who would testify about whatever; that the hypocrisy surrounding divorce, which you could only get for adultery, or for many years of abandonment and the suffering attached to that, was something that people from the right and the left agreed on was no good. No-fault divorce meant that if both agreed, or even one person agreed, that the marriage was not good, that legally it couldn't possibly be good. In other words, a marriage that de facto wasn't working should be dissolved and freely, with no accusations, and no meanness, and no fighting, and no whatever. It spread like wildfire throughout the fifty states.

Now, divorce is not necessarily caused by no-fault divorce. Divorce was rising and divorce has many very complicated routes. But the expression of the community and the change in the legislation came first in California.

Ringside Seat

I happened to come to California at that historic time, where I was in a ringside seat at a community mental health center. We got many telephone calls all of a sudden from agitated parents saying, "What am I going to do about my children? My husband and I have divorced, or are divorcing, and the children are aggressive. They're crying. They're acting up. They're not going to sleep. They're behaving in ways I've never seen before." The nursery school teacher called saying, "We don't know what to do." The calls came around preschool children. We looked at each other. It was a highly trained professional staff. I went to the library, being a scholar at heart, and I discovered that lo and behold there was no research, none, on the impact of divorce on children, despite, and I say ironically, our major efforts to change the family. We hadn't looked at this.

We saw children who were very frightened. There were sleep disturbances. Children who had never been particularly aggressive in elementary school and in preschool were hitting other children. The nursery school teachers and the elementary school teachers are saying these kids are out of control, and the only change that occurred in their lives had been the divorce of their parents.

We asked these parents to bring the children in, and we decided, at that point, to look at it. I went to a local foundation and said, "Look, this is where we are. Nobody's looked at any of this. We can't give these people advice. We don't know what to do. We have no clinical experience with it. We have no research experience."

I didn't have a lot of money, but enough. I hired some really experienced clinicians and I invited lawyers to send us families, and in return we would talk to the parents and hear them out. That's how the whole California Children of Divorce project started. The project is still the only one of its kind in the world.

We saw the mother and the father and the children at the time of the breakup, and before the legal divorce. We interviewed each family for sixteen hours at that time and recorded faithfully, and we really learned what the tremendous impact was that divorce was having on the children.

The Scaffolding of Their Lives

The children had a sense of loss, and anger at their parents. Their great fear was that they would be abandoned. I mean, this is a wealthy country. We had largely middle-class children who had never been hungry in their lives who were suddenly afraid that they would starve to death, that they would wake up in the morning and there would be nobody to take care of them. They were overwhelmed with frightening fantasies that had to do with the fear that the scaffolding of their lives was collapsing under them.

So we decided to take children aged three to sixteen, and we went back a year later. Since I was very much in accord with community opinion, I had no reason to doubt it. I thought everything would be fine. Okay, so the kids were upset, but they would be over with it. I mean, a year is a long time in the life of a four year old. It's 25 percent of her life, right?

Lo and behold, the children were worse. Parents were more worried. There were economic problems which were beginning to surface which people hadn't expected. Child support wasn't paid automatically. Parent-child relationships changed a lot.

This was one of our major findings, that divorce is a focal point of change in parent-child relationships because the adults are putting their lives together. That's very different than parents in an established family, who have made the decisions of their lives. I mean, these people are human beings. They're out looking for a new man, a new woman, a new love, a better love, and a more constant relationship. That's a time-consuming process. You're a little bit out of sync.

The children, who were born into an intact marriage and where the future was clear, are suddenly regarded as an obstacle, to be perfectly honest, to your need to put your life together. I get up in the morning because I have to take care of Mary Jane, otherwise I'd lie in bed. So the child assumes a whole new psychological meaning for the adult that the same child, at the same age, doesn't have in an intact, functioning family. And the children were aware of diminished parenting. They, in turn, became more frightened, crankier, more demanding, more difficult. The parents became more impatient. They had less reserves of energy. And they didn't have each other.

Diminished Parenting

Let me give you an example. You have a child in a functioning family, when suddenly there's a crisis in the family. Often divorce doesn't follow a long period of unhappiness. There are a lot of myths about it. Often divorce doesn't occur under conflict conditions. It occurs if there's a crisis. It occurs because there's been a death in the family, and people suddenly need more from each other than they've been able to give before. It occurs because of an economic crisis. Divorce rises when there's unemployment, because the difficulties ricochet into the family.

But most of the children have no idea that there were difficulties in the family, and that's still true. Now, when people are throwing dishes, or when they're hurting each other, they surely do, and they know it with great suffering. They may not necessarily be in favor of the divorce — children rarely vote for divorce — but they know that there's trouble.

Most of the children of divorce that I've seen — and I've seen overall over six thousand children at our center — do not know that there is a divorce coming down the pipe. So if you have a child in a middle-class family, often the mom is not working full-time, especially if that child is the third child in the family. When the child comes home from school, Mom's at home. Often this is a mom in a family where the mom's a volunteer in school. I mean, mothers put in endless hours volunteering and being part of their children's life. They fetch, they carry, they take the child to ballet lessons, piano lessons, marionette, whatever, library. Suddenly, that mom is in the marketplace. She's gone back to school.

This one little girl told me that at age four she used to sit outside the bathroom door, which her mother would lock. Her mother would be in there studying for an exam that she was going to have the next day. The only peace and quiet the mom could have from the three children would be locking herself in the bathroom. The child would sit cross-legged outside the bathroom door, waiting for the mother to come out. This was a child who had been the center of her mother's life and the father's life. The father had an economic crisis. He disappeared, really, in great crisis, and in great trouble. The mom was out working during the day and going to school at night. When I saw the little girl, she said to me, "I'm looking for a mommy. I need a new mommy."

That's a difference in a child's life. That is different. Is it poor parenting? I hate to call that poor parenting. It's diminished parenting. It's tragically diminished parenting. But this is clearly a mother and a father who under other circumstances were both devoted to this child. So it's a crisis in the parents' lives. It's not an easy-come, easy-go decision, which then reverberates into the child's life. It is experienced by the child as an abandonment.

Festering

I was able to keep this project going for twenty-five years, so these children who started it from ages three to sixteen years are now twenty-eight to forty-three, and I've known them all through this period. I've become sort of the tribal elder in their lives. I was there at all the major battles.

Why don't they get over it, because the divorced family is changed? This is a very important myth. It is not one divorce from which the child recovers. That probably would happen. Of my hundred children, only seven children had a mother and a father, both of whom had one, happy, stable remarriage. For most of the children in this study, and for most children, it's not one episode. It's not that easy in the middle of your life for two adults to put their lives together in remarriage.

One of the terribly sad findings is that the incidence of divorce and remarriage in subsequent marriages is much higher than in first marriages. But the original rationale was that people would undo the mistake of the first marriage and do it better. Well, that rationale didn't hold against real life. In real life, the second marriage collapsed faster. Men married much faster than women. So the children saw their father remarried, and then that second marriage collapsed, and there was a third marriage. So all along, the child had to get used to a stepmother, and then another stepmother. Only half of the women in my group re-married. Many of them re-divorced, but even those who didn't remarry had lots of boyfriends, their lovers. These people aren't children; they're adults. They're looking for a good sex life. They're looking for intimacy. They're looking for friendship. They all dread loneliness.

So I've called the post-divorce family porous. The walls of the family are not as clearly closed. More people come and go and life is different and harder to adjust to for the child of divorce, not only at the time of the breakup but all through. Now, where you have a really good re-marriage, that child recovers. But it's not that common a situation for it to be a good remarriage for the mom which also includes the child in the orbit. Many of the kids say to me that, "He's really good for my mom, but it doesn't matter for me."

Preschoolers: "Will I Be Alone?"

The age of the child at the time of the divorce is critical in terms of the child's experience and in terms of the response of the child. All children react in terms of being afraid. "What's going to happen to me? How is this going to affect my future? Who will take care of me?" But they re-act differently.

There are many differences by age and some by gender in terms of how children react at the time of the breakup. All of the preschool children are symptomatic, because for them there's often a disruption of physical care as well as the sense of the world becoming an unreliable place. They don't know what's going to happen and who will take care of them. They are afraid; they're genuinely fearful in a very concrete way that if one parent can leave another, what is to keep both parents from leaving them? And the logic is irrefutable. They develop a whole rash of sleep symptoms, because if I lay me down to sleep, who will be here? When I wake up in the morning, I will be alone. They lose what-ever their latest civilized achievement is. If it is toilet training, if it's go-ing to nursery school, if it's being able to spend some time alone, what-ever it is, there is regression. There's crankiness and irritability that drives their poor parents crazy, but it derives from the children's anxiety.

There is the sense in the preschool children that they did it. They do not understand logic and cause and effect — that the sun rises and sets. I mean, the sun rises and sets because Mom says so, and so on. And the issue of, "If I was naughty, or my dog was naughty," and, over and over again, "I didn't tell Daddy what I was supposed to, I didn't give Daddy the message that Mom gave me and that's why they broke up." I mean, the saddest reasons from these little kids who suffered the pangs of hell for having caused this rift and then felt helpless to remedy it. There was nothing they could do.

Often, of course, when the parents aren't getting along they will fight over the child. They will say, "You are responsible," "You're responsible." That just gives validity to the child's sense that "I did it." They suffer a lot in this blaming themselves. I mean, this is serious. I have children drawing themselves in the examining room, drawing themselves sinking into quicksand and so on, because they feel that they are so naughty.

So you are getting strong reactions, which can be taken care of fairly quickly if you restore care, you spend some time putting that child to bed, you say to the child a thousand and one times in many different ways, "I'm going to be here. Daddy's going to be here," you take the child to see where Daddy is living. It is terribly important. Because otherwise the vision is of Daddy like a Chagall figure flying over the roof. We don't have children who understand time or latitude or longitude. Five blocks is forever. I've had children who come back from a visit where they touch everything in the house to make sure it is still there. We are looking at a sense of reliability in the child that's been disrupted.

Ages Six and Seven: "A New Dog, a New Little Boy"

As we go up the developmental ladder to children of ages six and seven, the emphasis changes to the fear of being replaced, which is very sad. "Where is Daddy?" is a serious issue. Since daddies come in families, an issue I kept hearing over and over again was, "Is my daddy going to get a new mommy, a new dog, a new little boy?" So you are not dealing so much with the immediate feeling of abandonment, but "Where is my daddy? Will I see him? Just because I saw him last week, will I see him this week? And even if I see him every three days, am I sure that I am going to see him?" So the fear of loss of the mom or the dad is there; the little girls, who make wonderful use of what I call "Madame Butterfly fantasies": some day when he grows up, he will come back to me.

Ages Nine and Ten: "I'm Busy"

Nine or ten year olds are getting angry. The anger is that the parent is so selfish. "I need my parents to keep my life going. I'm busy on base-ball. I'm busy on the playground. I'm busy going to school. I'm busy. I'm busy. Why can't they just keep things stable and together, and why are they so selfish and preoccupied with their needs?" Obviously there are many differences among children. I'm talking in general.

Adolescents: "I Paid for My Parents' Divorce"

The adolescent says, "Who's going to take me to college? Who's going to send me to college?" Child support ends legally at age eighteen, and it's a very, very serious problem for these kids, because when they reached age eighteen, very few of them had the money for college. Only 30 percent of these middle-class children, sons and daughters of doctors and lawyers and business chiefs, had really substantial financial help with their college education. Across the street, kids in the same neighborhood from intact families who were their friends in high school, 90 percent of those children had substantial help from their families when they went to college. So that when these children reached age eighteen and were legally adults, they couldn't go out into the world with high-level skills from a high school. They said, "I paid for my parents' divorce," and they were appropriately grieved and un-fairly treated.

In adolescents, what you are also getting is a tremendous fear that what happened to my parents is going to happen to me. "Will my relationships fail?" What you are getting in early adolescence — real early, like eleven and twelve, especially among girls, but not only among girls — is taking over the care of the whole family, and giving up any responsiveness to their own needs. Doing so willingly, and doing so gladly, to take care of sometimes both parents, sometimes their siblings, but making sacrifices which they can ill afford of their childhood.

You get a lot of acting out during adolescence: "The day I discovered my mom's affair was the day I started my sex life." Thus, the very high level of sexual behavior — partly, again, because parents are not supervising as strictly as before. Adolescents need to feel there is somebody to fight with; they do not want to come home to an empty house. As a matter of fact, one of the youngsters in the study said to me, "Coming home to an empty house was how I got into drugs and sex."

It's Not Just Childhood

I've come to the conclusion that the major impact of divorce is really in adulthood. The early reaction is very painful, but it fades after a few years if the family is reasonably functioning. The average number of years it takes is about three and a half or four years, something like that. But the major impact of divorce on the child is in adulthood, when the man-woman relationship moves center stage.

Divorce isn't any old crisis. It's not a tornado. It's not a death in the family. It's a very specific crisis of the breakdown of the relationship between the main man and the main woman in the child's life. Children, I've come to the conclusion, identify not only with their mom and their dad as people, as we've generally accepted, but they clearly internalize the relationship between them. They spend all their time observing the relationship between them. I know all the details, especially from the children in the intact families that I interviewed, about how Mom and Dad get along. Do they kiss each other? Does he pinch her? Do they dance? Are they angry? Do they talk? Do they fight in the open? Do they fight behind closed doors? When the bedroom door closes, does that mean they are fighting? Or are they making love? So that's a tremendous source of knowledge for any growing child. They spend their whole life studying that.

There is nothing they study in school that they look at as carefully as they do the man-woman relationship in their family. Their parents may have successfully decided to divorce, it may have been the best decision of their lives. From the child's perspective, they failed. It's very hard for grown-ups to realize. It doesn't mean they've failed, it means from their child's perspective they failed. From their child's perspective they failed to keep it together. She failed to keep the man; he failed to keep the lady. And they failed in their child's view at one of the major tasks of life and, for the young adult's view, the major task at that point.

They have trouble in their third decade of life, in their twenties, in knowing what they are looking for in a man or a woman, in believing that they can keep it together, in believing that they can have a lasting relationship. Their fear of failure is very powerful — as powerful (and this is their conflict) as their intense wish to do better than their parents did.

Disassociate and Say, "I'm Me"

The tremendous inner conflict does and doesn't get resolved. This is their task in their twenties. They have to take that inner image of a failed man-woman relationship and disassociate themselves from it and give themselves another shot. They say, "I'm going to do it my way. I'm not my mom. I'm not my dad. I'm me." They acquire hope and confidence also from other arenas in their lives. So they have to learn from their own experience.

They are remarkable, really, in that they do for themselves what children really have a right to expect from their parents. They create their own morality. As one young person said to me, "Both my parents lied and cheated. I decided I'm never going to lie." They create their own morality, and many of them have a really very high morality. As one young woman said to me, "Sometimes I feel that I was brought up on a desert island. The idea of sex and love and intimacy all together is a strange idea to me. The guys I have a good time with, I really don't even like." But they put it together by the time they're thirty, thirty-one, or thirty-two. It takes them longer to grow up. They do it themselves, or it's the luck of the draw. They meet somebody. People change a lot in adulthood. They just don't grow up in childhood.

Lightning Striking Twice

The other residue in adulthood, which surprised me, because I didn't expect it, is the fact that almost all, and I say this very carefully, of the children of divorce, as adults, suffered with a residue of symptoms in which they were afraid that disaster would strike suddenly, unaware. The happier they were, the better their life, the better their job, the better their love life, the better their relationship, the better their children, the more frightened they became that they would lose it.

I think this is clearly related to what I said about the fact that so few of them expected the divorce when it happened. From their point of view, everything was going well and BOOM — the floor fell out from under them. We always tell everybody lightning doesn't strike twice because profoundly in our heart, we know it strikes twice. We all believe it strikes twice, so we reassure ourselves with false reassurances, and this is the fear of lightning striking twice.

Now, I'm not sure it ever goes away, in the same way that I'm not sure that a child of divorce ever fully trusts another person. I hate to say this, but I think it is true. I'm not sure a child of divorce ever fully trusts that another person will be there for them, will love them, will be dependable and will love them forever, whatever forever consists of. In some corner of their heart, there is the fear that that person won't be there in the morning, either will betray them or will abandon them.

I think people go into therapy for a while and get a lot of help with these fears. I think therapy is very helpful for a lot of these young people because they are highly motivated; they know what they want and they can use it. As a matter of fact, the first gain in therapy that some of the young women mentioned to me is that they can go to a party, and, if they don't like anybody, they can go home alone. So they suddenly feel they have the right to choose. They have the right to look around and they can be by themselves, because the fear of being alone is a direct descendant of their childhood fear of being abandoned.

A young woman was always afraid when she got into a quarrel that the quarrel would cascade. That's the other problem that these people have. Quarrels scare the daylights out of them because they think the quarrel won't be resolved. It isn't that they lack the social skills, as one of my colleagues has said; it's that they are convinced that once you have a quarrel, it will cascade down and destroy the relationship. That is what they've been seeing. That is what they know. They say it over and over again: I'm not prepared for marriage. I'm not prepared for a relationship. No one ever told me. I never saw a man and a woman on the same team together.

Any Such Thing As a Good Divorce?

There is a good divorce. A good divorce is when people have prepared for what is coming later. If the woman is going to be changing her way of life and going to work full-time, she needs to prepare herself for that during the marriage, so there isn't that radical change in her life and in the life of the children. In most of these women's lives, all of a sudden they had to go to school at night and go to work during the day. They really took terrible jobs for years until they could get up in the workplace and develop the skills to command something. I think the issue of being economically prepared for what's ahead is very important.

I think that to the extent that people can part without savagery, it's helpful. I think it is foolish to think that people will part without sorrow and without anger. I think that is impossible. I think it's possible to realize that that's a civilized feeling, anger and hurt and sorrow. We have to live with that. You live with that for a long time. You won't keep it entirely under wraps. I think the notion of a bloodless, totally bloodless, angerless, totally civilized divorced is not helpful. But within bounds I think that's better.

I think a divorce in which the parents are able to really maintain their parenting together is a blessing. I don't think a father in one home and a mother in another home is an intact family, but I think it is better, and I think it can be very helpful to the child to see their parents trying. Children are very aware of parents trying, whether they succeed or not, to maintain their loyalty.

The children are very aware of what they talk about as "My mom was so selfish. My dad was so selfish." Or "My mom makes sacrifices. My dad made sacrifices." They give their parents grades in terms of whether they were willing to give up anything for their children. If parents really can earn that, I think they will set a very good role model for their children and their children will appreciate that and love them.

I think that is as good as you get. I think those children will still have to struggle when they reach adulthood, but they can certainly have a protected adolescence, because there's structure in the family. When they reach adulthood, I think they would still confront the issue of, "Can I succeed in a relationship? Can I make it hold?"

Any Such Thing as Good Divorce Legislation?

Well, I can tell you where I don't stand. I don't think that limiting the exit from a marriage is going to make better divorces. I think limiting exits gets us no place. We should learn something from history. The move for no-fault divorce, even though it didn't consider the needs of the child and all the changes that would occur in parent-child relationships, was based on the wish to improve marriage. Trapping people in bad marriages or making the exit very narrow, I think, is very foolish way to go. I don't think it protects children.

I have seen many marriages where the parents didn't get along but where the parents maintained, at great emotional cost, good parenting for their children. Children did very well in families where the marital relationship was marred — not open fighting, but where the people were lonely and unhappy. Where their sex life is deprived, where they may have had affairs outside, I don't know how they solved all of these issues. But they maintain their parenting. The myth is that children always know when there is trouble. Children know when parents fight openly. They don't know if parents sleep in different beds.

Growing Up Fast, Growing Up Slowly

You have to decide where you look when you examine anything. If you look only at the outside, then children of divorce grow up fast. They handle money fast, they're independent fast, they can take care of themselves, they are street smart, and they know their way around, because they've had to. As several of them say, "I'm a child of divorce. I've had to take care of myself and I didn't want to listen to my mom and then listen to my dad. I learned to make my own judgment and I learned to make it very early and to trust myself. If I can get along with my folks, I can get along with anybody."

In terms of their emotional development, they grow up slowly. Then, you're looking inside. They make relationships slowly. They have a very hard time making a commitment in marriage or to a relationship. They have a great deal of trouble combining sex with love, which is an important part of maturation. You don't expect that of a thirteen and fourteen year old. You do expect that of a twenty-five-year-old. They have a great deal of trouble deciding whether they want to become parents. It's not a given. It's not a given for a lot of people; there may be a conflict between a career and being a parent. That wasn't the conflict for these people. It was a conflict about whether in having the kind of childhood I had, can I be a parent? That's a different kind of conflict. Many of them said that they didn't have the models that they needed in order to be a parent, or if they decided to become parents, in this very moving way they said, "I want my child to have everything I lacked." Then they spelled it out. "I don't want her to mother me, I want to mother her. I want her to have the childhood I never had."

The Very Difficult Dilemma

We didn't realize that divorce doesn't rescue children. Divorce is a good thing for adults. For a lot of adults, it changes their lives very much for the better. But except in violence, and not always in violence, divorce doesn't rescue children from the loneliness and unhappiness of a marriage that they usually don't experience.

Divorce in the life of a child is entirely different than in the life of an adult. For an adult, it is a remedy. It brings a bad chapter of my life to an end and opens the door, and hopefully, with any luck, I'll do it better next time around. Doesn't always work, but then life doesn't always work out. But for the child, it's not a remedy, it's the loss of the family, and there is no substitute for that family that's lost. Unless you have a very good remarriage, and that takes a lot of time and it's not easy to create.

The central moral dilemma of divorce is that in a whole lot of life's problems, what's good for a parent is good for children. Safety in the neighborhood is good for parents and good for children. A good lifestyle and enough to eat and enough to do, enough money, is just as important for parents as it is for children. But in relation to divorce, parents' and children's needs and wishes can often diverge. This is a very difficult dilemma. We have been reluctant to acknowledge it, let alone face.

Judge Helen E. Brown

Helen E. Brown is the Wayne County Third Circuit Judge for the family division in Detroit, Michigan. She is on the front lines of what she describes as a war zone.

No One Is Dead, But . . .

I tell people that as a family judge I feel blessed because I used to be a criminal judge. Someone was usually dead when those families came to court. Now, at least, everyone's still alive. That's a relief because there's hope. But it is shocking sometimes to find out how scary it is for the children.

The most common kind of abuse is the subtle kind where the child is really left emotionally and psychologically to fend for themselves. When the parents are arguing so strenuously, the child begins to think, "I have to figure out what to do for myself, myself." Some of the teenagers will actually leave home, live with another family, or live with a girl-friend, because they can't take being put in the middle anymore. Both parents have actually given up their role as parents and substituted the role of soldier in doing battle with each other.

When the parents are arguing, when they put the children in the middle, when they don't want to speak to each other, when they tell the child go ask the other parent for this or that, or tell him this or that, it's very painful and difficult for the child. It's an adult responsibility they're placing on children. They need to see how it's affecting the children. A lot of times parents don't realize it. They're not really thinking about things from a child's perspective.

The Kids

I really only see high-conflict divorces, because everyone else settles their cases. It's almost surprising that so many children in those high-conflict divorces are still able to be wonderful.

The children of the high-conflict divorce tend to be mature, more independent, more aware of what's going on. On the downside, when the conflict goes on for more than the six months it usually takes to get divorced — when it goes on for a year or even two years — these children tend to be very damaged. I see some aggressive, violent types of behavior, attitudes, feelings, and demeanor. They don't get along with their peers. If they have siblings, they tend to turn to each other a little bit more and pull away from one or the other parent. They tend to take sides against a parent. The parents tend to try to pull the children away from the other parent. The conflict becomes very ingrained emotionally and psychologically. These children are in trouble, and they really need to have counseling and intervention to turn them around.

It's hard for the children to see past the negativity, past the anger. They have so much anger. Mostly it's held inside because children are disciplined if they act out aggressively. They turn it inside themselves. That, I think, is really scary. Sooner or later that's going to come out.

Parents Don't Get It

The parents don't get it. They don't get it. In those high-conflict cases where the damage is really done, they continue the battle. They continue to feel that somehow if they're victorious it will make it all better. They don't understand that it's the fight itself that's killing these children. They don't get it. It is like a war zone. Everyday, people are in front of you arguing. The judge sits there day-in and day-out listening to arguments. It's a stressful kind of environment. You internalize some of it because you care about the children so much. I see my job as needing to change the environment from argument to discussion and to resolution. We have a conflict. How do we resolve it?

When you go to war there are victims. There's carnage. People get angry at their spouse or their former romantic partner and they want to punish them. They want to go to court and sic the law on them, as I sometimes say, and have the judge bring the hammer down on one person or another and then they feel victorious. But what's happened to the children through all of this? The children are actually the victims, because that just creates more hostility, more anger, and more resentment.

If the parents come to court and drag out all of their dirty laundry, then the other person is going to have increased resentment. They might take that out on the child. They may want the child to have less time with the other parent. How are you going to solve it?

So we really have to turn everything inside out in family court. We have to turn the aggression into some kind of resolution. These parents are going to be the parents after the judge is out of the picture, after the lawyers are out of the picture, after all of the motions are out of the picture. They're still left as parents. How are they equipped to proceed?

Sometimes I tell parents, "Well, when your daughter gets married, where do you think you're going to sit at the church? Will you sit next to your former spouse? Will you be in the back of the room? Will you not even be invited, because of the conflict?" "Even when they're little, when there's a piano recital, are you both going to be invited to this or is this going to be a source of some stomach churning for this poor child?"

So the better that the parents get along whether they're together or not, the better it's going to be for the child. But, frankly, it's always better for the child, except for some extreme circumstances — it's generally better for the child if the parents to find a way to stay together. That's the best-case scenario.

No One Says, "Never Divorce"

Of course, some people have to get divorced. I don't want anyone to think that I'm saying that no one should ever get divorced. But we've got a 50 percent divorce rate. I mean, clearly, 50 percent of the people don't need to get divorced if they learn how to resolve conflict and communicate better. If they make a commitment and stick with it, it's going to be better for them and better for the their children.

A Stranger in a Black Gown

Taking your divorce case to court is awesome and kind of scary because the court has the authority to decide, first of all, where the child is going to live and with whom. Second of all, the court has the authority to decide whether the child should be permitted to leave the state if one of the parents wants to move out of state. And, finally, if the parents can't decide, the court has the authority to rule on issues like parenting time and summer activities. I even had a case where the father wouldn't agree for the child to go to summer camp, and the mother had to ask me for the authority.

So, the judge can be very nit-picky. The judge can decide what time, where, and exactly what the child can do. I've never been invited to dinner at their home. I don't know their lives or their families. The parents are putting all of these decisions into the hands of a total stranger when they can't make the decisions for themselves. That ought to scare any parent.

John C. and Christina

John and Christina divorced five years ago and have a seven-year-old daughter, Francesca. John has not remarried. Christina is engaged.

JOHN'S STORY

A Slow Death

I don't think there are any good divorces. I guess there are just some that are better than others. It was about five years ago. Just like most things, I guess, it was a slow death. The timing was not good, everything, the circumstances surrounding it. We had my ex-wife's family living with us. That was two adults and three kids, so there were five people living with us and that's hard. They're good people, very good people, but it doesn't matter how good people are. When you're having problems in your marriage, it's not easy to have other people around.

There were all sorts of things going on. There were some financial chaos and communication problems. We were living in a house out in the suburbs. It was nice. It's never one thing that makes a divorce happen. It's a combination of things.

When Was It Really Over?

Well, there's the legal part of it. There was a separation, where you stop living together. We went through miniature separations, where I was out of the house for a couple weeks. It was scary, because you think once you move out it's just a step closer to being divorced, which I really didn't think we were going to do. She did more of the initiating for it. I thought there were still avenues we needed to explore.

Even after I moved out, I still thought, "Well, we'll see what happens." You really don't want to be married to somebody who doesn't want to be married to you. It wasn't peaches and cream for me either, but, again, you have a child, so you owe it to yourselves to try everything you can.

I moved out and moved into my apartment and I said, "Wow this is where I'm probably going to be living for awhile." It was shortly after that that one morning I woke up because somebody was knocking on my window. It was like 5 A.M. and I walk over to the window. It's a guy and he flashes a badge at me. I'm thinking, what is this? He says he's from the sheriff's department. I'm like, "Whoa, what?" I was barely awake. I know I was having problems sleeping during those times. He just hands me papers through the window and he says, "You probably know what this is?" I'm like, "No." He says, "Well, see you later." And he leaves. I look at it and they're papers, divorce papers. I'm like, "Oh, my God." I start reading them and legal language is a little, well, let's say it's not very pretty, especially when it's talking about the demise of your family. I was completely floored and that's when I knew, "Whoa, there's no going back now."

Only One Asset; It Was Two Years Old

Let me tell you, it was a very difficult time. I wasn't sleeping. I was waking up in my own place not knowing where I was. It's a horrible, horrible thing. It's completely traumatic for months and months. We really had nothing to divide. We had no assets. It was really only how are we going to parent our child throughout this process in a healthy way, and it was very difficult.

I was just speaking to my brother last night and he said, "Boy, I give you credit for pulling through." I've never given myself that much credit, because if I had not had the family and the friends that I have and still have as a network, you don't know. I was basically a zombie. I think I would go into work and just sit there twirling the telephone cord around my fingers. I don't remember doing any work or anything. I was just numb. That went by for months. We separated in August of 1995 and were officially divorced in June the next year.

I think we both found our own ways of telling Francesca, because we both had very different perspectives on why we were no longer going to be living together and why we were going to be divorced. I think it depended on the situation. What I remember is trying to deal with it on your own personal level, and then you have to have this whole other mindset operating so you can parent well. It's not easy. It's not easy when the other parent does not have the same perspective and their emotional tension is high.

There were some very unpleasant scenes in exchanging Francesca. It was very difficult to look in my rearview mirror and see Francesca, who at the time was two years old. I think it was just as scary for them. They didn't know what was going on. We all end the journey together. I actually can't think of what I might have told her. I've written it all down. I keep a journal, and I keep a journal with her, as well. A lot of those thoughts made it into those pages. It's amazing. You can survive anything. I think if I could survive that divorce, there isn't anything I couldn't handle, because that's how bad it was, even with all the support I had.

Family Court: Just Incredible

I had to leave court and believe me, court is just rough, family court. It's really the last resort anyone should have in settling family disputes.

Why did I have to go to family court? You're legally married, so you have to go through a judicial process to dissolve that union, and a child is involved, so you have to settle up what the rules are going to be. How is the kid going to be parented? How much support is going to be paid out of your paycheck? To me it was always just ridiculous that we even had attorneys handling this. It should have been her and I sitting at the table figuring out how we were going to do it, but we didn't have that luxury.

Why not? When somebody serves you with papers, you have to respond. Me not being an attorney, you have to hire somebody to do your bidding. Their interests are really not the best. The attorney is there to get the advantage for their client. That's their only interest. When there's a kid involved, it's an adversarial process. You have all these parties in disagreement. It's lengthy. It's expensive in a prohibitive way. It's just incredible.

Ah, Child Support

At first, the lawyers just took care of it. They contact your employer's payroll office and it's deducted. They go the safe way. A lot of the process is a complete invasion on you. At one point in the beginning, they were taking 40 percent out of my check. I pleaded with the judge. All I can say is, you don't know it until you get there.

I'm saying, "They won't do that. They're not going to do that. They wouldn't take 40 percent of what I make. I'll lose my car." You're just so naive in the whole divorce process. And that's exactly what happened. I said, "Wait, I need my car to work. If I don't have a car, I can't work; I can't pay child support." But they don't care. I know that sounds biased, but I do have my own opinions on how I think the courts treat families and men in particular.

Did my ex-wife have an alternative? Yeah, you always have a choice. There was no child endangerment or anything like that. Although, as I mentioned when I got served the papers, there was some language in there that just completely floored me, like, "have reason to believe that I would leave the state and kidnap my daughter." Just very ugly things like that. The courts have to consider that stuff very seriously.

All you really have to do is allege anything, and the courts have an obligation to follow up and consider it real. That's the language her attorney used, and it was probably under his advisement that those things go in there to make sure that she gets the advantage. She had the choice. She signed it. I remember my father telling me that he had a conversation with Christina. She said, "I didn't tell them to put that." But she signed the papers. I could sit here, and I can go through a whole list of what I thought was wrong in the process — things I feel she should have never done, actions she should have never taken. Lots of those.

Did I Expect This?

No, I just never thought. I just never thought. My parents are still married. They have been married forty-five years, something like that. So I just never could imagine myself in a situation like that. It's just mind-boggling. I could not imagine myself in that predicament. How am I going to live without my kid in the same house? How is that all going to happen? I never thought it would have gotten to that level. Believe me; things, like I said, were hard.

It would have been very easy for me to leave the marriage if I just looked at it from the point of, "Well, I'm not happy." But, to this day, we still have different perspectives on what happened and the reasons that led up to being divorced.

It's All about Being a Dad

You have to put a lot of things to the side, and you have to make compromises. You have to make sacrifices, just like in any situation, whether you're divorced or not, whether you're a single parent or not. I probably wouldn't be around here if I didn't have a kid. I'd like to travel. I might be living in another country right now if I didn't have Francesca.

I think the ingredients to being a good father, or just being a good parent, are always the same. Paying attention to your kid. Help them guide themselves to being a strong and healthy kid. You know, emotionally, spiritually, and morally. She's an incredibly well-balanced kid. I'm very fortunate. I don't know what I've done to contribute. I think there is some luck involved. I've got good health, so I'm able to do things with her.

What kind of things do I do with her? I'm pretty active, so we do a lot of camping, bike riding, roller-blading, and dog walking. I still play a lot. I'm like a kid myself, so we just play. We dance a lot. There are a bunch of instruments at home, so we have jam sessions sometime. We do a lot of artwork. I have always had a passion for being creative with paints and lettering. So I try to pass on what I know, just like my father passed on a lot of things to me.

Really, I don't have a lot of time with her. Her teacher spends more time with her than I do and has for the last five years. Right now I see her every other weekend and then a day during the week when she sleeps over. Then I have any extra days that she has, such as spring break. I'll ask her mom what we can work out as far as time. I used to have a lot more vacation time, too, but I'm in school now.

I totally blow off school when I'm with her. I blow off most things that I'm supposed to be responsible for just so that I could have time with her. I don't usually work on papers or other projects unless somehow I can involve her with it. We hang a lot, too, and she does like hanging.

For the first couple years we spoke almost every day on the phone. Now we don't speak every day when she's not with me. For the first three years I maintained some type of contact with her every day, whether it was by phone or dropping by her school for lunch or just to hang out with her for a little bit. Those first couple years were just re-establishing things, making it a new "normal." Because you're really still a family, it's just that it's rearranged differently, and you still have to communicate with everybody involved. We are fortunate. I get along very well with Christina's family, and her family gets along well with mine. We still are close in a sense. So I'm very fortunate.

Getting Past the Bitterness

I think it just takes time. After a short amount of time, I was able to really get a perspective: "Okay, this is the situation, and this is how we're going to do it." But it takes two. It really does take two. If she or I decide not to cooperate or have animosity, then it's going to spoil the whole thing for everything.

CHRISTINA'S STORY

When Did You Know It Was Over?

I can't say it was one thing. It was many different things. Gosh, all the memories. It was probably eight months before we separated. It was Christmas of 1994, and my sister, who lives down the block, was living with us. My sister, her husband, and her three children were living with us in our home. We had a home at the time. Their home was being remodeled, so they moved in for four weeks. They stayed four months. So I'm returning the favor now. That's why I moved in with her.

It was a very stressful time. Ironically, John's the one who was all for it. Oh yeah, because he's very family oriented. He loves to have his people at his apartment all the time. It's like an open house. So that's how he's been. We separated in May of 1995. I'd say November or December of 1994 is when I knew that I was just done. There were arguments, there were attempts to go to counseling and attempts to communicate, and they all failed. Timing is everything. Finally, when John realized that I was serious, he wanted to go to counseling, and by that time I was gone in my head. It was very difficult, a very difficult time. I can't label it as like a good or bad divorce, because I think we've struggled a lot, but we've come out the positive end of it really.

We Don't Stick to the Legal Paper

It's work. It's work. Even now, something happens that I don't agree with or whatever, and instead of grabbing the phone and saying, "Why did you do that?" I'll take a deep breath and maybe bring it up two days later, maybe not bring it up at all. I think another key for us has been not to let our daughter, Francesca, pit us against each other. She's so intelligent, she can very easily do that. She used to not speak up with her dad but then would want me to call him. She'd say, "Tell him I don't want to stay over that day, or tell him I'd rather do this." I don't do that anymore. It caused a problem when I did it for a while. Now I just tell her, "You know what? You've got to fight your own battles with your dad. You fight them with me. So don't be afraid of him." I think now everything is better because I stay out of that.

We're very flexible. We don't stick to the legal paper. You know how it says Wednesday after school until 7:00 P.M. and every other weekend. We don't do that. He's in school now, so he sees her Mondays and she sleeps over. He doesn't bring her back because we're too far for him to travel in traffic and bring her back. That would be unreasonable. At the same time, if there's a family function and it falls on his weekend and I'd like her to be there, you know, he accommodates and I do the same. We switched weekends just a few weeks ago because his Easter and my Easter were a week apart but they fell on opposite weekends. So we split the weekends for a few weeks. So that's the key for us is to put her first and to be flexible. It's a constant challenge.

Could Counseling Have Saved the Marriage?

Yes, I'm a counselor myself. If counseling would have been implemented when I wanted it to be implemented it could have saved the marriage, but he was unwilling. He was too angry. "I don't need counseling," you know.

I used to beg him to go to counseling. Crying, begging him, and he wouldn't. It was only when I served him with divorce papers that he said, "Okay, I'll go to counseling." By that time emotionally I was out. I was gone. There was too much pain, too much disagreement, and too much hurt. Looking back on it, the person I am today, we're not compatible to be together now.

What would have happened if we had gone to counseling? I don't know. I don't know. You know what my counselor told me? I don't remember how she put it, but she said that it depends on what you want to put first. Are you putting your personal growth first, or are you putting the growth of the marriage first, the commitment of the marriage? At that time, back then, I was done with the commitment to the marriage, unfortunately.

It's much too complicated to really be able to go through all the reasons. But there was a lot of arguing, a lot of crying, and a lot of drama. Once you have too much of that, I think it's very difficult to come back even in counseling. It got to the point, you know, where people would say, "You should stay together for your kids." Oh, that used to make me so angry. Stay in a marriage where I'm not happy, for my child — then what am I teaching her? Then I'm teaching her to be a martyr and stay if she's not happy.

So I was very adamant about not staying because of her. My parents divorced after thirty-five years, but they should have divorced after five. All my life I heard, "I stayed with your father because of you kids." So I would have never put that burden on her to be unhappy in my life, and to tell her that I stayed for her. You know, I think she's fine. She has her moments. Every once in a great while, especially if she's overtired, she gets more emotional and she'll say, "Oh I wish you and my dad were together." But overall she does great. She really does, and I really believe that.

She's excited about having a new brother or sister at some point. So I don't know. If I had to do it all over again, yes, my ideal wish would have been that he would have been willing to go to counseling early on.

Who knows what would have happened? But I think it's worked out just fine the way it is.

Our Friends, His Friends, No Friends

That's funny you should ask about mutual friends. We used to sit and look at our friends and say, "I wonder twenty years from now who is going to be divorced." We never thought it was going to be us. We got married before a lot of our friends did. We had a lot of mutual friends — or so I thought they were mutual friends — from college, none of which have I remained friends with. None. It was "poor John." "Poor John got divorced. I can't believe she did that to him." So, yes, I didn't stay friends with anybody.

I was very hurt by that. I felt like, boy, you really learned who your friends are. They weren't really our friends, they were his friends and I was his wife. I think people had a hard time. They think they can't be loyal to one and still be friends with the other. I think it takes an exceptional person to be able to stay friends with both people, set boundaries, and not get in the middle of things. Unfortunately, none of our friends from college did that. If they see me — and I've run into maybe a handful of them in the last five years — they're polite with me and ask, "Oh, how are things?" But I think divorce is not in a vacuum. When you get divorced, friendships change too. John just meets you once and he's your best friend, which used to really annoy me when we were married. But now he can do what he wants because we're not married. So in answer to your question, my life totally changed because I had to cultivate all new friendships.

I Was Angry in the Beginning

If I look back on it, I say, wow, we really did well with everything we were going through. I think we just rose above a lot of things that were going on, but it was difficult. When I got married, my parents didn't want me to marry John because he wasn't Greek and they felt he wasn't ambitious, he wasn't serious about a job, and he was a vegetarian, and they thought that was weird. So they weren't supportive in the beginning, but then they grew to love him. When I was getting a divorce, my father didn't want me to divorce him. I said it wasn't in a vacuum. It was reactions by everybody, family and friends. I was very angry in the beginning. I didn't want him around. I didn't want him to come if there was a family function. I didn't want him to come even if he was close with my family. I felt like, "Hey, your loyalty should be to me. I'm the family." Now that we've worked through everything, I have no problem with him being around.

Francesca Counsels Her Friends

In the last year and a half, the parents of two of Francesca's best little girlfriends have gotten divorced. Francesca has been able to help them through it. I think it has helped Francesca not to feel like she was the only one in her class, because even though it's the year 2000, in a Greek Orthodox school the rates of divorce are not as high. I mean it's getting there, but it's still not.

So she was the only one in her class until a year and a half ago. In one of the divorces that involved two little girls, the mother remarried really quickly and they changed schools three times in a year. That I think was really difficult for those girls. Francesca would come home and kind of tell me what her friend said to her in school. Her friend was embarrassed, and she doesn't want to tell her other friends. When she first told Francesca she said, "Shhh, don't tell anybody else that my mommy and daddy are getting a divorce." Evidently she was able to tell Francesca because she knew that Francesca's parents were divorced.

The other divorce is just recent now. I don't think either has been really ugly, but I also think that because the children are older that they haven't adjusted yet the same way Francesca has. For Francesca it's kind of old news.

David Royko

David Royko is director of the Marriage and Family Counseling Service for the Circuit Court of Cook County, Illinois. He says that it's too easy to have a bad divorce and discusses ways parents can make the process easier or harder for their children.

We See Only the Most Stressed Parents

It's incredibly stressful for parents in the court fighting over the children. We see the most conflictual 10 percent of the parents who are in divorce court. We only see parents that are fighting over custody or visitation, and those are the cases that have the highest degree of rage, the highest degree of conflict, and, really, the highest degree of stress for everybody involved, the parents as well as the children.

The attitude of "I'm the only one who should have custody" is very typical of what we see. What parents bring into mediation often are issues that are really unrelated to the children or at least not directly related to the children. When they come in and say, "I want custody and my husband doesn't deserve custody, he never was around, he never did anything for the kids," what is often being played out is the conflict in the marriage. It isn't really about custody of the child. It's really about leftover issues from the marriage.

All a court can really give you is the legal divorce, but the emotional divorce is the much tougher divorce to get. The parents that we see are nowhere near getting the emotional divorce. Typically, they are very involved in the conflict, very invested in the conflict, and what is really being fought out are issues regarding their relationship and not necessarily what's going on with the children.

Do Children Really Need Two Parents?

That's not a dumb question. There are many reasons why children need two parents. One reason is that mothers and fathers are very different in many ways. You can just see it when parents are interacting with an infant. I am using sort of clichéd and stereotypical terms here, but the mother will be the one who is the most nurturing and the one that's most concerned with the comfort of the child and making sure that the child is happy and comfortable. The father will be the one who will pick the child up and be bouncing the child on his knee and throwing him up in the air and giving the child a little risk-taking thrill. That's sort of a good example in a very superficial way, but I think a very significant way, of the differences between mothers and fathers.

For a child to develop in a healthy way, it is very important, if at all possible, to have both parents involved. As the child grows, one of the first things that a child will come to realize is that they are part mom and part dad. If one parent is missing, then there is always going to be a hole in that child's life, a hole psychologically in that child wondering what was it about that parent or what was it about me that made that parent absent from my life? Why was it that that parent didn't stick around? Is there something wrong with me? Is it because I'm unlovable?

Some people say children may be upset for a little while, but they get over it. That would be very nice, but it's not true. Divorce is something that stays in one way or another with somebody through their entire life. It doesn't mean it ruins their life. It doesn't mean that it affects their life negatively from here on. But the impact of divorce is one of the most significant events that can happen in a child's life, and something of that significance will have an impact on a child's life well into adulthood.

How the parents handle the divorce, how the parents handle their relationship with each other and with the child during and after the divorce, will have a lot to do with how well the child will adjust. Problems can stay with a child indefinitely if the divorce is handled badly for a child. Ideally, what you want to see is the child work through the grieving process and come to some sort of resolution and not have lasting wounds — open sores, in essence, psychologically, for years to come. However, how much of a scar is left really varies from child to child.

Easy to Have a Bad Divorce

Professionals are saying, "Divorce is a reality. Whether or not it's good or bad, it's always going to be there." What I think is by far the most important piece is how the parents handle it regarding the children.

There are a lot of ways to have a bad divorce. It's too easy to have a bad divorce. The first way is to keep fighting, to keep the conflict going even though you're divorced. If you want to have a bad divorce from the standpoint of the children, put the children in the middle of the conflict and have the children be the messengers. Pass messages back and forth through the kids. That is a great way to have a bad divorce and mess up the kids because then they get to experience the wrath that's really aimed directly at the other parent.

Another way to have a bad divorce is to bad-mouth the other parent or to have family members bad-mouth the other parent to the child. Put the child in the position where they either have to defend the parent or they can feel guilty about not defending the parent. Put the child in a position where the child has to be the parent of the parents or where the child feels the need to be the savior or needs to offer emotional, psychological support for one parent or the other. Keeping a custody or visitation conflict going is another way to really make problems for a child, because a child going into a divorce typically feels like they are, at least in part, responsible for the divorce. When the conflict continues over custody and visitation, that in essence is confirming that, "Look at this, my parents are still fighting over me. All of this is my fault." So, those are some very basic ways you can make a bad divorce for a child.

The Child's Reaction

You're better off, in fact, in a lot of ways if you see a child's reaction to a bad divorce. If a child is crying, well, right there you know it's a very clear sign that there are some problems. What you run into more often with a child who's really being stressed is the child isn't going to share it with the parent. The child doesn't feel safe sharing it with a parent. Not necessarily that the child doesn't feel close to that parent, but because of the way the battle is being fought, it is not necessarily safe to talk about their feelings about the divorce with one parent or the other because of the kind of reaction that the parents might have. It also depends on the age and the sex of the child. Girls tend to talk more than boys do about their feelings. Girls tend to express their pain more directly verbally than a boy will.

There can be depression. A child really looks depressed. Another way that depression in a child can show itself is through anger, through acting-out behavior, through fighting or defying authority, through getting in trouble at school.

You also will see if a child is really being affected negatively by a divorce, you will see problems with drug and alcohol use. You can often see promiscuity with children who are caught in a bad situation involving divorce. Grades can drop precipitously. They can drop very, very quickly. A straight-A student one semester caught in a bad divorce situation a semester or two later can be pulling all D's. These are not, unfortunately, uncommon.

Children Are Going to Learn

Children learn from their own childhood and their own experiences. Whether or not it's a good thing or a bad thing, children are going to learn. They see divorce in their own family and in other families that divorce is just one more option. The divorce itself is not necessarily something that is frowned upon.

I think the bigger problem though is the problem that society pays when it comes to the aftermath of high-conflict divorces. When divorces create problems for the child, you increase the likelihood of divorce with these children, as well, especially if their model for the marriage and the divorce has been a very unhealthy model.

The fact is, divorce can be a learning experience for children. Just because Mom and Dad are divorced doesn't mean that they have to be enemies. They can still work together and they can still get along for a common purpose. If all the child learns is that Mom and Dad are enemies, the child may grow up wondering if marriage is worth it.

Often Hard for Parents to Appreciate

Most children don't talk about the divorce fondly. Children do not like divorce. Children don't enjoy divorce. You do occasionally get a child who appreciates that it's more peaceful at home now. They don't have to hear the fighting. That is a good example of parents who've been able to do a good divorce, because you often get children who say they fight just as much now as they ever did when they were living together. That's awful for kids.

When it comes to a child's experience of divorce, children don't want to see their mom and dad get a divorce. It's the foundation upon which children have built their entire lives. The one thing that most children will take for granted, even if their mom and dad don't get along, is that they will be together, that they will always be living with Mom and Dad. Young kids often don't even like the idea that they will grow up someday and move out of the house. Their idea is that they will always live with their mom and dad. So when this breaks apart, it's devastating to a degree that I think is often hard for adults to really appreciate. There are very few things that will hurt an adult as much as a divorce will hurt for a child. The pain can be unthinkable.

Mom and Dad Are Flabbergasted

It's still remarkable to me when interviewing children whose parents are getting a divorce or who have gotten a divorce how insightful children can be and how articulate they can be about the experience. Often they will see things about their parents' relationship that you would think only a trained therapist would see. They will point out interactions and patterns of interactions between Mom and Dad. When I report back some of these things to the mom and dad, they're often flabbergasted, because they can't believe that their child has been so aware of what's been going on between them. They thought that somehow their children had not noticed.

They will notice facial expressions. They will notice body language. They will notice how their parents act like children. They will often draw analogies between children fighting and arguing at school and children not wanting to share toys. They say, "Just like my mom and dad, they don't know how to share me. They don't know how to share the house. They don't know how to share the dog." Whatever it is, they will often draw analogies, and very perceptive analogies, about how Mom and Dad are acting like children.

Sometimes the children will say things along the lines that they feel that they're maturer than their parents are. The sad thing is that often children who've gone through something like a divorce, something very traumatic, have had to become older than their years. They come across as older than they really are because of the pain that they have gone through. So couple this with the need to express what's going on and you often hear very, very revealing pictures of family life by children.

The Courtroom: So Much Exaggeration and Grandstanding

A courtroom is by nature adversarial. You've got one side pitted against the other side. It's sort of a civilized battlefield, and not necessarily always so civilized. The whole nature of divorce is unfortunately adversarial most of the time, and this gets played out in the courtroom. The whole nature of what a child needs is not adversarial. What a child needs are parents cooperating in the best interest of the child.

So much of what goes on in a courtroom is exaggeration, is grandstanding, is trying to, at all costs, to represent your clients to get what your client needs. So often parents go into a situation already angry with one another, and what happens in a courtroom is that parents share things that have been said and people are testifying about them. It makes what they were feeling before they went into court seem like a stroll in the park. A litigation involving the family can leave them so twisted emotionally that they're in worse shape than when they started. How does this affect the child when their parents hate each other even more, when they're even less equipped to cooperate, and when they're more geared up for battle than for cooperation?

What I often will try to get across to clients is that you don't have to be friends and there are plenty of people in the business world that hate one another. They hate each other's guts. They're not friends, but they're great business partners. They somehow manage to put together a business that's thriving, and that's the way to look at it if you're getting a divorce. You don't have to like one another, but you're business partners with the mutual interest being the child and the thriving of this child.

Can There Be a Good Divorce?

For a good divorce, first off accept the idea that this person that you're divorcing is no longer a part of your life in terms of who you are. They are separate from you now. However, when it comes to the children, you must cooperate. If there's anything you have to do that might involve disagreement, that might involve arguing, such as working out details of spending time with the children, finances for the children, school for the children, do this away from the child. What you want to do at all costs is represent a united front with a child. You want to present them with the idea that Mom and Dad are still always going to be there. Mom and Dad can cooperate for the sake of the child.

For a good divorce, it's important for parents to get help for themselves as well as their child. You know, it's funny; you will often tell parents your child would do well being in some sort of support group or getting some sort of help for what they're going through and so would you. However, nine times out of ten what I'll hear a parent say is, "I agree with you my child needs this, but I don't have time for myself. I'm doing fine." What I try to tell the parents is that the child is not going to do that well if you're in bad shape. It's like when you're flying on an airplane, and the flight attendant gives you the instructions of what to do if there's an emergency. They always say that if the masks drop from the ceiling, which is a terrifying image, you should make sure your own mask is secure before tending to the child. The idea being that if you're a mess, if you can't breathe, if you can't even take care of yourself, you're going to be of no use to the child. If you're a psychological or emotional mess, if you don't get help for yourself, you're going to be that much less available and that much less helpful to your children.

How much the kids suffer will often be directly related to how much the parents are doing right or wrong. Often that comes from parents putting the children in a position where they do not feel the freedom to love both parents. A child who has to start thinking about how anything they say or do will affect the other parent, whether or not it will hurt the other parent and whether or not it will bring the parent's anger toward them — what that child really needs is peace in their lives. They don't need to hear the conflict going on and on and on. How much a child suffers is really up to the parents most of the time. Now, all children that I've ever talked to suffer, because they're children and because their parents are getting a divorce. I've never talked to a child who expressed no pain, but I've talked to many children who really are able to move past the divorce and settle in to a life that to them feels quite okay.

Olivia and Adam

Olivia and Adam are teenagers, and their parents recently divorced. The divorce made them much closer, but they don't like being caught in the middle and used as messengers.

Remember the "Divorce Talk"?

Adam: Yeah, I do. I was pretty broken, but I could understand it. They have gone through some rough things, and I thought it would be a good idea for them to do that. Since then, things got harder. But there's not as much fighting, stuff like that.

Olivia: We knew it was coming. They were at counseling and things weren't going too well. Like Adam said, I think it is better that they split up, because there'd been a lot of arguments and a lot of tension under our roof. Also with my brother and I, we would fight all the time because of that, and lately, in the past year, it's been that we've been a lot closer.

Adam: Definitely.

The First Signs?

Olivia: Two years ago in winter, I just remember my mom was in a really upset mood. She got very upset and sad, and I just didn't think things were going well between them. They'd just been fighting. They'd been fighting for a couple of years.

Adam: Yeah. I could also tell that sometimes when they used to spend lots of time in my dad's office talking about things, trying to make things better. But it just didn't work. Sometimes when I overheard things, I knew that it wasn't going well.

Olivia: I wasn't surprised. I knew that it would be coming eventually with the way things had been around the house.

Adam: Definitely.

Olivia: Big tension and a lot of arguments.

When You First Heard the Word "Divorce"

Olivia: I was upset. Having your parents live together for the fifteen years of your entire life, and you know it's not going to be the same.

Adam: Yeah.

Olivia: They split up and one moves out of the house. It's sad, but at the same time you have to be thinking about how it's better for them.

Adam: Definitely, there's that. It does help a lot even though it is hard to have your parents split up. At first it wasn't really a divorce. They're still separated now to this day, but it's basically the same thing. Divorce is just a word for the legalized stuff, so it's sort of the same for me.

Ever Think It Was Your Fault?

Adam: Never.

Olivia: No, my parents made it very clear that it had nothing to do with us. They did a good job of that, and I don't feel responsible for what happened.

Any Way to Make It Easier?

Adam: Well, the parent can respect their children, because their children are a big part of this. If they don't have children, it's probably a better thing, because the children are a big part of this. You can really hurt them if you do the wrong thing. You want to tell them what's going on so they don't get any wrong ideas.

Olivia: But don't get them too involved with it, 'cause custody can sometimes be a big problem. It's better, I think, if they live closer to each other so it doesn't have to be an issue. Sometimes it can get all ugly, and I don't think it should be that way. Kids shouldn't be involved in that at all. It's just between them.

Feeling Caught in the Middle — What to Do?

Adam: First, you probably want to start by telling the kids what they want to know. Then they will know what is going on, and they won't feel like it's their fault or that they're caught up in the middle. Then you should have the kids say what is making them be caught up in the middle. Then maybe the parent could try and fix that and make it better.

Olivia: Like right now, my brother and I are switching off times between our parents. It's not exactly equal between the two of them, but we're trying to make it. If we spend the same amount of time with both parents, it helps a lot. Try to even it out on both things, both parts.

Adam: Yeah.

Olivia: I think that one way parents could make it easier on their kids would be to divide their time up equally between the two parents. Just to let them see enough of both parents, so that it doesn't feel awkward. At least try to make it as natural feeling as possible because it can become difficult, especially if the parents move away from each other, far away.

Can Parents Talk Too Much?

Olivia: Yeah.

Adam: Yeah, sometimes there are things that the kids don't need to know. I figured that out myself and it's rough. Sometimes just a little information is good enough.

Olivia: The details sometimes . . .

Adam: aren't the best.

Olivia: You don't want to hear. I told my parents that I don't want to know exactly why or what happened. But they gave me the basic idea of it and I'm satisfied with that. I know that it was better that they did split up, and that's what is.

Clues to When Enough Is Enough

Olivia: Just ask them.

Adam: Basically asking them can help a whole bunch. Cause if you ask them, then the parents can see what is wrong and know what is wrong, so they can help fix it and make it better.

Olivia: There's not always something that the parents can do. There are some kids who just don't talk and express their feelings. They'll eventually get over that I think, but, for the time being, it's sometimes better to be left alone. Hopefully if things aren't going well for the kid they'll eventually say something about it. There are some quiet kids that don't express themselves too much.

Advice

Adam: Our parents kept the fighting and arguing away from us. They'd bicker sometimes and act like little children. I know that's very immature. I think that they should just keep that away from us.

Olivia: Just to understand that it's not the kids' fault and that it probably is better that their parents are splitting up. There's not much that they can do about it. Some kids think that they can stop it.

Adam: Yeah.

Olivia: Like *The Parent Trap,* trying to get their parents back together.

Adam: Let me say that doesn't work. I mean, it would be great if they were to come back together, but I know it's not possible. It sort of gets out of your head after a year or so. Afterward, everything will be better. That's also some advice to other kids that I have — it will all be good sooner or later.

Olivia: There will be tough times when things aren't going exactly right, but you can get through those. Things will work out in the end and it's not their fault that their parents broke up. Although things might get rough at times, always look forward to the better times and think of the better times in the past.

Adam: Because it will get better; even though there is probably no way to fix it, it'll get better sooner or later.

Ever Used As a Messenger?

Olivia: Yes, I don't like that at all.

Adam: Too many times. "Tell your dad this"; "tell your mom this." Blah, blah. "Take the mail, it's your dad's." Blah, blah to you, Mom. "Drop this off to your mom." "Drop this off to your dad." I don't like it at all. It's not our responsibility to do that, and yet we do it because we love them.

Olivia: I don't like it either. Just don't let your children be the in-between. That's one of the problems. That's one of the reasons that kids can think that they are a problem, because their parents communicate through the children.

Adam: Definitely.

Dad?

Adam: It's just nice to be with him. Any time with him is well spent. Sometimes we play some cards or rent a movie. We have fun. My dad and I play on the guitar sometimes. I like being with him.

Mom?

Olivia: Because we're with her a lot more, I think we do less things and she's got to work.

Adam: Mom is — she's looking for a job, so it's sort of hard to spend lots of time with her. But as much as we can, we do.

Holiday and Birthdays?

Olivia: Switching off.

Adam: Yeah. That's the hard part.

Olivia: For birthdays, it's more like half a day with Mom, half a day with Dad. Maybe a birthday dinner with Dad, and then birthday cake with Mom.

Adam: Yeah, Christmas was a little odd.

Olivia: Because it was our first Christmas without both of our parents.

Adam: We're all sort of separated. So we had Christmas with my dad two weeks actually before Christmas. It worked out fine, though.

Olivia: They try as much as they can to compensate for this divorce.

Adam: Yeah.

Ever Get Tired of the Shuffle?

Adam: Yeah, actually that happens a lot. Sometimes it'll be that I'm out with my friends or something like that and it'll be like, "Adam, time to go to your dad's," or "Adam, time to go to your mom's." I don't really like that. I think that we should be able to choose when we have to go. Most of the time, we can choose within a couple hours when we want to go or how much we want to stay. But it should be a little more lenient than that.

Olivia: Sometimes it's more a problem with my dad 'cause I see him less, and so he wants to spend more time with me. The weekends are usually when he wants to see me. I like to go out on weekends. So he might ask me, "Oh, you want to come and see a movie with me and Adam tonight?" And I'm kind of hesitant 'cause I want to go out with my friends. It becomes a problem sometimes. But he understands, and I try to see him during the day more. We might go shopping one day and then go, I don't know, go to a park or something.

Wish Anything Had Been Done Differently?

Adam: Actually, no. They're very good to us and I really respect them for that. They've treated us right. We've grown up to be very good people because of them. Well, so far, at least.

Olivia: Yeah. At the beginning they were handling it well, but lately there's been a lot more tension in that they're not getting along too well.

Adam: Yeah.

Olivia: I think they're through the divorce and they're not being very giving toward each other.

Adam: Greedy.

Olivia: Greedy, a lot of greed, and . . .

Adam: A lot of greed. And sort of like little children bickering about stuff.

Olivia: Yeah.

Adam: So, very immature sometimes.

Olivia: I tell them that they are acting immature. And they are like, well dah dah dah.

Adam: Blah, blah, blah, yeah. Little pointless statements that don't matter.

Olivia: They sound like, "You started it." "No, you started it."

Anything Good about This Divorce?

Olivia: Well, yeah. I mean, my brother and I have become closer.

Adam: Definitely.

Olivia: There's not as much tension and a lot less stress. Like when I was in school and they're fighting a lot, sometimes I would do worse. I just felt uncomfortable where I was and what was happening. It's easier not to have it.

Advice for a Family Starting a Divorce?

Adam: You want to be able to understand the other people in your family — what they're trying to say and what they want to say. Because then it'll be easier for them to understand you, and then everybody can sort of, you know, get along.

Olivia: Make sure the line is clearly defined between family and the kids and the legal issues and the things that shouldn't be told to the children. Just make sure that there's a clear definition between the two. What should be said and what shouldn't.

Abbie

Abbie is a junior in high school. Her parents divorced when she was in the fifth grade. She wishes that her father hadn't had to live so far away, and that she hadn't been separated from her brother.

We Watch Out for Each Other

My parents and my stepparents would do anything for me. I know that they would. They're always very careful to make sure that they're not stepping over any boundaries, especially now that I'm older. I can tell that my parents are letting go of me more, and they are giving me more freedoms. I can always talk to them about things and they're not judgmental. We watch out for each other.

The most important thing with my parents is that I know I can come to them with anything. Even if it's something that I know they might not approve of or something they wouldn't agree with. They still love me the same. They don't look down on me for it, and they don't get upset with me for coming to them with something that's hard for me to talk to them about.

Well, my mom is one of my really good friends 'cause I can talk to her about things. But she is still a parent 'cause I know that I can't talk to her about everything that I talk to my friends about, and she'll still punish me and things like that.

What kind of parent would I like to be? I think I'd want to be the same kind of parent that my mom is, especially with my daughters. I have three brothers, and I know my relationship to my mom is really different from what her relationship is with my brothers, because I'm the only girl. I think I'd want to make sure that my kids knew that they could talk to me about everything and that I would be here for them.

But I'd still let them know I'm their mom and they can't be disrespectful and they can't break rules without getting punishments.

The Divorce

How did my parents tell me they were getting a divorce? My parents got divorced when I was in fifth grade. We had just moved away, and we'd only lived in Oklahoma for a year. Before we moved there was talk about them getting divorced. They had talked to me and my older brother and my younger brother, who was only three at the time, about them maybe separating and my father moving away without us. Then we all moved together.

Then they would just sit down and they had several talks with us about things that were going to happen, and my dad moved out of the house. They talked to us about what that meant and everything. Then when they finally got divorced, they just talked to us. They told us it wasn't going to change our relationship with them, they told us it was just because they had grown apart, and things like that. I just remember they sat down with us a lot and talked to us a lot about what was going on and made sure they were walking us through each step.

I was sad and I was frustrated because I was the only one of my friends whose parents had been divorced. When we moved to Oklahoma I thought that it was the divorce capital of the country, so I was really mad at them for moving there. I thought it was because we moved there that they'd gotten divorced. I was only in fifth grade, so I didn't really understand. I just knew that my dad wasn't going to be living there anymore and that my mom and my little brother and I were going to be moving back to Chicago. I was really mad at them, but then I started thinking about it. I knew they were a lot happier, and it really didn't change my relationship with my dad, even though he lived far away. So I wasn't mad anymore. It still makes me sad, but at the time I was really mad.

I was really mad at my parents for like three years. It was hard for me to talk to my dad, especially about being mad at him, because I didn't see him. So, if we got into a fight on the phone, he wasn't there the next day to make up with me. I didn't always want to talk to him about how I was feeling. But then when I finally did, I felt a lot better. For a long time I was really, really mad at him. I felt like it was his fault for not moving back here and things like that.

I wasn't surprised by the divorce, because I kind of knew it was coming. I was in denial though, 'cause I didn't really realize what it meant and I knew I didn't like it. But I wasn't surprised. My parents hadn't been arguing where we could hear them, but just little things like we weren't all sitting together at breakfast anymore. They'd been talking to us for like a year and a half about them thinking about getting separated and everything like that. Both my parents are ministers and since we moved to Oklahoma my mom wasn't able to find work as a minister there. I knew my mom was really unhappy in her job, and that kind of sparked different problems with my parents, I think. I think my mom was really unhappy. So when they told us that my mom wanted to move back here, I wasn't surprised at all. They kind of had to get divorced, since my dad had a job and she didn't.

Anything They Could Have Done to Make It Easier?

No, I don't think there's anything my parents could have done to make it easier. It wasn't that hard for me. They talked with me a lot, and they were going to let me stay there if I wanted to. But I really didn't feel the need to. My older brother did. But I don't think they could have done anything. Except, maybe, I wish my father hadn't lived so far away, and that they hadn't split up my brother and I. My older brother stayed in Oklahoma, 'cause he was a junior in high school. That was probably the hardest part, not living with my brother and living five hundred miles away. That was hard.

I am really excited that my dad is going to move back to the Chicago area. I'm sad, because it is so close to when I'm leaving for college. But I'm really happy for my little brother, 'cause he's the exact same age that I was when my parents got divorced. I think it will be really good for him to have my dad living so close. All of the rest of my family lives here, so it will be good for my family as a whole, I think.

It will make Dad more like a frequent part of my life, because right now I talk to him on the phone, but I feel like I'm always filling him in on things. It's hard to explain. Sometimes he comes over and I feel like he's a visitor. Do you know what I mean? So it'll be better, because it'll feel more like I have a normal relationship with my dad.

Wish Anything Had Been Done Differently?

Just not splitting up my older brother and I. Sometimes I feel they shouldn't have ever moved to Oklahoma. We visited there once and my mom knew what the work was going to be like, and what the treatment was going to be there for her. They moved anyway. So I wonder if we had never moved if they would have gotten divorced. But aside from those two things — splitting up my brothers and moving there in the first place — I think they did everything they could. I know they tried really hard to work it out, and they were honest with my brothers and I. They didn't hide things from us. So I think they did everything they could have.

The divorce made my older brother and I a lot closer. When we lived together we fought all the time, because we're five years apart and I was always really jealous of him. When my parents divorced I was eleven and he was sixteen. I guess we had a pretty normal relationship. We fought a lot and he beat me up. But now we're really close, and I talk to him about a lot of things. I'm not sure that that's because of my parents' divorce or just because we're older now. He's twenty-two now. But we're really close and I talk to him more than I talked to him when I lived with him. I still feel that I missed out on some of the things about having him live with me. I have friends that have older brothers, and their relationship with their brothers is a lot different than my relationship with my brother. We missed out on a lot of the fun stuff. We had to do a lot of the more mature stuff.

For a little while I felt some responsibility for the divorce. I don't anymore. But I did at the beginning because I didn't understand why else they would break up. It was easier for me to blame it on myself than it was to blame it on them. I could deal with it better then.

Parents should just say that it is not the kid's fault. Parents don't divorce because of their kids even though, like, they might fight about their kids. It's not because of the kids that the parents are getting divorced. It took me a while to realize that because it was hard. It was like a hard thing for me to understand and so I just figured it must be my fault. But I know now that it wasn't. I wish that I had known that in the beginning.

I think the parents need to be educated about how to deal with their children when they get divorced. I think that when the parents tell the child that, "We still love you, and this has nothing to do with you," that's the most important thing. I think that my parents did that, but they didn't do it enough. They could have told me more that it wasn't my fault, and they could have explained to me why they were getting divorced. I think they were a little scared of telling too much. I wish more parents told their kids that it wasn't their fault and talked to them through the whole thing, so that the kids knew that it wasn't their fault.

I don't think parents should tell the kids personal things, like if there were intimacy problems or whatever. The things the kids don't want to know, the parents shouldn't tell them. But if they have questions, I think the parents should be honest.

Advice for Other Kids?

Do I have advice for other kids? Just to not think that it was their fault, and to talk to their parents honestly about how they're feeling about it, and not feel like they are not supposed to tell their parents when they are upset with them for it.

I know that telling my parents when I was mad at them, and telling them I was frustrated with them and that I didn't understand, made it a lot easier for me. Then they knew when they had to explain things to me. I think that if I'd been more closed with my feelings toward my parents, I wouldn't have been able to get over it so quickly. They wouldn't have known what to talk to me about. So, I think it's really important that kids remember that their parents are still their parents even though they're divorced, and that you're still going to be able to go to either of them; that it doesn't change *their* relationship with their parents just because their parents' relationship changed.

Awkward Moments?

The most awkward moments are when my stepparents and my real parents are all around each other. That's probably the hardest thing to deal with still. I've totally coped with my parents' divorce 'cause it happened like six and a half years ago. I've been able to adapt around it, but the awkward moments are when my dad comes to pick me up and my stepdad is there. It's not because they don't get along. They do. But it's just because it's a little awkward where their boundaries are with each other.

Like, when I graduated in eighth grade, all of them sat together: my stepmom, my stepdad, and my mom and my dad. That was a little weird. I think it's hard right now because my dad lives so far away and he doesn't make a lot of the normal parental decisions that I'd like him to make. Sometimes that causes arguments in my house. My stepdad has the authority to be a parental figure because he's a parent in the household. But sometimes I get very frustrated, because he's not my dad, and I don't want him to be able to punish me the way my dad would.

So, it's hard because my father lives so far away. He doesn't have say in things like, just basic things, like how long I'm going to be grounded, whether or not I can use the car, and things like that. I'm not sure the awkward moments ever go away, because there's my stepdad and my dad, and I have a really close relationship with both of them.

I don't feel like those awkward moments are my responsibility at all. I just kind of let my parents feel awkward, 'cause it doesn't bother me. I can tell that it bothers them sometimes when they're greeting each other and things like that, but I pretty much let them deal with it.

I think my dad will want to have a more active role when he moves back to the Chicago area, and I think that's going to be really hard. I know he's moving back here to feel more like a daily influence, and I think because he hasn't been a daily influence for so long that that's going to be where the most awkwardness comes in. He's going to want to have a say in some of the decisions that he hasn't been able to have a say in because he lives so far away. Our family — like, the one I live with — has gotten into certain routines with parental responsibilities and things like that. When my dad comes in, it's kind of going to alter some of that. I think that's going to be the most awkward moments for our family.

I'm older and I'm not at home very often and the communication that I have with all of my parents is pretty much equal even though I live with my mom. But my little brother, I think, is where like it's going to be weird. My dad is going to want to see him more often, and that will be the problem. It'll be like wanting to pick him up from school and go to parent-teacher conferences with my mom. Things that he hasn't done since my little brother was in kindergarten. I think my parents will work it out. I just think it will be uncomfortable for a little while.

Did the Divorce Change You As a Person?

When my parents got divorced, my little brother and I moved back here. My mom was a single parent for about a year and a half, and so I had to take on a lot more responsibility with my little brother. I think it forced me to grow up a little too fast. My dad is always telling me that I don't have enough time for fun. I know that I'm really responsible with school and everything. I started cooking dinner for my brother and babysitting a lot and doing things like that that I wouldn't have had to do if I had two parents. But since my mom had to work so often, I had to take on a lot more responsibility.

I think it just made me aware of responsibilities really young and gave me a lot of responsibilities that I wouldn't have had at such a young age. I think in a lot of ways that it kind of developed me more. My older brother was really bad at dealing with the divorce and so I kind of talked him through it, which was weird, because I was younger than he was.

Anything Good Come out of the Situation?

Well, both my parents remarried and they both married people that I like a lot. My mom and stepdad had a baby, so now I have another little brother that I love a lot. Those are really good things. I wouldn't want them to take it back, even if they could, because my relationship with both of my parents is a lot stronger; and, if they took it back, then I wouldn't have my little brother.

My mom's happy now and I know she wasn't, especially when we lived in Oklahoma. Both my parents are really happy, and I have my little brother.

Patrick Murphy

Patrick Murphy is the Public Guardian for Cook County, Illinois, and sees problems with the way government has dealt with the "underclass."

Children End Up Being Wasted

The types of children that we deal with are abused and neglected. They don't have fathers. The mothers have basically reached a wall, where they're unable to care for them financially or emotionally. What you have is neglect, abuse, and the inability of the government to either assist the parents properly or to take care of the kids properly. So the children end up being wasted.

You're talking basically about children of the so-called underclass. That is probably 95 percent of what we see. The other 5 percent are rich and poor kids who are sexually abused or physically abused. The culture of the so-called underclass is children being born to very poor people, children whose fathers are uninvolved and whose mothers are teenagers. By the time the mothers reach twenty, they have three or four kids by different fathers. The fathers are not involved. The mothers turn to drugs. It's the only reasonable way of taking a vacation. Ultimately everyone ends up in the system.

That's not to say that most poor people are like this. Most poor people, in fact, are not like this. One thing that always bothers me is the patronizing that goes on from some groups. Most poor people, most black people, are not like this and are not members of the so-called underclass. It just so happens that the predominant members of the underclass happen to be very poor. But most poor people are not members of the underclass.

"The Next Time You Get Pregnant"

Your typical cases are young girls who get pregnant. It's almost expected of them to get pregnant, because no one's talking about motivation and high school. The best example involves one of the lawyers who recently went to pick up a kid, a fourteen-year-old kid from the inner city, who just gave birth to a child. She happened to be a ward of the courts; she was in our system. On the way out the social worker said, "The next time you get pregnant, get prenatal care."

Well, the simple fact is, had that kid been a fourteen-year-old kid from the suburbs they wouldn't say, "The next time you get pregnant." They would say, "Don't get pregnant again, because it's going to ruin your life." Have an abortion, have birth control, abstinence, whatever it is. Indeed, if it were a kid from the suburbs, she probably wouldn't have been there anyway, because chances are very good she would've used birth control or had an abortion or been involved with abstinence.

What ultimately happens is that many poor people like this find that they simply are unable to raise their kids. They don't have enough money. They don't have any resources. They have no education. They can't get a good job. They cave in under the pressures, they turn to booze or drugs or both, and they come into our system. Then what happens is the children are taken away. We give the mother help from a psychiatrist or psychologist, and she gets better. We give the kids back, and then she goes back to the same high-rise housing project and looks out the window and gets depressed. It's a reality-based depression, and everything repeats itself.

Politics, Politics, Politics

Why are these young women getting pregnant in the first place, and why are there so few marriages? I think there was a whole culture which in part was propelled by our previous welfare system. I like to think of myself as a liberal; even a liberal-left Democrat. Most liberal-left Democrats consider me conservative and Republican and most Republicans consider me a liberal-left Democrat.

The simple fact is that our previous welfare system set up a whole group of people, basically patronizing them and giving them a small amount of money. No matter how much welfare is, it could never be enough to get them by. Then a lot of lawsuits, brought by people like myself, solidified the system back in the '60s. So a culture was set up wherein it was understood you would have babies young. You would get apartments given to you by the government. You would have no man around. And this would repeat itself, so that we have grandmothers in their early thirties, great-grandmothers in their forties, and everyone considers this okay.

It's like you say, "Let's change it." Oh no, you're being racist or sexist. It's okay for girls to have babies, and if you try to interfere with them, there's something wrong with you. The problem with this is that you get hit from the right and the left. The right says, "Don't go in there and talk about abortion with these young girls; let them have their babies. That's good." And you can't even talk about birth control if you're far enough right. The left says, "Oh, don't get in there and tell these kids to have an abortion. They have a right to use their bodies the way they want to." In the meantime, the only people who are really getting shafted are the young mothers and their babies.

I've been in this business since 1968, and there's a stage where you say, "Wait a second, it ain't workin' the way it's supposed to work." At that point you either change or you become a whore to the system and you say, "Hey, I'm getting paid, everyone else is getting paid, let's go and ask for more money to help poor people." And you set up this big Poor Bureaucracy consisting of white, middle-class liberals and now black, middle-class liberals which ain't doing nothing for the people in it.

And I think the point of welfare reform was to get the message across that the government ain't going to be there for you. You better get your high school diploma, you'll hopefully go on to college, and so on and so forth.

I'm Really Optimistic

I think things are changing. We're sitting here talking at a point in time where I really am optimistic. For years I was pessimistic, but I see the birth rates are dropping amongst both white and black teenagers. Since '95 they've been plummeting. As long as that happens, I think that we're going to see a real turnaround.

But for years almost every government program unconsciously or inadvertently encouraged women not to be involved with their men. At the same time, the culture was so poor and so discriminated against and so chaotic in the real inner, inner, inner city. I want to emphasis that this is a very small group of people, even amongst the poor. It became cultural and it became natural in a large part because of government programs and in part because of segregation, discrimination, etcetera. But the good news is, I really think that's changing.

I think that what's evolving in our society is great. I think that fifty years from now we're going to be so different than we were twenty or thirty years ago. Gay marriage is going to be recognized, as it should be. There will be different kinds of families out there. There'll be some "*Leave It To Beaver* families," and you'll see working moms and dads staying at home and working part-time. It's going to be just a whole different situation out there. It's going to be a lot better, I think. I'm really optimistic. For a long time, I wasn't. I just think we've gone through some hard times and we're emerging, and it's going to be a great society.

What Do We Do Now?

The first thing is that abortion should be available to poor and rich alike. I consider myself a Catholic, although I don't know if the pope considers me a Catholic. But I think that if abortion is legal, it has to be available to everybody. Not that you encourage abortion. I think that when it comes to abortion in the first six months, basically, it should be available on demand. After that, I think we should look very carefully at it. I think they're nuts at both ends of the political spectrum.

I also think that I would try to resolve problems of the poor without bringing the courts and judges and lawyers into the process. We lawyers think we have the solution to everything, but to the degree we can keep them in the community with master's-degree social workers dealing with these issues and problems we should. The court should definitely be the last resort, because we don't have the answers. It'd be cheaper. Lawyers, whether driven by financial considerations or whatnot, always want to get involved and want to encourage litigation. If it can be done outside of court, and it's pretty possible, I would certainly encourage that.

Looking for Love

Who knows, we may be together for many, many years and never take that final plunge into marriage. I think a lot of it has to do with financial issues. We want to be able to have a nice wedding.

ANTONIA

I want the one person who's going to love you no matter what, even when you come home and smell like a dog that's been ran over three times.

RICKY

People who presumably believe in the sanctity and permanence of marriage will nevertheless preface any question they write to me with the phrase, "It's my first wedding." And I think, "It's your first wedding? People used to say, 'I am getting married.'"

JUDITH MARTIN (MISS MANNERS)

Marriage is not important. Relationships and commitment and love are important.

COLLEEN

We now live in a world where it's already presumed that they're sharing a bed. Now that they've decided to share a kitchen, where's the shock? The stigma is gone.

LARRY BUMPASS

We started to pull out our handy dandy Palm Pilots and figure out when is the next time we can go out, and it ended up being like three weeks away on Thursday between 8:30 and 10:30. It's kind of crazy fitting it into the time schedule.

SCOTT

The American experience today is that people are not marrying until their mid-twenties or even later. Putting off marriage may help people make wiser choices, but for many young singles, it is not always easy to know where sex belongs in dating relationships. Although the church says to wait to have sex until marriage, the reality for many today is that sex doesn't wait.

Not only are people waiting longer to get married than in the past, but for young singles today the pathway into marriage has changed. People used to marry so that they could live together. Now people live together so they can figure out whether they want to get married. More than half of first marriages today are preceded by cohabitation.

One reason living together is so popular is that young people are acutely aware of the risks of divorce. They think that living together before marriage will reduce the likelihood of divorce and increase their chances of having a successful marriage, but in cohabiting relationships the balance of power tilts to the partner who is less committed and more likely to walk out. Some also believe that sharing living space will give them the advantages of marriage without the legal commitments, but that isn't the case according to experts like Linda Waite.

Other couples delay marriage until they can afford the wedding of their dreams. But in the meantime, a growing percentage of these couples also have children. This places their children in greater jeopardy of family breakup than kids born to married parents. Fully three quarters of children born to cohabiting couples will see their parents split up before they reach age sixteen, compared to a third of those born to married parents.

When we first met Antonia, she and her boyfriend John had just found out they were going to become parents. They are living together, but as for marriage? . . . For the moment, it isn't in their plans.

Antonia and John M.

Antonia and John live together and are expecting a child. Antonia is studying at the Art Institute of Chicago. John is an emergency medical technician and a real estate appraiser.

ANTONIA'S STORY

I was married before. I was twenty-two when I met and married my husband. I was married for about three years. I've been separated for a year, now divorced. I'm actually going through the legal proceedings right now for a divorce. I met him in New York City. I had just gotten home (I was traveling in Greece), and I thought I'd met Prince Charming. I romanticized a lot of it and we had a very short courtship, only a matter of months, and then we got married.

Getting married was a last minute, spontaneous decision. I remember we were out listening to a band, and I said to him that he was going to marry me. He looked at me and said, "Oh, that sounds like a good idea." That was about the extent of it. There wasn't any planning involved.

I don't think I had thought as much about marriage as I had about commitment. Marriage was something that wasn't on the top of my list of importance. I'd always been an extremely committed person in relationships. I had never had a problem with loyalty and making these long-term commitments, but marriage just wasn't something that struck me as being inevitable or a next step to anything. I just loved him with all my heart at the time, and I felt like I wanted to do something right. I wanted to for once take the appropriate steps and actually make the legal commitment. So it was very spontaneous.

Our Directions Just Changed

It was so subtle. Marriage didn't really change anything for us. We had an excellent friendship. We both enjoyed traveling, so we spent the first two years of our marriage traveling around the United States. We would go from place to place and we'd get menial-type jobs. I'd paint and he'd kind of just bum around or write. We just thought that was the lifestyle that was the most appealing to me, sort of the beatnik lifestyle.

My ambitions took hold of me, and I really decided that school was where I needed to be. My painting needed to be fine-tuned. At that point, we began to grow apart. He still wanted to live this childlike lifestyle with no responsibilities. I became sort of the maternal figure in the relationship and held things together. Our directions just changed.

Was it a surprise? It was gradual. It wasn't so much a surprise as it was a feeling that from the beginning I always played this motherly role in the relationship. He was a little younger than I was, quite young when we married and not long out of his house. So he'd gone from one nest to another.

I guess when I was younger I felt very comfortable in that role because I grew up taking care of younger siblings. That maternal role gave me security. Me taking care of him made me feel important. But as I got older, I needed a partnership and I needed him to display some mature, masculine responsibilities, some characteristics of adulthood. I realized that you can't change a person. You can only love them for what they are or move on. He's a great person, but just not for me.

I wasn't soured on marriage. I guess I was hopeful for the future. I just knew I had a more concise view of what I didn't want. I knew upon looking for somebody again, which would take time, that I'd look for somebody a little more mature and a little more down to earth and a lot more responsible.

We Decided to Live Together

I met John when he was bartending. I was out on a date and we decided to have a bite to eat. I had never been in the area before and we found this little Italian restaurant hidden away. John was my bartender and the rest is history.

Did I get his phone number? No, I don't think I'm quite that audacious. I thought about it, I have to say. My gentleman friend got up to use the bathroom a few times and I wondered, "Gosh, do I have enough time to get my number on a napkin and slip it to him?" But it wasn't a respectful thing to do to the guy I was with. So I waited and I took a matchbook from the restaurant so that I would remember the address. I hung on to it, and a few weeks later I went back looking for him.

We decided to live together when I got pregnant, which was about four months after we had started dating. That was about three and a half months ago. I'm expecting a baby, so John and I decided that it was a good time to make the move. I needed a lot of help around the house, and I was quite sick the first few months of my pregnancy. His support was really essential for me, and financially we needed to relieve ourselves of the burden of an extra rent.

When I found out I was pregnant the thing on my mind was school, to be honest. I had my heart set on attaining this degree for so many years, and I'd finally braved going back to school. I finished high school, and I decided to take an alternative route of life and travel and experience things before I went to school. The years began to go by, and I got older. I noticed a lot of people within my age group were already finished with school, and that was very intimidating for me. Finally, I just sort of bit the bullet and said this is something I really, really want. It doesn't matter my age. I'm not getting younger, so I need to do it. When I found out about the baby, the first thing I thought was "Goodness — how am I going to finish school and have this child at the same time?" But I think having the baby gave me extra initiative to finish, because now I have somebody depending on me to provide things and to set a good example, to be a role model.

John's Reaction to the Baby

He was a little nauseous, I think. He was scared. It took him a few days for the idea to settle in. I think he really accepted it when he saw the first ultrasound. That was about a month and a half after I took the test and found out I was pregnant. He was there with me in the hospital room and he saw the baby on the TV monitor. He was just like, "Wow, that's our baby. This is so real." It was tangible for him, and I think that was important. That really locked it in for him.

Marriage: I Don't Know

I know we'll definitely be together and both playing equal parts in taking care of the child. Marriage, at this point, I don't know. We'll have to wait and see. I'm not against it, by any means. I think our main concern right now is being financially prepared for when the baby's born. We're going to go through some tough times the first few years of the baby's life. Both of us are in transition trying to finish school, trying to work. We don't have a lot of extra time for each other, even, right now.

So that's going to be difficult, and I'm prepared for that. But I know that the love is there, and the support is there, and encouragement. Who knows, we may be together for many, many years and never take that final plunge into marriage. I think a lot of it has to do with financial issues. We want to be able to have a nice wedding. Maybe when the baby gets a little older, and he or she can experience it with us. That might be nice.

I think I'm a strong person. I persevere. I need somebody that's equally as strong. I become bored quickly in relationships if I'm not learning anything from the other individual. So I like people that want to experience new things and want to live life and have an open mind to learning. You know, outside experiences.

My Ideal Family

I suppose everybody has their own vision. Definitely two parents, a lot of love. Not necessarily a lot of money, but I would like to be able to live in a safe neighborhood and provide my child or children with the basic necessities without having to worry and scrape. I'd like to be a good role model and not be a hypocrite, to be able to tell my children these outside influences are there, to be able to talk openly with my children. And for my children to know that I am behind them and supporting them and that my husband is also.

It's really hard. I want to say white picket fence out in the country, a whole lot of land for my dogs to roam around, animals (a lot of animals), but who knows? I guess my version of ideal is always changing as I'm getting older. I do know that having a career is important to me. But, I think, especially being a woman, that my role in my child's life is so vital, and I think there's a real fine line between being goal-oriented and being a parent. I want to be able to invest as much time, if not more, in my children as I do in my career.

I think the United States is very capitalistic. People are much more geared toward making money these days. In the 1950s, my grandfather owned a little drugstore and was basically a soda jerk. He supported a family of seven on that meager salary. Today, that would be virtually impossible. Because of the economy, both parents are forced into careers or working. Because of the sexual revolution, women are much more geared toward having careers and competing in the career world.

I think that leaves children at times on the outs — lot of latchkey kids, and a lot of kids that don't have as much time with their parents as they probably should, and a lot of single parents. Forty years ago, being a single mother was shocking, especially in small towns. So now it's just the norm.

JOHN'S STORY

It's kind of funny. Antonia came into my restaurant. I was bartending, and she was on a date. I don't know. We just had kind of a chemistry. I wasn't trying to intrude on her night, but I definitely felt something for her. I hoped she'd come back, and she did. She came back about a week later and she missed me. She came back again and I was there. That was probably two weeks after she had been in the first time. We dated immediately. Two days later, we had our first date. We went to the Shedd Aquarium, which was very fun. I hadn't been there since I was a little kid. It was pretty cool.

I had no plans to get serious about anybody at that point. I like to take things one step at a time, but I definitely felt some feelings, some strong feelings, and I was ready to pursue that avenue.

Finding out that I was going to be a father was very scary, very exciting. It was something I wasn't expecting, but something I'm ready for, you know? Something I definitely see as a positive thing. It has really changed my life already, and it's only been a couple of months. In a lot of positive ways, I feel like I've grown up a lot in the last few months, redirected my life in many ways. I was content with being kind of laid back and easy-going and kind of a slacker. This has given me a lot of focus, pursuing some things in life, bettering my life, finding a career, which I had kind of blown off for so many years. I really didn't know where I wanted to go, and this has kind of pushed me into choosing.

Marriage? We're going to live together. One step at a time, you know? The baby's first right now. That's our main priority, and that's our main focus. Down the road, I definitely think we will get married. But there's no date or no pressure on that situation right now. We don't want to distract from what's going on now with the baby.

My Family

They're happy. At first they were shocked, but they're very happy. Now they're really excited. They're really happy for us.

My family was a good family. I love my brothers and my sister very much. We're very close. My brother Danny, in particular, because we're a little closer in age. We spent a lot of time growing up. We were kind of best friends for many years and still are. When I was fourteen my parents got divorced, which changed things. But I remained friends with both of them and did not let their problems get in between my relationship with either of them. It was like any family. It had its dysfunctions, but on the whole I'd say I grew up in a really good home.

I knew that my parents fought and they had problems. So it was no real big surprise when they got divorced. It was no big shocker to the family. I was probably a little more shocked than the rest of my family because I was the youngest. But I dealt with it pretty good. I knew that they had to do what was best for them, and we were old enough to accept it.

Marriage: When We're Ready

I don't know. I think traditions are changing. The new generation is not quite the same as the old. Where before you get married, have babies, you know, it's a progression. Nowadays I think it's a little different. It's like marriage doesn't seem to have the value that it used to have. It seems to me in a lot of ways it's just a piece of paper.

We've gotten away from the real structure, the family structure, I think. We've gotten away from what marriage is supposed to be about. You know? The commitment, the vows. It seems that people take vows and they don't really mean it.

I don't have many friends who are married. I can really only think of two or three. I have a few friends that live with mates. No marriage though. I think there's more people living together these days. I think there's a lot more wait. People are getting married at a later age. They date a longer period of time.

Why are more people living together than getting married? Oh, man, that's a tough question. I really don't know. Maybe people are afraid of that commitment. Maybe they want to try a person out and see how compatible they are, how they live with them, before they actually commit to marriage. See how they travel with people and things like that. I don't know.

I guess it all comes down to a commitment of locking yourself in to one person. A lot of my friends are just gnawing on that. They've had some really good girlfriends that I thought would have been perfect for them, and they kind of decided to wait and wait and wait and wait. I think it was just that fear of being with that one person for the rest of their life.

We've definitely talked about getting married, but not too much. I don't think I'm going to wait until Antonia asks me to get married. I think I will wait to do it right. To make it a special, special day. When we're financially ready and emotionally ready. When I can take her on a vacation of her dreams, you know? That's one thing I'd love to do and to do that now. I can't do that. It wouldn't be that dream day that she may have thought about for so many years, or that I have thought about for so many years. I kind of want it to be as perfect as possible.

It would be friends, family, and just a celebration. Just having fun with all the people that I love, and I just think it would be a great experience. I'd like to do something outside, I think. I love the country. I would love to do it on a beach somewhere with the ocean and the sun setting behind us. I think it would be beautiful, but I don't know if that's how it's going to work out. I guess we'll see. One step at a time. We haven't gotten there yet.

Right now, like I said, our focus is on our baby. That's all we need to focus on right now. We know we'll be together. We're partners. We don't need to put pressure on going through the whole ceremony right now just to make other people happy and to do it traditionally. That's not fair. We're going to do it our way. We'll do it when we decide that's the right time. It might be a year from now, or it might be a couple of years from now. I'm not sure, but we'll know. We'll know when the right time comes.

Larry Bumpass

According to Larry Bumpass, family instability has increased in recent years despite the constant divorce rate. He discusses the role cohabitation has played in this.

Sharing the Kitchen

When we look at all this dramatic change and ask why is this happening, there's no simple story. But there's a story that can be woven together that I think makes some sense. That's why I have discussed the increased acceptance of sex outside of marriage on the part of young people and the fact that with delayed marriage this has become just very much a part of our culture.

Sex was one of the benefits of marriage to the extent that sex was confined to marriage. When you think about cohabitation and go back two or three decades, it was very negatively regarded and described in pejorative terms of "shacking up" or "living in sin." The reason was quite obvious. It was simply an open admission that this unmarried couple was having sex. Well, we now live in a world where it's already presumed that they're sharing a bed. Now they've decided to share a kitchen, where's the shock? The stigma is gone. So there's little reason for a couple not to cohabit if want to.

Very similar things, I think, are going on with respect to unmarried childbearing. I know at the outset that divorce probably has played some role in this for two reasons: One, in reducing the stigma against single-parent families themselves. They become common and less stigmatized through this creation of single-parent families by choice. Also, given the high levels of divorce, when a young woman finds herself pregnant, the pressure to get married to someone she may then very likely divorce right away just makes little sense. So many go ahead and have a child.

Now, the same argument I was making about cohabitation, I think, applies very quickly to unmarried childbearing. Once again, it was a matter of great shock when a young woman was found to be pregnant when she was unmarried, because it was blatant evidence that she was unmarried and sexually active. Once again, the stigma is gone, because the presumption is she's probably sexually active.

Now, I keep emphasizing that these patterns are related to one another in very complex ways. The fact that couples can cohabit without being married makes it much easier to put off marriage. So delayed marriage can be seen as in part a consequence of increased living together, increased ability to live together without being married.

The Plot Thickens

One of the primary reasons that these changes in family life are as important as they are is that children are involved at every turn. Cohabitation tends to be thought about as something college students do while they're in school. But, in fact, the trend in cohabitation was led by the less educated rather than college students. More importantly, most cohabitations involve children, and indeed many cohabiting couples have their own child in that relationship.

This is another point where all of this starts to weave together. We tend to think of unmarried childbearing as creating single-parent families. But a substantial part of unmarried childbearing in the U.S. and even higher levels in countries like Great Britain occur in two-parent families. That is to say, they're cohabiting. They're unmarried, but the child is born into a household with both their mother and their father.

So, the plot thickens. There is this relationship between living together and having children and yet being unmarried. In fact, virtually all of the increase in unmarried childbearing in the U.S. over the last decade, and I believe the same is true in Britain, occurred among these kinds of families. That is where the mother and the father are living together and the child is born into a two-parent family.

It's a complicated situation. Many of those who have a child while living together do get married. Many cohabiters do get married. Many break up before the marriage. There are some very complicated stories there that are worth our exploration. But they're hard to tell because much is often made in the policy discussions, especially from those who emphasize family values in more conservative positions, that couples who live together before marriage are more likely to break up. Now that's true and I'll come back in a moment to how that's related to the stability of children's family lives. But the important thing is that the best researched evidence available suggests that it is not living together that causes the higher instability of the relationship, but rather a *selection*, to use a technical term. It's the kinds of attitudes and values that are brought into cohabiting relationships, as opposed to those who marry directly. To put it simply, someone who would never think about cohabiting is also likely to be someone who would not engage divorce as an option, except under the most extreme circumstances.

So you get something of a sorting into two populations. The one that would find divorce more acceptable is also the one that's more likely to begin a relationship by cohabiting. It's also likely that those who begin a marriage directly without living together are more certain of their relationship. Couples who want to try out their relationship — and that's the reason young couples often give us — do so to find out whether it's going to work. Well, if those who cohabit include those who were less certain about their relationship to begin with, they are likely to include some who are, in fact, in less stable relationships. So the divorce rate is higher and the stability of cohabiting relationships is lower. But I don't think it's causal.

There is a very interesting relationship between cohabitation and divorce that I think is not as widely accepted, but I believe it to be true. Going back to the long-term trend in divorce, the divorce rate has been constant in the U.S. for the last twenty years, coincidentally leveling off at about the time cohabitation began to increase so rapidly. Now, to the extent that couples are living together who would in the earlier regime have married, then when these couples break up without marrying, these would've been divorces under the old system. So it's family instability that falls outside of the statistical accounting system. We think the divorce rate has been constant but, in fact, children's family lives have become less stable over this time period because of these changes in their family relationships that are outside of a statistical system.

Increased Instability

If you include the cohabiting families as well as married families, the increase in family instability is much more where you would've expected it to be on the basis of the trend line. There has, in fact, been a 27 percent increase in disruption rates and family instability over this time period where the divorce rate was constant, simply because of the cohabitations that are not in the system.

It's great fun to a demographer to try to patch together all these different components and their rates and proportions. But I think the broader picture can be described as about half of all marriages do end in divorce, and a higher proportion of all unions if you include those that began as cohabitations and break up before marriage. About half of all children will spend some time in a single-parent family. That is either because they are born to an unmarried mother who is not living with the child's father or because the family unit they were born into breaks up, and then they usually live with the mother or with the father alone. So the level of instability is about half or somewhat higher, and children are spending less time in married families.

Children and Transitions

Children are experiencing more transitions in their family lives, and there's evidence that the number of transitions that children go through is important for their life outcomes.

It seems to me there are about three things that we ought to focus on in talking about this. There is an array of theories about why it is there are negative outcomes on children from these many transitions. One of the most important components is simply income. As children move from a two-parent family usually to a mother-only family, given the lower income of females, they experience a reduction in economic well-being. Often we talk about poverty and ignore the fact that this reduction in economic well-being can have a very significant effect on a child's life even if they're well above the poverty line.

A second component of this is the kinds of residential moves that often accompany those economic changes. There's a change in neighborhood, a change in peer groups, and a change in housing that can have negative effects on children's lives even if they're well above poverty. This is not just a low-income thing.

Another point is that there is evidence that children who've had disruptions, multiple disruptions, in their family lives are more likely to have children while unmarried themselves. They're more likely to have sex at an early age, at a very early age. They're more likely to experience the breakup of their own marriage. They're less likely to complete high school or college. So there is an array of objective negative outcomes that one can measure.

A Terribly Important Point

But there is a terribly important perspective on this because those results are often seen as laying guilt on the parents, who were involved in the disruption. A very important perspective on that is to realize that we're talking about average levels. On the average, children from broken families do less well across an array of domains. But at the same time a great number of children do quite well, thank you. It's not a uniform deterministic kind of thing. Many children from intact families do very poorly. So it's a difference in average levels. One of the more interesting results relating to these family background factors is the finding that children who come from intact families where the parents have rather poor relationships with one another do every bit as badly as those who come from single-parent families. So there's much more to the dynamic that also includes the parenting and emotional tenor of families with conflict and not just the divorce itself.

Linda Waite

Linda Waite is a professor of sociology at the University of Chicago. She has studied the positives and negatives of marriage and cohabitation.

Cohabitation: Depends on What People Want

I think it very much depends what people want. It's not marriage for most people, and if people are expecting marriage-like benefits without getting married the evidence suggests they don't get the marriage benefits. If what they want is a roommate with sex, then cohabitation is fine. It's easy exit, and cohabiters, unless they are engaged and they have the hall rented and the dress bought, tend to lead separate lives. They tend to have separate social lives. They tend not to co-mingle finances. They don't have a joint checking account. They don't co-insure. They don't say, "Listen, if anything happens to you in twenty years, I'll take care of you, I'll be there." They very much don't do that.

So a lot of the things that people get with marriage, you don't get with cohabitation. What you get is freedom and independence. So it depends on what you want. If you thought you were getting security, commitment, dependability, fidelity, you're much less likely to get it with cohabitation.

Just Together on the Bus

I'm not talking about all cohabiters. The cohabiters who are getting married look on lots of dimensions like people who are already married. I'm talking about people who don't have any plans to marry. They tend to lead much more separate lives than married people do. Their social lives are more separate. Their financial lives are more separate. They're much more likely to have a second sexual partner even though they say they expect their partner to be faithful to them. When you ask cohabitaters if they expect their partner to be faithful to them, they report "yes" as often as married people. But they don't do that. So, yes, it's a different agenda.

Is that because of the trial nature of cohabitation? I think that's true, especially if they don't have plans to marry. Sometimes I think it's just convenience. It works for now and let's not worry about what's going to come. But there's some recent research suggesting that, especially for women with children, cohabitation leads to fairly high levels of depression, mostly because they're unsure about the future of the relationship.

So in that situation, cohabiters definitely don't get the emotional benefits of marriage, especially for women with children who come with some feeling like this person's going to be around for a while, that they're committed to you, that they're working for you and with you and you're working as a team. In cohabitation, you're not working as a team. You're just sort of together on the bus.

Benefits, and Cohabitation vs. Marriage

When cohabitation first came on the scene, we saw it as something that college students did. But in the last thirty years, there has been a fairly substantial change. Now cohabitation is more common for couples with relatively low levels of education and less common for couples where the partners are college educated.

When social scientists first started studying cohabitation, they thought, "Oh, well, it's a way to gather information. You should see if you're compatible, if this is a good idea, if you're a good match. The people who find out that they really don't like living with this person should split up." So the only people who should go to marriage would be those who found out this was really what they wanted. They liked it. They liked this person. This was going to work.

So they ought to be less likely to divorce than people who married not having this information, right? Those marriages ought to be more stable. In fact, every research project that's ever looked at the stability of marriages that were preceded by cohabitation has found that people who lived together before they get married are significantly more likely to divorce later. It's true in Canada. It's true in Sweden. It's true in the U.S. It's true wherever we've looked. So for some reason, living with somebody is just not a guarantee.

Regarding marriage, there certainly are marriages that are horrible, and nobody would suggest that people stay in those marriages. You can't. But, in fact, the chance that a man becomes an alcoholic or a career criminal if he has a tough adolescence goes down if he gets married. You can look at men's drinking patterns — say, follow young men during their twenties. Some of them get married at twenty-two; some of them get married at twenty-five. You can look at their drinking patterns and see the chances that they drink to excess declines as they find someone, become engaged, and get married. You see the same thing with criminal behavior — that if men who are serious delinquents as adolescents find someone to marry, and it works, then that often turns them around, which is pretty amazing.

So, on the one hand, if anybody in the marriage has really substantial personality problems or problems with violence or problems with addiction, it's not good for the individuals involved, and it certainly wouldn't be good to stay in that marriage. But that's relatively rare. I can give you examples on domestic violence, because I'm just looking at that now. About 5 percent of married men and married women say that arguments between them became physical in the last year and ended up with somebody pushing, hitting, or shoving. Seventeen percent of cohabiters with no plans to marry and 14 percent of cohabiters with plans to marry reported that happening. This is once we take into account age and race and gender and education. Big differences. So, the chances that there'll be violence in your relationship are lower for married people than they are for people who are cohabiting.

Probably Different Kinds of People

There is a strand that runs through all of this. The people who choose to cohabit are probably different people than the people who choose to marry directly. For example, people with strong religious values would be less likely to cohabit, more likely to marry directly, and probably more committed to the institution of marriage, however they feel about the particular person. Investments in your marriage, even if it's because you think that marriage is a sacrament, improve the quality of the marriage. So if you take two couples and one of them commits to marriage and the other one says, "I'm with you as long as we're good together," the couple with the commitment over and above just their relationship will commit and invest. Those investments will improve the quality of their relationship. So they'll end up with a better relationship than the couple that just sort of said, "Well, let's see what happens. As long as it's good, we'll stay together."

Marriage Changes People

I'm a sociologist, so I see things from the perspective that marriage is a social institution and, as a social institution, it changes people. It changes the choices they make. It changes their behavior and makes them better off in the process on a whole range of dimensions. There's a wealth of literature, much of it on fairly academic studies, that focuses on one little aspect of well-being, but I don't think people have put it together in the past. I see a very large picture of changes, improvements in well-being, brought about by marriage across a range of dimensions.

The dimensions that I'm sure of include physical health and length of life — improvements for both men and women — emotional well-being, sexual activity and sexual satisfaction, career benefits, outcomes for children across a range of dimensions, domestic violence, and wealth and assets. What else is there left except maybe beauty?

This is one of the areas where I think our popular conception is really a misconception. When I talk to people about the work I'm doing on marriage, one thing that very often pops up is, "Oh, marriage is good for men and bad for women, right?" But, in fact, the evidence suggests that that's just not true. I feel very strongly about this that, in fact, the evidence suggests that marriage is good for men and good for women. The dimensions may be a little different and the mechanisms may be a little different, but I think it's very hard to say that one gender benefits more than the other.

One thing, as a caveat: It's probably true for physical health that men get larger benefits than women do. For career benefits, I'd say men get career benefits from marriage and women don't. Women don't pay any penalties, but they don't get any career benefits. There are other dimensions where women seem to get more benefits than men.

What benefits do women get? Money is one. Let's be frank. I think money is underrated. One of the things that women get from marriage is they get financial support for themselves and especially for their children. If you look at poverty rates for single mothers, they're quite high. One of the things that's clear is what women do with the financial resources that men bring to marriage. They devote more of their time to their kids.

One could argue that it's one of the things that often women want to do. They want to spend time with their kids, especially when kids are young. Being married allows them to do that. I think one of the reasons that marriage doesn't give women career benefits is that some women trade off higher salary and career advancement for time and attention to their kids. The financial resources of the husband allows them, if they want to do that.

Does Divorce Impact Men?

Absolutely divorce impacts men, and it's very clear in the data that men who get divorced or become widowed tend to — not all of them — but too many of them experience fairly substantial declines in physical and emotional well-being. That's partly because for a lot of men, their wives ran the household and sort of organized their life. They made sure that meals were on the table, often negotiated medical bureaucracies, kept track of their health, and kept track of their emotional well-being. Another thing that women tend to do in families is to organize the social life.

Men often say that their wife is their best friend more than women say their husband is their best friend. Men tend to focus their emotional friendship networks around their wife, or she manages those networks to a much greater extent than women focus their friendship networks around their husbands. So when their wife dies, they can't cook, their household life falls apart, they don't have any friends, they don't have their best friend, and they don't have their emotional support. They eat poorly, they sleep poorly, and then they die.

"Jeez, Am I Doing the Right Thing?"

Is divorce better if parents are not getting along? That's probably true, but it has to be high levels of conflict pretty much in front of the kids. There's a very interesting study that came out a couple of years ago where a team of researchers followed families and the kids over a fifteen-year period. They had measures of how everybody was getting along. Some of these couples divorced and some stayed together. They followed the kids and looked at how many of them went to college, their emotional well-being, and what kind of families they formed themselves. They had many indicators of how the kids were doing. When the divorce ended a high-conflict marriage, the kids were never worse off, and on some dimensions better off. When the divorce ended a moderate or a low-conflict marriage, the kids were never better off and often worse off. That all sounds perfectly reasonable. What they found was only 30 percent of the divorces ended high-conflict marriages. So 70 percent of the divorces made kids worse off.

I think the truth of the matter is that maybe the parents have a relationship that's boring or not emotionally satisfying, but they're good parents; or the parents have a conflictual relationship but they're able to keep it private, and their relationship with the children, each of them, is good. Well, the child, in fact, loses. It's clear that children lose the resources of their father pretty often when parents divorce, and the family has less resources anyway because of the divorce. So as parents divorce, kids are less likely to finish college, for example, and it's clear a lot of it is just there's not the money to pay.

The truth is, children in two-parent families have a lot more resources and it's not just money. They have two people that they can call on for help, for time, and for attention. You want to get a science project done, you have two chances that somebody's going to be able to help you. If somebody is having a bad day, there's somebody there who might not be having a bad day who might be able to help you out.

So parents in two-parent families spell each other. They back each other up. When one of them can't do it, maybe the other one can. They give each other emotional support in their parenting role. So I think, "Jeez, am I doing the right thing?" If you have someone else to bounce the ideas off of, to back you up, to talk about it, it's easier to be consistent, it's easier to follow through, and it's easier to do a good job.

And How about Sex?

I think that sex is really important. Social scientists are doing a lot of research on sex and it's an important part of life. It's an important part of marriage, and I think we do a disservice to pretend it's not something that people cohabit for and people marry for. This is my research that's coming out soon in a journal: Married men and married women report higher levels of sexual activity than dating men or dating women who are sexually active. They report slightly lower levels of sexual activity than otherwise comparable cohabiting men and women, but they report higher levels of satisfaction, emotional satisfaction from sex.

When you take into account the differences in sexual activity, the differences between married and cohabiting people get bigger. Each sex act is substantially more satisfying to married men and married women. A lot of it for men has to do with just the amount of sexual activity and what they do. For women it seems to be just being married. When you take into account everything else you can think of about them and about their sexual practices, married women still show significantly higher satisfaction with sex than cohabiting or dating women, unless the dating women are engaged.

Sex is really about bonding, about connection. It's partly a physical connection, but it's partly and probably primarily emotional connection. When people are committed to each other, when people have a satisfying relationship that's long-term, that's ongoing, they can relax and be themselves and have a good time in a way that maybe you can't if you just met the guy.

Ricky

Ricky lives with his girlfriend, whom he met while working in a hotel. He wants to have a committed relationship, but he is not sure when he will be ready to get married.

How We Met

My girlfriend and I used to work together at a hotel. I was a salesperson and she was a lobby bar waitress. We actually hated each other. I thought she was the most stuck-up girl in the hotel and she thought I was the most stuck-up salesperson in the hotel.

In New Orleans, it's a big party town. You do a lot of drinking. One night we went out, and I realize that she's not that bad after all. One thing led to another and two and a half years later she moves to Chicago.

We were together for about three months when I left New Orleans and moved to Chicago. We dated for about three months long distance. It didn't work. We broke up in March or April. We kept dating. Well, we weren't dating, but we were friends. I was dating other people, she was dating other people, but yet we kept talking to each other: "I'm dating this girl, what do you think?" "I'm dating this guy, what do you think?" Eventually, we realized that we were just meant to be together. So she moved out here and we got back together Memorial Day weekend. It's been a little roller coaster ever since. But it's been good.

The Proposal, the Hurt, the Eight Hundred Square Feet

I proposed in Mississippi when she lived down there. We were talking about it. It was a done deal. We were going to be married. We were going to be married in January. We were just going to elope and go to Mammoth, get married over the rocks. Nice, nice little wedding thing. Small, intimate, family, nothing major. Then she got scared in December. She'll probably kill me for this, but she gets scared, she runs and says, "Ricky, I can't do this. I'm out of here. I'm looking for a job going closer to the Mississippi River." So we stopped talking for about two weeks. My heart is broken. I'm dying. Here I am finally saying, "Okay, I'm going to do the whole marriage thing, I'm giving up all this bachelor life," and she runs on me.

It hurt. It hurt real bad. Hey, it crushed that male macho stuff that you go through. That just died. It hurt real bad, hurt real bad.

Why do I think she was scared? Big commitment. She was married before and didn't want to have to go through another divorce. I think that's the reason why she left or, rather, why she ran. No, I haven't been married. I decided to wait for the right one. When I think I get the right one, she leaves on me.

But, it turns around for the better. She moves to Chicago. Yeah, she dumps me in December; in January, she's living here. She takes a job with this company, and it gets a little interesting from there. She takes a job at this company, making about fifteen thousand dollars more than what she was making in Mississippi. She was probably there for about three weeks. The guy realized it was a bad mix for each other. He says, "You're not good for my company," and she says, "You're not good for me." They part ties.

So now she's in Chicago, been in Chicago for three weeks, no job, no home, and we weren't living together. She was living about thirty miles from me. She's like, "All right Ricky. What do I do now?" I'm like, "Oh God, here I am. I was going to marry you in October, you dump me." I'm still a little bitter, but what are you going to do? So she ends up moving in with me. Into my one-bedroom, eight-hundred-square-foot apartment that I lived in for the last two and a half years very comfortably by myself. That's been a little interesting. It's gotten better, but the first three weeks were pure hell, just pure hell.

My Mom Found Out

I never considered cohabitating before. No, no, not with my upbringing. My dad is a pastor, so from a religious point of view, you can't do
that. It's just that I was brought up old-fashioned. You can't shack up.
You can't get the milk before you get the cow and all that stuff. So that's
not an option. Or it wasn't an option. My brothers and my sisters kind
of kept it from the family that Ricky is now living with his girlfriend.
But eventually Mom found out, and life got interesting with the family.

Another Person Sharing My Space

Truthfully, it was uncomfortable. It was tough because I was very comfortable in my world, my eight-hundred-square-foot apartment, comfortable in my world. Now all of a sudden there is another person sharing my space — one bedroom, small kitchen, and small bathroom.
There's no place to run and hide. No place to get that extra space. So,
now she's here, and we have to make it work. She can't move back
home, and she didn't have any other place to go.

   At that time I think our relationship was platonic. We had broken
up. She had dumped me. I was still bitter from that. So I'm like, "No,
we're not in a relationship." But we have the talk where, "No, I'm not
seeing anybody else." She's not seeing anybody else, but we're not together. I think it was just that male ego thing, saying, "No, I'm still my
own man." Truthfully, she was my girl. I just didn't want to admit it. But
eventually I had to succumb.

I Escaped the Big Bullet

Now I'm a little gun-shy. I want to get married, eventually. I believe that
I will end up marrying her, but to say I'm going to get married now, tomorrow, or this year, I don't think so. I don't think so. I look at it almost
like, I escaped the big bullet, you know? That big gun that was shooting
out of the cannon, "I have to get married." I'm out of it. I offered, she
said no. I'm done. So I don't have to get married right now, at least for a
little while. Until she says, "Ricky we're going to break up or else. Let's
get married." Then I'll probably end up marrying her.

My gut right now says that something big will happen once she gets settled in Chicago. I think she might run again, so I don't want to take the chance of putting my heart out there and then her running. I just don't want to take that chance. But I think time will help with that. But today it ain't gonna happen, or this month.

But, I'm Tired of Being Single

The single life was good, but I had enough. Now, I'm at the point where I'm tired of just dating everyone. Makes me sound like King Stud. I'm tired of dating. I'm tired of being out there just dating one person this month, another person next month. I like to have that one person that I can count on forever that I know through thick and thin is going to have my back. I can come home and celebrate my success stories, and I can tell her when I screwed up and say, "Oh, my God, I might lose my job," and she's going to say, "Okay, baby, it's going to be okay. Don't worry."

That's what the relationship is all about to me. I think when you're just dating out there, you don't really have anybody like that. You don't have anybody like that. I want the one person who's going to love you no matter what, you know, even when you come home and you're smelling like a dog that's been ran over three times. She's still going to give you a kiss when you walk in the door. She'll give you a kiss and say, "go bathe," but she still gives you that kiss.

A Little Interesting

I'm black. My girlfriend is white. That's been a little interesting.

Why? Because we're taught as we're growing up that color isn't an issue, especially in my generation. You're not supposed to see color. Love the person you're with, everybody loves everybody. Well, in the politically correct world, yeah, that's correct. We're supposed to do it. But in reality, it's still very much a black/white world.

In the closed doors when you're with your family, "are you sure you want to marry somebody that doesn't look like you?" She went through the same thing. She grew up in the South, so you can only imagine how her family was, bringing home a black guy. I grew up on the West Coast and my dad is a pastor, and at one point he was with the Black Panthers, so, am I sure I want to bring home a white girl?

I believe you fall in love with that one person and regardless if she's white, black, Korean, or Asian it's kind of hard to say, "No, I'm not going to love you, because you don't look like me." Truthfully, it's almost like you don't see the color. You just see that smile. The smile she has just lights up my heart.

Scott

Scott, a graduate student at the University of Chicago, dated a woman for seven years and lived with her for eight months. He didn't want to commit to marriage because he didn't want to be held back.

That Trip to Mexico

As I got out of a very serious relationship, it took me a little bit of time to get back into the dating scene, and I'm not quite sure if I'm all the way there yet. I am looking for somebody that's going to make me take that next step and form a family and relationship.

I dated a girl for about seven years with one stint in between. We started dating in college pretty early. I think I was twenty-one when I started dating her. She's a wonderful girl. I cannot say anything bad about her. She's beautiful and very intelligent. We had a lot of the same ideals with religion and family. But it came down to the fact that I got into graduate school in Chicago, and I had to make a very harsh decision. I wanted to put my career in front of a relationship. I think I had done that the entire relationship and really not given myself 100 percent to it.

In daily life, I would make a decision based on what was going on at the job, rather than what I had planned for her. One example: At work we we're coming down to a deadline, and we had planned on a trip to Mexico, just her and I. Basically the day before the trip, I called her up and said we've got a deadline, and asked her to cancel the trip or push the vacation back. It didn't quite win me any points, but it was just exactly what I did every time.

We Need to Talk

We were living separately for most of the time until the last about eight months. We started to live together. Did she think that was a premarital relationship? She did, and, at the time, I did. I thought it would definitely lead into marriage, or a way I would feel like I was ready to get married.

Ending the relationship was agonizing. Absolutely agonizing. I was traveling back and forth for my job, and it was probably one of the hardest weeks I've ever gone through. Once I found out I got into graduate school and realized that I didn't want to be slowed down from my career, I decided that I wanted to end it and put that behind me and go toward my career. It was a hard, absolutely a hard decision, and a decision I've questioned every day.

The actual day was kind of interesting. I received an acceptance letter to graduate school at home; she read it and gave me a call. She said, "You got in." I turned around and said, "Well, you know I have to go." Obviously some tears were shed, and she said, "We need to talk." When I got back, it was either get married and she would move up here with me or I would end it and go alone. I said, "I can't get married, I can't move forward with a relationship," thinking that she would slow me down in what I wanted to accomplish in this stage of my life.

Since the Breakup

It has definitely been an emotional roller coaster. The highs are very high and the lows are very low. It's amazing at the very low points that emotional pain can cause physical pain. I had never experienced that before in my life. Definitely a lot of sleepless nights, questioning did I do the right thing? Did I give up the best thing that's ever happened to me? Definitely, the thoughts come in spurts. When it first happened, it would be almost daily, and then it would move to kind of weeks. They say time heals all wounds. I think this is the same situation. On the flip side, the highs are very high. Where I'm either dating a lot or I'm very busy in grad school, I'm trying to juggle fifty million different things, and it really just occupies your mind and takes your mind away from the pain or thinking about her.

She cut off all communication. I've actually tried to communicate with her several times by e-mail and one phone call when I was back down at home in Atlanta. But she obviously did not want to speak to me. She was obviously very angry with me. So she said that she's moving on with her life. I need to also.

Dating Again

I think dating definitely has changed even in the past five or six years from when I was dating in college. I'm after different things. Then, it was to have a good time. Now, it's like I'll make my decision right off the bat. If I'm clicking with this girl and I want to date her more, I'll pursue that. Truly, I think it means having a little bit more stakes right now. For example, I went out with a girl last week and we had a very nice time, it was good conversation, but I knew there were no sparks and it was nothing I wanted to pursue. So as I left, it wasn't like, "I'll give you a call sometime," and never call. It was like, "I enjoyed the date. Have a nice life."

How else has dating changed? Well, the first thing is time. I think we had a lot more time when I was younger, especially in college. Right now, it's hard enough dating one person at a time. I went out with this one girl, and we wanted to go out again. We started to pull out our handy dandy Palm Pilots and figure out when is the next time we can go out, and it ended up being like three weeks away on Thursday between 8:30 and 10:30. It's kind of crazy fitting it into the time schedule.

Marriage?

Not initially. I don't think that's the first thing that comes up. You've got to find out if you're compatible, and then I think the next stage is seeing if you're compatible with your religion and family and ideals and what you want. Even right now, I don't think my ideals have changed that I'm right now putting my career first. But I think I need to find a person that thinks the same way and will be able to be with me as I progress in the career.

I think it's kind of professional and personal. Personal, I definitely think I need somebody who is going to want to have a family; maybe not a large family, but I'd like to settle down and have a family eventually. On a professional level, I definitely have to have somebody who has their own career goals as well as someone who wants to form professional goals with me. I would love to be able to start a business and either incorporate my wife into the business with me or we do it together. So I definitely have to have professional and personal goals.

My Family

I lost my mother when I was about a year old. She was actually pregnant with a little sister at the time, and I think that really affected my father deeply. I don't think he every truly got over it. Never truly loved again. I think I was probably the only person he really loved and lived for. But he got remarried when I was about nine years old, and with that we formed another family. I had two stepbrothers and a stepsister. I was close to them at the time we were growing up, but we were not alike. We were very different types of people. Finally, my father divorced my stepmom, the mom who I grew up with, about two years ago. It really separated the family and took a toll on the family. Just recently, I've tried to re-form a relationship with my stepmom and my stepbrothers.

Marriage May Not Be Worth It

We always read the statistics that 50 percent of marriages end in divorce, and obviously that plays a part in being very weary of marriage. I'd rather be single at twenty than single at fifty. It makes an extremely big difference. You know, if there's any question that a marriage may not work, it may not be worth it to get into it. I think everyday that that plays a deep part in people my age.

People are a little bit spoiled these days, even with what they want out of life and career. I think we all, especially in America, expect to have the white picket fence and the beautiful house and make a lot of money. Maybe fifty years ago people were really struggling a little bit more than they are today. I think that carries over to what we expect out of a relationship. I'm definitely an example of that. I don't want to settle. I want to have all those things; it's the entire package. Therefore, people are looking for more out of their spouse as I am. I'm looking for the entire package, and I don't want to settle for anything short of that.

I'm hoping also that I provide the total package to somebody. I don't want somebody else to settle for me. I want to be that person that they put on pedestals, as well as, I want to put them on the pedestal and idolize that person.

I completely agree that it is quite a job. What's the old saying? — there are two questions in life: what you're going to do with it and who you're going to spend it with. I'm going to a graduate business school. I don't think I have to worry about what I'm going to do in my life. I feel that I'm going to be successful no matter what I do on that side. The more difficult question is who I'm going to spend it with. I think that's going to be the harder thing to do. I think the harder you work in school and work, the more successful you can be. In relationships, that doesn't always work.

Next Trip to Mexico?

What happens the next time there's a trip to Mexico and a demand at work? That's definitely a difficult question. I guess the other thing you always say is it's lonely at the top if you don't make some of the right decisions. I hope that when I finally get married and I put this person on a pedestal and they put me on the pedestal, that it's a situation where I will want to make that decision. I don't want to have to put my career before everything in a relationship. So when that decision comes up again, I hope I make the right one, which may be going to Mexico.

David Popenoe

David Popenoe is a professor of sociology at Rutgers University and co-director of the National Marriage Project. He conducts focus groups with young people across the country and sees some disturbing trends.

Our Focus Groups

At the National Marriage Project at Rutgers, we decided to concentrate most of our efforts on looking into the mating and dating and marriage ideas, patterns, and behavior of today's pre-married young adults. That means mainly kids in their twenties. We know a lot about the Baby Boomers and what they did to the nation. The Generation Y kids are today's teenagers. They're of interest, but they're not fully formed. We have this big group, sometimes called Generation X, which really does represent something quite different from the Baby Boomers. So that's what we're looking at, and it's quite remarkable what's going on out there.

The Baby Boomers grew up in strong, intact families, and they had enough family security, in my opinion, of course, that they were able to go off in a highly individualistic direction and get away with it. They still had family back there that they could turn to. So they went to the extreme.

Today's Generation X are the children of the Baby Boomers, and they've grown up for the most part in crummy families, in which you've had a tremendously high divorce rate, if you even had marriages to begin with. These kids are kind of shell-shocked. They're like deer caught in the headlights. First of all, they desperately want a long-term marriage more than the Baby Boomers ever did. The Baby Boomers had come from these strong families and felt they could do something else. Today's generation knows that that's important but they don't quite know how to go about it. They certainly haven't been taught how to do it by their parents. And the popular culture, the entertainment industry and so on, which is the single most important thing in their lives right now, is about as anti-marriage and anti-child as you can get. So these kids are floundering.

A Sexually Charged Scene

For the first time in history we have this long period of life called young adulthood in which people are living apart from the families in which they grew up and they're not yet married. This is a sexually charged scene. It goes on for ten or twelve years before they eventually marry. The idea is that this is a good way to prepare for eventual marriage and children.

Most of these people, especially the women, still want to have children and they all want to marry. So the question is, "What does this say about preparation?" The fact is that I think that if you were to design a life that was maladapted for what's to come later this would probably be it. They're not thinking about marriage in any realistic or close sense. They're certainly not thinking about children, and they're leading a lifestyle in which relationships become very fragile and involve all sorts of serial connections with other people. That's the kind of attitude one would think you wouldn't want to have when you're married, having children, and wanting to stay the course.

It's interesting in our focus groups that they don't quite understand marriage as an institution anymore. It's a relationship. You know, you have a pal that you can take around with you for life. We ask questions about, "What the heck is the marriage license for?" Their view is that they can't answer it. But in general, they think that maybe it's just a way to raise taxes or something.

Men Are Optimistic, Women Aren't

Do we need marriage anymore? The reason we need it is because children, when they come into this world, have a mother and father biologically in most cases and they look to this mother and father to care for them. It has always been that way. Marriage is the thing which holds those two people together. Or to put it in a more biological or historical way, marriage is the institution which holds the father to the mother-child bond. That's no less important today than it ever was in the past. Now, if you want to just rid yourself of the whole thing and go to some alternative scheme to raise children, fine. But history is not on your side. There has never been a better solution than a mother and a father staying together and raising their own kids.

There's a whole other new body of evidence that's coming forth about how important marriage is to the individual. Somehow in binding yourself to another person for a long period of time, you get all sorts of personal benefits that people are not fully aware of. You live longer. You're healthier. You're happier. All the studies tend to show that. When you stop and think about it, the thing that you want to avoid is the lonely person who's cut off from all ties to others. Of course, the Baby Boomers never thought of anything like that, but maybe the Generation X'ers are beginning to think a little bit more about that.

All of our couples, by the way, do want to have this pal for life or this partner, although there are some striking differences between the women and the men. The men really are very optimistic about the future. They think they're doing all the right things by delaying marriage, by living with a woman first (which they regard as kind of insurance that the marriage is going to be successful). The women are much more pessimistic about the future. They don't think that there are good guys out there. They don't like the idea of cohabitation. They don't want to wait so long to marry, because their biological clock is ticking.

The biology was never enough to hold a father to the mother-child bond. That's why every society has set up the institution of marriage — virtually every society — and they did it for this purpose of holding the father to the mother-child bond. They realized that the outcome for the children would be better. Of course, in times past, where you lived in large extended families in small communities, the extended family pressure was enough to hold the marriage together. Today those ties are gone, and it's kind of left up to the father's own whim as to whether or not he wants to stick around. In fact, there are all sorts of people telling him that you can have a whole lot better life with some chicks down the street. And, sure enough, that's what he picks.

A Ghastly Scene

If you want to get into evolutionary psychology, all of this goes back to the very different biological and sexual strategies of men and women. I think that if you do away with the institution of marriage, you are still going to have the mother-child bond, because that's the strongest relationship in humankind. But I believe the father-mother-child bond is going to weaken, and the fathers are going to have a tendency to pull away and set up new families of their own, letting the mother take care of the first kid.

Evolutionary psychology is now the "in" field. Ten years ago it was almost unheard of and you would get hooted by an audience if you brought it up. Now it's front-page stuff in the newspapers. The fundamental issue is that the mother has a very, very strong tie to her own child, and she knows that that child is hers. She has a limited number of children that she can have in life, and she's got to take care of them. The dads can go one of two ways. Either they can stay with that mom and help her raise this child and help that child become a successful adult, or they can go off and spread their seed widely and have little children all over the place. Therefore, you have a very different sexual strategy. The woman is trying very hard to get a man who will stay with her and settle down and care for the kids. The man is, at least at some stages in life, trying hard not to be tied down so that he can still, at least unconsciously, keep this other option open.

Today, in the young, pre-marriage adults, you see that the women are very concerned that they're not going to have the guy. The guys seem to be footloose. The girls tell you that there's a meat market out there, that none of these guys seem to be serious. The girls all want to have a child, and, by the way, more and more of them are saying that if the right guy doesn't come along they're going to have it on their own. They can do it now, because you've got support from the state and so on. Now the guys, on the other hand, they're kind of unconcerned about all this in a way because they know that when they get to be thirty or so they can find a woman. Or, if they don't want to marry, they can stay loose. They can just have a whole series of girlfriends or they can marry. This society is not too worried. They can dump the person if they want to and start a new family if they find someone better. It really is a kind of child-oriented point of view or a human-relationship point of view, but in my view it's a ghastly scene.

Why a ghastly scene? Because I think what people want more than anything else is close relationships with others. If you ask people late in life what has brought them the most meaning and significance and value to their lives, it's going to be close relationships that they have had with others, either marriage or relationships with children and close friends. That's why the family has always been so terribly important.

What happens when marriage is not in the picture anymore? We are headed in that direction, and if you project trends you end up with an even more ghastly, to use that word again, scene than we have now, in which children are raised mostly by their mothers and the fathers are roaming around.

The state has an enormous role in stepping in where the father has stepped out. You might try to have parenting contracts, as some say, so that you can at least get the money from these fathers, but look at what's happened today following divorce. Try to hold all of these dads to good behavior. It's extremely difficult, and I think a parenting contract is, frankly, kind of a joke. If we get to that stage we're finished.

When Children Are out of the Picture

Children are rapidly going out of the picture, and that's one of the big, big problems of our time. The main thing that happens is that the whole reason for the institution of marriage virtually collapses. If it's just a question of adult relationships, I don't think the state would have a big concern; the church, a religious institution, wouldn't have the whole thing institutionalized.

It's a tremendous benefit for people to have a whole lot of close friends, but we don't have the state involved in trying to organize close friendships. Marriage obviously will hang, because there is a benefit in staying with one person. I think removing children is probably the straw that's going to break the camel's back.

I would just point out that with each year we are having fewer children. In the middle of the 1800s, about 75 percent or 80 percent of households had children. Today it's below one-third and maybe pushing 30 percent. So, in other words, the average household in America doesn't have children, and we're gradually talking about a society in which children are an afterthought. Now some people who have children think of them as having a trophy child: "Oh, let's have a child. That might be fun." It's just something that is brand new in history. Life has always been focused before on the prospect and issue of having children.

The Child Arrives and All Hell Breaks Loose

I think it's always nice to have a marriage which is deeply fulfilling for parents. But I think from the child's point of view, they're just happy to have two parents there who are taking care of them.

One of the interesting findings of recent years is that most marriages break up today just out of a kind of boredom. Many people get tired of each other. There's not really the kind of severe conflict that used to break up marriages in the past, and should break up marriages today. You would hope that adults could learn that marriage is important, that many problems can be worked out over time, and that there are all sorts of tools now that people can turn to for help with their marriages.

When the first child comes, you enter a phase of the marriage which is probably the least happy of any phase of the marital life cycle. That's something which is a very serious problem today. Young adults live a pretty happy kind of lifestyle, free and easy, and if they have a mate that's a pretty equal situation. They're both working and have free time and so on. Then the child comes and all hell breaks loose. People just are not prepared for that as they once were. Therefore, it becomes a very difficult scene in so many families. The guy isn't getting his sex anymore. The woman isn't getting the help she needs, and she's had to change her entire life. Now she has this child. Something you could do to help marriages a lot is by giving people a lot more parenting education in advance, so they would know what's ahead and know how to prepare for it.

The Entertainment Industry and Mass Culture

One of the most corrosive influences today, in my view, is market commerce leading to a consumer view of marriage promulgated by the entertainment industry, which has become the dominant force in popular culture, especially among young adults. If you're to analyze television, music, movies, and the rest, this is the most anti-marriage and, I might say, anti-child barrage of information that one could imagine. There's nothing you see very often that has anything to do to help you have a marital commitment or be good to your kids. It is all focused on freedom and autonomy and spending money and changing products, including personal relationships. That, by the way, is a far more important phenomenon in explaining where we are today than government.

Stacy

Stacy is a thirty-year-old, single, African-American woman who is pursuing a Master's Degree. She thinks her independence threatens some of the men she dates, and she struggles with the Church's teachings on sex.

Marriage — Just a Piece of Paper?

I think seeing it in black and white on paper just kind of reinforces the commitment. But I think that walking down an aisle and having a ceremony is just pomp and circumstance. That's just something people need to validate that it's actually taking place. My parents have been married for thirty-one years, but they just had a courthouse wedding. My sister's getting married. I'm the oldest. She's having a big wedding. This wedding is turning into my mother's wedding and my aunt's wedding, and it's turning into my sister's future mother-in-law's wedding and so forth. It's kind of out of their hands now. I think that happens a lot.

Men Tell Me I'm Too Independent

Black men do respect me! But I know I'm different. I come from a two-parent household with a father I've had all of my life. I think that's one reason why it's hard for me to stay in a long-term relationship. I've had men tell me that I'm too independent. It's not that I don't meet men, but I don't want a man to become my father. I want a man to become my mate. A lot of times I think black men don't know how to differentiate the two. One guy I really care for a lot basically told me, "You've had a father all of your life, you really don't need me." Well, yeah, my father is still at home, and he doesn't even condescend to me the way that guy did. He wasn't like that.

I don't know why the communication is so bad. You can go in a lot of different areas as far as what made that happen. You can take it real far back through historical accounts, too. I think that has a lot of hogwash to it. I really think it has to do with a person's upbringing and their spiritual grounding, their spiritual relationship with God. That's something that I'm starting to learn. I didn't grow up going to church. My parents had it forced down their throats. They said, "If you guys want to you can. If you don't want to, we're fine with it." So, I'm going through this new awakening and processing things for myself. As a result, it's causing me to consider things differently. Consider things from a safe and spiritual perspective that just wasn't there before.

Are Men Threatened by Your Independence?

They shouldn't feel threatened. Right now, I have an apartment that's practically empty. They shouldn't feel threatened, and, if they are threatened, then that makes me know that that's not the one for me. I don't think being such a strong personality comes from the fact that I'm an independent woman. I think it comes from my upbringing. I'm the oldest child. I always had to set an example. Set a precedent. People who know me, my grandparents, will always say, "Stacy was never a child."

I can't speak for a lot of other women who are independent and self-sufficient. All I know is that, yes, I have been a threat to a lot of men. They shouldn't be, but they are. Why is it a threat for someone to be able to say no and mean no? Why is it a threat for someone to be able to express how they feel and convey it so that people understand and there's no room for asking, "Does she really mean that?" To say what you mean and do what you say, why is that a threat? Anywhere else, that's a good leader. That's a charismatic person. Any other arena outside of relationships, that's what you want in a person who's representing you. So it shouldn't be a threat. But it is.

Manhood

Yes, a lot of women are earning more than men and raising children without them. Is there an impact on men's view of their manhood? Yeah, but if you really wanted to say who took away what from whom, women didn't take it away. Black women did not take away the black man's manhood. If you look at white men, white women, black women, black men, the black men are at the bottom of the list, but not because black women put them there. You go into a lot of sensitive areas, but to blame their black women for that is not their fault, because they have to survive, too. And a lot of times they'd have to survive without the help and assistance from their black men.

Dating As a Thirty-Year-Old

It's hard. It's hard. There are so many things to struggle with. I'm going to church now. My biggest struggle is sex. The church says you're not supposed to participate. My thing is I'm a thirty-year-old sexual being and I like it and you're telling me I can't do it? That's very hard. When people meet, physical attraction is there, and the church wants to try to make that the last reason for two people to come together. It's usually the opposite of that. How do you juggle that? It's very hard.

I'm not going to lie, some of the relationships have just been about sex and some of them have been about emotional attachments as well. But it's hard. Then there's all of the other outside factors. Yes, there is the risk of pregnancy. More importantly, there's the risk of AIDS or HIV. That's the very scary stuff. So it's very hard.

Do I think I'll get married? I don't know. I was telling someone not so long ago that out of all the serious relationships I've had, I didn't feel marriage-minded to any of them. I take that back. I felt marriage-minded to one, briefly, when I was sixteen years old. Did I think that by the time I was thirty I would be still single and childless? No. No. I thought I would follow in my mother's footsteps, marriage right out of high school.

Our frame of reference is very different. When my mother left her parents' house, she went to her husband's house. A lot of times she can't understand what I go through being a single woman. She thinks I'm not practicing good people skills, as far as having a stranger come over for dinner or going out with a stranger. There is no pressure from my mother to get married. Her whole thing is that a lot of times she can't relate to me being single, because she's never been single. She's never been single. She's never had her own place. She grew up differently.

Just like everything else, you have to make a mistake. You have to fall. You have to get burnt. You have to suffer small defeats to win. That's the optimist in me. I really believe that. It's just a matter of, are those two people, at the same time, ready to be successful together? That's what I mean when I say I'm still being processed. Bishop Brazier talks about the reason why you haven't met your mate. It's because you're not ready.

Nothing is wrong with you because you're thirty years old, you're single, and you're childless. It's just that you are still being processed to meet your soul mate. Both of you have to be evenly yoked at the same time, at the same place, in order to succeed. So, okay, I'm still being processed.

What about Living Together?

I don't really agree with the living together for long periods of time. I think living together should be done a year or less, an engagement with a marriage right around the corner. I don't understand when people live together for more than nine months or a year if they're not going to get married. I don't really understand that.

My thing is that if you live together, you might as well get married. You share the finances. You share the household expenses. You live together as husband and wife, so do it. So, I know for myself I couldn't live with someone for more than a year. I would want to be married to him. Either I live by myself or we get married. That's why I haven't lived with a man. I lived with my family. Then I moved out on my own.

Marrying within Your Race?

That's hard for me. I've been kind of struggling with that myself. I've dated outside my race, and I'm learning how honest I can be with certain people about that. That's very hard. I know that what color he is doesn't matter. If I'm strong enough to deal with how society will respond and if he's strong enough, we can make this work. But then you start talking to family and your peers and other people around you who just can't fathom, why would you want to go outside your race?

Black men have a hard time finding out and knowing that this woman they're interested in, this educated, attractive sister dated a white boy? Oh, no. No. No. So I had to keep that a secret. It has caused me to ask myself why am I dating this white man, or why did I date that white man? I am a strong activist for my own ethnicity. I know I'm a black woman, and I support my black community. At the end, how do I fit this white man in that equation? Yeah, it gets very hard to justify. I haven't come up with the answer yet.

Bishop Arthur M. Brazier

Bishop Brazier is pastor of the Apostolic Church of God in Chicago, Illinois, which has thirteen thousand active members. He finds that many couples today focus more on their own individual happiness than on the needs of the family.

Happiness

It seems to me that as I give counsel to a lot of married couples, I have noticed that they tend to center on their desires, their wishes, their needs. When I say "their," I mean the individual seems to be more concerned about how they can be happy in life; how they can achieve their particular goals. Sometimes it comes into conflict with the needs of the total family. There is not that interaction.

I don't find that give and take and the need to make compromises. Some people look at the word *compromise* in a very negative way, as if you're giving up something for nothing or someone has taken advantage. But compromise really is the art of meeting each other, meeting the other party halfway. I find that lacking.

The option for leaving the family relationship is so easy, and there are no really negative repercussions. There is this tendency to separate and to end the marriage in search of this elusive thing called happiness. Sometimes, individuals seek that thing called happiness even at the sacrifice of the welfare of their children. Sometimes, I notice that the couples are so locked into an adversarial position that the children are not really thought of.

A Sense of Freedom, a Lack of Control

In the African-American community, there was never this concept that women or wives were oppressed. Certainly the men always considered themselves the head of the home, but we didn't have this concept that women were oppressed. In fact, in the African-American community there was much more of a matriarchal society than probably in the white community. But there is no question that women, across the board, have felt a sort of sense of freedom. They are better educated today than they were in the past. Jobs are more available, and sometimes men have been unable to adjust to the fact that when your wife goes to work you lose a modicum of power and authority.

Obviously, not being a psychologist, I really don't have a fix on what really goes on in the minds of men other than my own personal observation, which is that there is a certain sense of loss of masculinity that, "I'm no longer really in control." That "I'm the head of the home and my wife should do what I want her to do."

There's no question that there are a lot more single mothers, and I have met women who have adopted that point of view that they have no intention of getting married but they want to have children. In fact, I have met women who made it very clear that they wanted to have a child by a certain man, but they didn't want to have anything to do with the man after the pregnancy took place. She was through with him. I think that is an indication of the moral lapse in our society today. I think that our American society has lost its moral values. We've lost our way in relationship to morality. We're living in a whatever-feels-good society.

It's that elusive thing that I referred to earlier called happiness, and people will do almost anything to try and satisfy themselves. Since our sexuality is such an important part of our lives, the loss of moral sexual values has permeated our society. Fifty years ago a female movie star who would get pregnant outside of marriage was almost assured to have lost her position in the studio. But today when women in the motion picture industry have children, it's plastered in the magazines and newspapers, everyone's happy, and it is totally acceptable in society. I think that here again that is a real problem in relationship to marriage. People feel that if I'm not happy in this marriage I can get out of it, because it's the modus operandi in America today.

A Trail of Children

What's happening to the kids? Here again, I think that it's a negative for children. This is not to say that a single woman cannot raise children. They do. Generally speaking, the single parent is the mother. We have some men, but that's sort of rare. I've seen women do extremely well with raising two or three children, and I've seen these children go on to college and do very well. But, by and large, without two heads in the family you have a breakdown in the family structure and it's very difficult for a woman. It's very difficult, in my opinion, for a woman with two or three children to get up in the morning, wash them, comb their hair, get them to the babysitter or a Headstart program, and then go to work, work all day, pick the kids up, and come back home. Her work is not over. Now she's got to clean, she's got to cook, she's got to do the homework with them. I don't understand how they do it. They have got a tremendous amount of strength. But obviously you can see that that's not good for the family.

Colleen

Colleen is a marketing executive in Chicago. She is single, and she isn't interested in getting married.

I'm single. I'm single. I'm as single as one can possibly be. I was dating someone for about a month and a half and that ended. Thank God, in some ways. We were way, way too different. He was younger than me, if you can imagine that. It wasn't that he was immature, he was just at a different point in his life and we are complete opposites. He lived a very, very simple lifestyle. He hated the city. He still lived with his parents. I mean, I should have known. He's a good guy nonetheless. It's just that we are way, way too different and he wasn't completely honest with me. When I found out, I confronted him and he lied. Then I confronted him again and then he told me the truth. It was really too late.

Looking for a Relationship?

Sure. Who isn't? I don't think you look for relationships. I think they just kind of happen. Most of the relationships that I have had kind of evolved. I wasn't looking. I think that when you're looking, you almost look so hard that you pass up opportunities. If you're looking, you're not going to find it. It's going to happen when you're not looking. That's just been my experience, I guess.

I think it is so important to women in some ways to be with a man. It's almost like a job title. A man kind of gives you an identity: "I have a boyfriend." It's so funny when you meet people for the first time and within five minutes they bring up their boyfriend, like, "I'm not alone." What's that fear of being alone? I mean, if you can't accept who you are and be able to deal with yourself by yourself that is not good. It's like you let someone dictate who you are.

Do serious relationships lead to anything? Well, not in my case, because I don't have a ring on my finger. So I don't know. I'm in my mid twenties, and I think you kind of go through a change. You've already been in the work force for a few years and you're just trying to figure out what you want. You have to be with someone who's been through it, so they understand the struggles you're going through and the questions you're asking. Then you go through it together. The stress of first jobs, the hours, the whole thing.

I really believe I've changed tremendously. More so probably in the last two years than the first three that I've been living downtown and working. For me that's where it is with relationships, and that's why maybe I haven't had something lead into something bigger, because I was maybe coming to this point in my life now. I'm not too concerned about it. It's not something that I'm looking for and it's not important to me right now, if ever.

I never had an issue with monogamy. I have an issue with being trapped. That's my thing. I've always said that I never thought I would get married, because I don't think I would ever be able to find someone who would understand what I mean about being trapped. I've been trapped. I've felt trapped before. It stunts your growth. It compromises your lifestyle and your independence. That's my thing.

I refuse to be in a situation like that ever, ever again, where I need my boyfriend or husband or whoever it is to make my plans for me. It should be like a complete compromise. It's not that I want to control the thing. I want it to be equal, and I just don't want to lose who I am, because I enjoy who I am. I want to be able to have that freedom to just go out and have fun and do my thing.

What about Living Together?

I guess it depends on where you live. It's obviously what's happening. It's the norm. If you lived in a small town and you were living with someone for ten years and everyone else was married, you might have a little bit of pressure. I think that in the city it's a whole different mindset. A lot of people do it, and a lot of people have been doing it, especially if they were married before. Then they're like, I don't need that piece of paper, or the ring on my finger, for commitment. I have it because the person is here and is committed. I don't know. It's a gamble. You know nothing is forever.

I don't want someone to take care of me. I can take care of myself, but I want someone to have fun with and have conversations with. I lived with someone and I thought he was the one. I was twenty-one. Divorce is a big pain in the ass. Divorce, to me — I don't want that failure. Maybe I have a fear of failure. So, it's like, if I don't get married, I won't get divorced. Why would you want to go through all of that?

I'm self-sufficient: I mean, like, that's why I didn't have to date someone when I wasn't working. I mean, it was just like I didn't want someone taking care of me. I don't want to be in a relationship where someone feels that they are obligated to take care of me. Do I think that's what marriage is? I don't know. It seems like everyone I know that's married is like, the man is taking care of you. It's not like I'm this feminist; it's just that I am a very independent person. I have been for a very long time, and it's really important to me to be able to keep that. That's what I fear about getting married: that I won't have my own bank account, even though people do. But it's like I won't have that. There's this whole joint thing. It's a very conflicting thing.

Marriage is not important to me. Relationships and commitment and love are important. You can have that, and I know people who have that who aren't married. You hear these stories about people who have been together for ten years, and they get married, and they divorced two years later. That's probably the type of person I would be, because maybe you have to give more. Maybe I'm not willing to give that. Am I selfish? No, I'm just honest. I'm willing to give 100 percent to the person I love, but that extra 10 percent, I don't know. I don't know.

Fear of Losing My Freedom and Individuality

My parents are together, so it's not like I have an issue about this because of divorce. Almost everyone in my family is together. I just have this fear of losing my freedom and losing my individuality. If someone I loved truly said to me that it is really important to get married or I will leave you, I'd really have to think about it. If I really truly care about this person, that would be really hard, because he's not respecting my beliefs. But at the same time, I love this person. I don't see myself living without him, but I don't know if it is within the confines of a marriage. I don't know. It's a really hard take. But marriage is not important to me, and I will stand that ground forever. I've decided that I don't ever see myself getting married; I never have seen myself getting married.

It's definitely different now, and women do not need to get married to be successful and to be self-sufficient. I can say it time and time again. I do not need a man. If I want a man, I will have one in my life. I'm very lucky to have someone that I really enjoy being around, and he respects me for all my ideals and all the things I believe in, and it's really nice. It's a nice change of pace. I'm someone who does not to want to be taken care of but wants to share and share. It's sharing.

Judith Martin

Judith Martin, better known as "Miss Manners," is a nationally syndicated newspaper and Internet columnist who writes about etiquette. She believes the trend for couples to postpone marriage until they can afford a lavish wedding reflects a fundamental misunderstanding of the purpose of weddings.

Weddings: Greed, Selfishness, and Showing Off

What has changed and what is under attack is that the need for ceremony and tradition seem to have expanded in highly unpleasant ways. It is not merely the fact of two people joining their lives and two families becoming joined. It has turned into people's need to show off. The need to raise money for themselves. I'm not talking about people who need money, but greed and selfishness. All of these things have gotten incorporated into the modern idea of the wedding, which I would think would horrify somebody marrying a person who exhibits these tendencies. If someone is easily overcome with the idea of being the center of attention, in total command, and able to demand behavior and tributes from everybody else, why would you want to join your life with that person?

It's not only extravagance. This show-business idea, which of course is a great basis of American popular culture, has very much entered the marriage ceremony. It is treated as a play. You cast people. You want to cast a male as the person who gives the bride away, even if she has not seen her father since before she was born, rather than focusing on the meaning of it: proudly her mother has reared her, and therefore her mother should give her away.

People want their bridesmaids to match as if it were a chorus line.

Fine, hold auditions; you can probably get a bunch of people who are the same height if that's what you're after. They have all that show-business mentality. And then they want to film it more than they want to enjoy it. They want to make sure that it is recorded. But that is a whole other aspect other than the greed factor that has taken over. I think there is a poverty of ceremony and formality in people's lives, and they see this as the one huge opportunity to be the star in a play that they've written.

I'm the Star, You're the Audience

Of course people want ritual. The peculiar part of what's happening to-day is that they want a kind of ritual that, first of all, is associated with the marriage of a young girl leaving her parents protection to enter the protection of her husband. Never mind they've been married four times and they have six children and all of that kind of thing. They want that. And I'm not totally scornful of this. Tradition has a strong pull on people, as well it should; but it is something that is supposed to adapt somewhat with the times and the circumstances. There is that delicate balance between observing tradition, which some people throw to the winds, and writing their own ceremonies and doing everything in a "to-tally original" way. It never really is original, because where did they get their ideas? It is a balance between using the tradition and recognizing what the actual circumstances of the situation are.

In the wedding trade, which I certainly do not consider myself a part of, writing the vows means personalizing the ceremony. There is that whole idea that it is about us. I disagree with this. There are plenty of aspects in marriage that are highly personal, but this is about the couple entering into the tradition of the society; of the religion, if it is a religious ceremony, but certainly of the civic society in either case. So it is not about them in the sense that it is their opportunity to brag about how much in love they are and to share all the details of the courtship, which people might find a little less appetizing than they imagine. This is part of the "this is our moment in the spotlight" attitude with which I disagree.

I am all for beautiful, meaningful ceremonies and making them as pleasing as possible, but it is not supposed to be, "I'm the star and you're the audience." The couple is part of the community, and they are bringing this very public declaration and legal and religious vows into the society.

The weddings that we should deplore attempt to turn the wedding into something other than a solemn occasion. Whether these are small things or large things they are the ones I find offensive. They may be little things that people haven't given much thought to, like, for instance, the wedding dress has changed just in the last two or three years.

The wedding dress was a ceremonial thing. It only dates from Queen Victoria. She started this business about the white wedding dress. She got married in white and then everybody had to get married in white. Before that, people just got married in their good clothes, but they were not costumes. But in any case, since Queen Victoria's time it has been something which combined beauty with a certain amount of dignity and modesty, covering the arms, certainly not highly décolleté, that kind of thing. In the last maybe two years at most, the wedding dress has turned into the debutante dress and it's a ball dress. It's probably strapless. It's certainly sleeveless and all that. What does that symbolize?

Why do I care what people get married in? As I say, I think the nicest was when they just got married in nice clothes as opposed to a costume. The reason I care is it shows where the focus is. People think of a wedding as a party. Well, there's a celebration afterward, and that should be fine, and if the bride wants to take off her jacket and wear a party dress to the party, fine. But the wedding just seems to have become a tedious prelude to having a party, as opposed to the reception being a celebration of the fact of the marriage.

But the ceremony itself, which should be at the key of it, is often lost in there. So you ask what do I deplore? I deplore the idea of treating it as a spectacle as opposed to a ritual. I deplore the idea of subverting the aspects that are important there, such as talking about your sex life during the ceremony as opposed to your assuming the responsibilities of marriage as defined by your religion or by the state. I also deplore turning it into a version of the Academy Awards or of a child's birthday party, as opposed to what it's supposed to be.

I was going to say the extravagance varies according to income level, but unfortunately it's not matched to income level. People will borrow and scrimp and otherwise put themselves in debt to give weddings way beyond their normal means.

So yes, they've gotten very extravagant, and they're planned from the wrong point of view. People will decide what kind of wedding they want, and then they'll marshal their resources to find out how many people they can afford to have, as opposed to what one would think would be the sensible approach, which is, whom do I want to have with me? And then, what can I afford to feed them? That should be secondary.

Religious Weddings with Religion Edited Out

For years I have gotten letters from clergymen and now clergywomen complaining about the idea that nonreligious people want religious weddings, and they want the religion edited out. They may only be getting married in a house of worship because they think it's a pretty setting and they treat it like a film location and so on. They boss people around, and they do this, and they do that.

I ask myself, what are these clergy people doing about it? Why aren't they the ones saying, "No, I will not marry you in this church or in this synagogue if you want to shoot a film or if you want to eliminate God. Go get married someplace else"? I am sympathetic about the awful things that seemingly nice people pull on them by surprise during the weddings. There are plenty of stories like that. But if it is clear from the start that they think of a house of God as a film location that they can come in and arrange as they wish and put on their own play within, why are the clergy allowing this?

It's My First Wedding

The purpose of the wedding is to bring into the society, in a legal and often religious way, the joining of this couple and the establishment of a family. Whether or not they have children, the other people involved become related to one another. The idea behind it, barring unfortunate mistakes, is supposed to be permanence. But people have thrown that aside, and I am struck by the fact that people who are presumably getting married because they believe in the sanctity and the permanence of marriage will nevertheless preface any question that they write to me with the phrase, "It's my first wedding." And I think, "'It's your first wedding'? People used to say 'I am getting married.'" This is very indicative. They think of it in an impermanent way even when, if you backed them in the corner, they would say, "Yes, yes, this is forever."

But that is not really the idea. People will very often have children before they marry each other. Very typically, people who have a child but think the sanctity of the wedding requires them to be able to afford to feed such and such a menu to so many people will therefore put it off. The interest of the child in legitimacy and being born of a permanent union or one, at least, intended to be permanent is not considered important. I mean, that's the kind of thing that rather shocks me. Failure, social failure and romantic failure, doesn't shock me nearly as much as the low aspirations.

David Blankenhorn

David Blankenhorn says that marriage is a public institution as well as a private relationship and talks about the importance of the marriage vow.

The Importance of the Vow

Ask yourself, what makes a marriage succeed? What are the determinants of success, predictors of success? Some people say compatibility, good communication skills, willingness to compromise, active listening, a sense of equal gender roles, or a sense of flexibility within gender roles. There are certain skills that we can teach people. There's also choosing the right mate, sexual and erotic attraction that binds people together. These are all very important issues. But I think some of the research shows that a lot of what determines whether a marriage succeeds or not is people's understanding of the promise they're making when they get married. Marriage is a public institution as well as a private relationship. There is a reason why we do it in public. It's a social thing. We make a promise. You look your intended in the eye, and you make a promise, and she makes her promise to you. There are witnesses, and you're expected to keep the promise.

It's good if you know what the promise is. It's especially good if you take it very seriously, if it's not just a piece of paper, not just some words to make your parents happy. The vows are not just some sort of beautiful literary content or historical resonance, but a serious, dedicated promise.

I think the vow is really so critical to whether the marriage succeeds or fails. Essentially in this generation, we the adults have told young people getting married to make the vows up themselves. You decide what the vow is. Two interesting things can be noted from this trend. One is that the issue of marital permanence is now off the table. People by-and-large don't say anything about forever. It gets left out; and "for better or worse" tends to get left out. It tends to just be a celebration of the intensity of the love. The notion that I will be with you forever, the flat-out promise, falls. Some of the vows even say, "Well, as long as love shall last." I have a friend who says that whenever he goes to a wedding like that he sends as a wedding gift paper plates. Most of the couples today simply leave the promise of forever out. But what does this tell us when the promise itself no longer includes the promise of permanence? Is this interesting or what?

Now, the second thing, I think, is even more interesting. We now communicate to the next generation that they create their marriage. They're the gods of their marriage. They're bigger than their marriage. The marriage, as represented by the vow, is a subjective creation that comes from them. They define it. They put their own individual stamp on it. They say what it is. They announce to the pastor who's marrying them and the relatives in the pews and the friends, they say, "this is our marriage, we unveil it for you now." And it's usually very smarmy about how much they love each other and what a wonderful couple they are, and how sexy and handsome they are.

That's the way I was, when I was young.

What gets lost in all of this is the notion that there's something bigger than the couple. Instead of the couple creating the marriage, the marriage creates the couple. What about the notion that the promise is bigger than they are? It's something that they ought to conform to, rather than to see it as something that they invented. What about the idea that lots of other people have used the same words to make the same promise, and lots of people in the future are going to use the same words to make the same promise? It's something that they can aspire to, can learn from, can take strength from, can figure out what it means to be married by reflecting on this promise that's bigger than they are. That's what's missing. Now, it's kind of a party.

When I got married in 1986, we made up our vows, and I think they were pretty beautiful, but you know what? I can't remember what they were. I remember the basics. I remember that we promised certain things about love and a good sense of humor. They were nice, and we thought about them and took them seriously at the time. I don't mean to trivialize them for us, or to trivialize them for millions of other couples. But it represents a real failure of the society and of the couples to really understand the meaning of the promise.

What's Happening to Us?

Surely we have the capacity to see the consequences of what's happening to us. I think we have considerable evidence that doing away with the institution of marriage and the notion that marriage is something bigger than the couple is not a good deal for kids. It's not a good deal for the happiness of the people doing it, and it's not even a good idea for the notion of a free society.

Cherishing freedom and a free society doesn't just come from nowhere. It's dependent upon certain ways of thinking and living. The founders were very clear that a free society cannot exist without some notion of virtue among the people and certain ways of living that are based on responsibility and cooperation. A very interesting question is, how do men and women find a common life together, and how do they raise the next generation? If we're unsuccessful and we don't produce competence and character among the rising generation, then the notion of freedom itself becomes jeopardized.

Looking Back

This idea that the family did not really exist until modern times reflects a great lack of knowledge. It's also a great exercise in hubris.

STEVEN OZMENT

The marriage litigation docket was full of instances where the woman thought she was married and the man thought he was not married.

JOHN WITTE JR.

It's certainly undeniable that Christian marriage has shared in many of these patriarchal institutions and assumptions. At the same time, Christian marriage has always tried to mark out a greater sphere of equality for spouses than typically existed in the surrounding culture.

LISA SOWLE CAHILL

You would have a clandestine marriage, but months later the young man might say, "I don't remember promising to get married. I understood this as just a little sex on the haystack."

STEVEN OZMENT

Many times children were betrothed even before the age of reason when they were infants or toddlers, and then the marriage was completed and consummated later.

LISA SOWLE CAHILL

The problems between men and women may seem new, but they are as old as humankind. Marriage evolved as an alternative to constant warfare between the sexes. But it took centuries of struggle to transform marriage from a political arrangement made by patriarchs to a relationship based on the free choice and mutual consent of the couple.

In the centuries that followed the fall of the Roman Empire, marriage was a mess. The Roman Catholic Church made an important contribution to marriage in the Middle Ages, helping to define marriage as a matter of free consent between husband and wife rather than as a contract between families. Basing marriage on consent was an accomplishment for the church in the Middle Ages, but it also led to ambiguities, misunderstandings, and sometimes legal disputes.

In the sixteenth century, both Protestants and Roman Catholics tried to correct the confusions of secret marriage by making marriage more public. It was during this time that the state became a full partner with the church in certifying and protecting marriage. This was a historic watershed in the creation of modern marriage.

But by the eighteenth and nineteenth centuries, marriage was beginning to change in the modern mind. The enlightenment idea of contract had elevated the rights of the individual in marriage, and marriage was no longer viewed as a sacrament or covenant with broad public meaning but as a private legal contract.

Marriage has never been perfect, and it has often been terribly imperfect. Very few people would want to turn back the clock to an earlier time when couples were trapped in unfaithful, cruel, or abusive marriages, and most people would agree that divorce is sometimes the best remedy for a bad marriage. But over the long arc of its history in the West, marriage has a record of accomplishments that many have forgotten. It was able to strike a delicate balance between the desires of adults and the needs of children, between the church and the state, between a legal contract and a sacred covenant. Many wonder, have we lost that balance today?

Lisa Sowle Cahill

Lisa Sowle Cahill is the J. Donald Monan Professor of Theology at Boston College. She discusses attitudes toward marriage in the New Testament, arranged marriages in the Middle Ages, and the Catholic view of marriage as a sacrament.

Some Backward Steps, Some Forward Steps

The most distinctive thing about Christian marriage from New Testament times is that it does not put a large emphasis on procreation. The place in the New Testament which constitutes the longest discussion of marriage would be one of the letters of St. Paul. That's some of the earliest literature in the New Testament; it even antedates the Gospel. In his first letter to the Corinthians, chapter 7, Paul talks about marriage and some of the obligations of marriage, but he doesn't mention an obligation to procreate at all. He does say that if a Christian is married to a pagan their children are holy, so that kind of assumes the family context, but he doesn't hold up an obligation to have children.

In that letter, Paul does a number of interesting things. The first is that he says that husband and wife, men and women, have equal rights to one another's bodies. So it sets up a context of sexual reciprocity and equality that would have been fairly unusual for either the Greco-Roman or the Jewish culture of the time. However, that difference should not be excessively emphasized, because even in the larger culture there were emerging egalitarian tendencies with regard to marriage. But the primary emphasis of Paul is on the relationship of the couple and their commitment, not on their obligation to have children.

One of the other things that Paul does in that letter is to talk about celibacy or virginity as a possibly preferable state to marriage. But you notice there that the reason is not because sex is bad but, rather, as he says, if you have a husband or a wife, you'll be interested and dedicated to making things go smoothly with that spouse. Paul says instead, "what I want you to have is single-hearted devotion to the Lord, so that single-hearted devotion to the Lord is the thing that governs all of Christian life, including marriage." In fact, because of that he even says that if a Christian and pagan are married and if the pagan refuses to live with the Christian, then the couple is not bound to the marriage permanently, because Christ has called us to live in peace.

A little principle of biblical interpretation also emerges in that text, because in saying that the couple is free to part, Paul also says that that's not what Jesus said. He said the message that a couple should stay together and, if they separate, they should not remarry comes from Jesus. But he says with regard to this Christian and pagan possible friction, he's going to offer his own opinion, and he concludes by saying, "I think I have the spirit of the Lord." So the principle there is that we have authoritative teachings from Jesus himself, and yet even St. Paul realizes that those teachings may need to be adapted over history.

If you look at the history of Christian teaching on marriage, that, in fact, is what we see. We see a long process of adaptation, accommodation, improvement, refining, some backward steps and some forward steps, as Christians attempt in their various cultures and historical positions to understand what it means to live as a Christian in the marriage state.

Personal Relationship vs. Social Institution

Even though the relation of the couple was more important to Paul, the importance of family and parenthood has also continued to be important for Christian marriage, just as it has in the other cultures of the world, historically and now. So we could say that the distinctive thing about the Christian approach, especially back in the first century, was that it emphasized the relations of partners. But still it shares with the institution of marriage worldwide the emphasis on intergenerational continuity, passing on the traditions of a community and the wealth and property of a family to the next generation.

The problem for Christian ethics and Christian marriage has always been *what's the relation of those two things?* How can we keep them together in an appropriate balance without giving excessive priority to either one or the other, so that marriage is just a personal relationship between you and me and not also an important social institution? On the other side, does the social institution and the ecclesial institution control the relationship of that couple to such an extent that their own freedom in their own commitment really becomes marginal or unimportant? So I guess I'd have to say that, historically, procreation did become more important in Christian marriage than it was in the New Testament. In that way, Christian marriage accommodated or reflected a larger social pattern, and that was certainly true up through the Middle Ages and even up to the modern period.

In the Catholic tradition, for instance, we have had a lot of debates about the necessity of procreation as one of the most important purposes of sex (hence the debates about artificial birth control). But if you look at the Christian tradition as a whole, all Christian theologians — including the Protestant Reformers, Augustine, and Aquinas — all of them would have said that, in fact, procreation is the primary purpose of sex, that it's necessary to have the intention to procreate to fully justify a sexual relationship, and that the context for that is committed marriage because committed marriage provides a context for raising children.

Marriages: Alliances of Families and Kinship Networks

During the Middle Ages we didn't have a separation between Protestantism and Catholicism. We just had one Christian tradition, although with Eastern and Western dimensions to it. But in the Middle Ages procreation was in fact very important. It was seen as a project of the families, who came together through the marriages of their young people to join forces, as it were. So marriages were often alliances of families and kinship networks in order to consolidate property, political ties, and to move the family interest as a whole forward to the next generation and through the next generation.

Individual spouses were often very young, particularly in the case of girls, who could be married at age fourteen and frequently to men who were significantly older, although not always. Men were sometimes married very young also. Those young people entered into marriages that were arranged by the elder members of their kin groups, and the personal consent of the individuals contracting the marriage was not a key; in fact, it wasn't really required. Many times children were betrothed even before the age of reason, when they were infants or toddlers, and then the marriage was completed and consummated later.

Another important thing to realize is that those marriages, just as they came into being at the demand of the family, so they could be dissolved in order to pursue family interest. If a young daughter of a wealthy family was married to the son of another noble family and the political relationship between those families deteriorated and the family of the girl decided that it would be better for her to be married into another kin network, then that marriage would be dissolved. That girl would be remarried to someone else. Marriage and divorce were not a matter of personal decision as much as they were a matter of family discretion, often taking place for economic and political reasons. So you had both the sort of impermanent marriage, and, also, you had the decision to marry as a group decision that wasn't focused on the individual welfare of the spouses.

This situation was exacerbated in Europe from the fourth to the eighth century after a series of invasions by the Germanic people. The Germanic tribes brought with them customs that were even more inimical to the basic Christian insight that it's the relation of spouses that's really key. For example, the Germanic tribes put even heavier emphasis on the responsibility of the whole kin group for any one of the individual members. That's why there was a lot of family revenge for perceived insults to the honor of the family, an obligation to kill the members of other families if they had infringed on the dignity of one's own members. Similarly, brides were obtained by purchase, sometimes by abduction and rape, and not necessarily with the consent of the bride or even the groom.

So medieval Christian Europe had quite a challenge in attempting to Christianize these people and to bring them within the scope of the marriage practices that had been developing from New Testament times and now were threatened or at least destabilized by this influx of other people. That is why in the tenth, eleventh, and twelfth centuries the Christian churches in Europe began to develop more careful laws about consent to marriage and about the permanency of the marriage bond once the individual couple had consented to it. If you look at the Catholic Church today, we still have those two requirements, although they aren't as broadly shared in other Christian denominations. I think all Christians assumed that a marriage will be entered into on the basis of the consent of the parties, but there is much more flexibility across the denominations on the question of indissolubility.

The reason for that is that in the twentieth century many of us have the experience of seeing marriages that are maintained at the expense of the happiness of the spouses. Sometimes the requirement that marriage be permanent can seem very oppressive. Certainly one issue that's much more in our consciousness today is the possibility of abuse within marriage and the family, whether sexual abuse of children or domestic abuse and violence toward women. So again, we see good reasons to dissolve a marriage. I think we sometimes fail to appreciate that the development of indissolubility historically was a way of protecting the freedom and equality of parties to a marriage to enter into that state on the basis of their consent and to have their relationship uninterfered with by interest formed outside.

So those values are things that I think we would want to protect, even as we reconsider some of our traditional practices. Today we have a big question about how much latitude there should be in dissolving marriages, and especially in North America where up to 50 percent of new marriages are anticipated to end in divorce. I think very few people think that that's a good situation, even though we might not want to return to a very rigid approach to prohibit divorce.

Sacrament and Covenant

In the Catholic tradition, marriage always has been and still is today considered a sacrament. So let's look at that very briefly in relation to the New Testament origins of Christianity and then looking forward to the Protestant Reformation.

The Bible does not define marriage as a sacrament. I think the most we could do is to say that there is a sacramentalizing tendency in the New Testament. There's one biblical text that is often used to ground the idea that marriage is a sacrament, and it's Paul's letter to the Ephesians, chapter 5, where the love of husband and wife is compared to the love of Christ and the Church. But Paul does not say that the love of husband and wife somehow is or mediates the love of Christ and the Church, but he just draws an analogy.

In the tradition, the idea that marriage is a place where God is experienced and that marital life is holy was really the foundation of the developing theology of marriage as sacrament. To say that marriage is a sacrament is simply to say just that, namely that God is present in marriage, that marriage is one of the basic human events in which there is an invoking of the divine. Although the doctrine that marriage is a sacrament is something that characterized Catholicism and was rejected at the time of the Protestant Reformation, there is an analogous concept in Protestantism, which is the idea that marriage is a covenant, that it is an agreement of woman and man to enter in upon a relationship that somehow reflects or shares in God's covenant with his chosen people. So the covenantal and the sacramental notions of marriage do have some points in common, although they're certainly not the same.

The theology of marriage as a sacrament in Catholicism is closely linked to the idea that Christian marriage requires consent and is indissoluble. The thing about a marriage that is the sacrament is the bond of the couple. It's not procreation. It's not that they have children; it's that they make a commitment to one another. So in making consent the most important requirement to initiate a sacramental marriage, the Church also picks up on that interpersonal dimension and prioritizes it over procreation.

There is a little glitch in the tradition, however, because although the Church taught that consent is what you need to have a sacramental marriage, it still has always permitted marriages to be dissolved if they were never consummated, even if they were entered into freely. So that's a bit of an inconsistency in the tradition. Maybe on the positive side it reflects the flexible nature of the tradition and the need for interpretation. But the consent and indissolubility requirements were ways of protecting that unique bond of equal partners, and it's through their relationship, their personal relationship, that God is present in marriage. That again opens out into an institution of family, an intergenerational network that also is very hooked into society and its requirement.

Repression of Women?

Marriage as a human institution cross-culturally and worldwide has almost invariably been structured along patriarchal lines, so the institution of marriage very frequently does place women in a subservient domestic and childbearing role. Domesticity and childbearing are of great human value in themselves. However, their value is not always equally respected in marriage because they're brought under the authority of men and not accorded as much social respect. So in fulfilling only these roles and being confined only to these roles in marriage, the contributions of women in other spheres have been limited or cut off. Also, the worth and the appreciation that women get for these roles, even in the marriage and the family, is lesser than it should be.

Now let's look at that human reality or that social and political and economic reality in relation to the Christian tradition of marriage. In the first place, it's certainly undeniable that Christian marriage has shared in many of these patriarchal institutions and assumptions. At the same time, Christian marriage has always tried to mark out a greater sphere of equality for spouses than typically existed in the surrounding culture. We see that in Paul's letter to the Corinthians. We see it in Ephesians 5 and a comparison of Christ and Church to husband and wife. We also see it in the evolving canon law on marriage, which required that marriage is entered into with the consent of both parties and that the families or elders or patriarchs in the families had no right to interfere with the consent once it had been given.

So there are both kinds of tendencies in the Christian institution of marriage, historically. There is a patriarchal element — women have been seen as lesser than men — and yet, at the same time, there's some protection of women's rights that's embodied in the theology of marriage as sacrament, the theology of marriage as covenant, and the expectation that consent and permanency will characterize Christian marriage.

The State and a Human Institution

I think that the state does have a role in marriage and family. I add that qualifier "and family" because the reason that I believe the state should have a role in marriage is that it is a human institution. It's not just a matter of individual welfare. It's a matter of social welfare. A marriage relationship is a form of social relationship. It's a basic institution of most societies, including our modern society.

That's especially true when you see the connection between marriage and families. There's the extended family out of which the married couple comes. There's also the family that they generate in having children. Therefore, the state should have a role, because it's interested in the welfare of society in general and the common good in our interdependence with one another and our mutual rights and duties and our duty to support one another. The state does have a duty to try to enhance the ability of individuals and couples to form strong marriages and families.

Can Marriage Be Reformulated without Losing the Religious Meaning?

Yes, it can be reformulated without losing its religious meaning, but for me the question is, what's the full meaning of marriage? What are the parts that you have to have there to really have a marriage? The traditional three parts are sexual intercourse, commitment of the spouses, and children. Today all three of those are being challenged.

I think most would want to retain sexual intercourse as part of what a marriage means; also commitment, although the permanency of the commitment is more on the table. Another dimension that is brought in is whether that commitment is a commitment of man and woman or can it be a same-sex commitment. That leads into the third variable, which are children. Do children have to be part of this?

Now, I don't know exactly how to handle this in the best way. I have to say that directly. I think that it is still important to hold up as some sort of human ideal — which is almost too strong a word, because it seems condemnatory of everything that falls outside of it — but there's some sort of human attractiveness to the heterosexual committed relationship to which children are born. Does that absolutely mean that nothing else can be respected as a form of Christian, sexual, and personal or even parental commitment? I think the answer to that is no. There can be other forms that are similar to this traditional form in some ways and not in others. What we're struggling with as modern Christians is how we see those other forms, how they're related to the traditional form. In some ways they bring a valuable critique of the traditional form, and, yet, is there something in the tradition that still needs to be speaking a critical word to all these new variables that we're seeing? With that, I will leave the topic.

Steven Ozment

Steven Ozment is the McLean Professor of Ancient and Modern History at Harvard University. He discusses clandestine marriages, the decision to make consent the basis of marriage, and changes in marriage patterns that went along with the Reformation.

Marriage Was Having a Rough Time

The late medieval period, roughly between 1200 and 1500, saw a lot of warring and feuding that took men away, decreasing the male population. It was also a period in which many men were drawn into the Crusades and left the West to recapture Jerusalem. These journeys to the Holy Land drained potential husbands. In addition, the celibate life was very popular at this time. Many men were drawn into the Catholic Church and into cloisters, and whether they were secular or religious clergy, in a parish ministry or confined to a cloister, they were celibate clergy. This was a rule of the Church. One of the incest prohibitions of the Church was that a cleric could not marry. This was, of course, a central prohibition that the Reformation would challenge.

Women found themselves in a situation where there was a shortage of males. In addition to that, even couples who wanted to marry had difficulty saving money sufficient to provide for a family. The difficulty of providing for a household prevented many from marrying early. Later, this would change, and the Reformation occurs at a time when marriage is becoming the dominant lifestyle, having been a minority position in the later Middle Ages, when the majority of people were single and society organized on their behalf.

Straws in the Wind and Secret Marriages

Figuring the percentage of people who were married in the centuries before the Reformation is rather tricky. There are those who say that perhaps 50 percent of women were married or in some kind of relationship akin to marriage. There were certainly women living in concubinage and virtual marital situations with clergy at this time. Often those marriages went uncounted. So virtual marriage, which was very real, was not deemed as serious marriage.

One of the things that changes this is that after the Black Death, guilds in cities and towns were very concerned about limiting competition. To this end, they made legitimacy one of the requirements for entering a guild. This, of course, was designed to keep outsiders away and to let the guild members promote their own sons through the guild. Controlling numbers and personnel was also a way to maintain a trade monopoly. But it was only one of several straws in the wind in the late Middle Ages that begins the shift from a society in which celibacy, or an unmarried life, was the dominant lifestyle to a society in which marriage was the dominant lifestyle. There was also a movement toward marriage among clergy, many of whom lived in concubinage, at which the church winked. It's certainly true of the Protestant Reformers: many of them were living with virtual wives, having children, and paying penitential fees ("cradle taxes"). Long before the Reformation, there was a move among the clergy to end celibacy and to have legal clerical marriage.

This was also a time of clandestine marriages. These so-called secret or clandestine marriages were contracted between young adults without parental consent, more or less in private. Young people made vows of marriage to each other, and the Church recognized them as a true marriage. If you promised you were going to marry someone, or if in their presence you took her as wife or or him as husband, you had contracted a legal marriage in the eyes of the Church.

Parents were very concerned. On the one hand, if a daughter had gotten pregnant in the process of exchanging vows and consummating them with sexual intercourse, the parents were very concerned that the liability of illegitimacy not encumber their daughter. She would lose her value in the marriage market if she had been, or even if people just thought she had been, active sexually before she was married. Sexual purity, especially in towns (less so in the countryside), was a very important part of the value of a woman in the marriage market.

Not Sitting around in Hair Shirts, Biting Sticks

The Catholic Church, very interestingly and very enterprisingly, declared that consent was the basis of a marriage. Two people, whether they were sitting at the dinner table in the presence of parents and witnesses or on a haystack alone, were married in the eyes of God if they exchanged vows of marriage and consummated those vows. One thing the Church was very intentionally doing was injecting itself into married life. It was very important to the Church's mission that it have a position of moral authority within married life. By being able to say that a marriage is a marriage under certain conditions, and to approve and bless marriages that had occurred apart from parental knowledge or consent, was the Church's way of establishing its moral authority on issues directly within the family.

On the other side of the issue, there's also something very interesting and positive. There was a great world of adolescent sexuality in the later Middle Ages. People were not sitting around in hair shirts, biting sticks. A lot of sex was going on. We know this from growing numbers of foundling homes for illegitimate children in this period. The Church is telling these young people, "If you're going to have sex or if you're going to be in a virtual marital situation, you're going to have to accept the responsibilities that occur from it." So, in that instance, this was something very positive.

Some people would say the infiltration of Church influence into the family was a sinister move, others that the Church was trying to bring order and discipline to family life and, through family life, to society as a whole. The Church also defined impediments to marriage, conditions under which one could not and should not marry. The Church declared itself the arbitrator of marriage formation. It defined the conditions under which marriage could occur and under which people could stay together or separate, and it could even bring the children of those parents into a marriage relationship even without the approval of those parents.

The Reformation Comes Along

The Reformation came along and said, "We have to have consent of parents and witnesses to make marriage valid. Marriage has to be public." The Reformers were reacting in large part to the many contested clandestine marriages. Imagine the situation: you would have a clandestine marriage, but months later the young man might say, "I don't remember promising to get married. I understood this as just a little sex on the haystack." So there was serious social disruption in some areas of family and moral life that led to the courtroom and to litigation.

Both the Catholic Church and the Protestants were very much concerned to address this. Protestants did it with more conviction, vigor, and success. They led the way in insisting that there be a public side to marriage and a blessing of the wedding in church so the marriage got registered and became a surer and more stable estate. Then, litigation over whether or not legitimate vows had been exchanged could be addressed when a contest reached court.

The other area in which the Church definitely and effectively injected itself into the family was by forbidding divorce. Real divorce had existed in antiquity and through the Middle Ages. Men and women could separate for real. It wasn't the Catholic "separation from bed and table," but never to marry another. Before the Church imposed its will, people could separate and then marry again. And this would be what the Reformation was intent on establishing.

I think it's fair to say that clerical marriage and the end of clerical celibacy was as important to the Reformers in the early years of the Reformation as were their doctrines of justification by faith and Scripture alone. All of the theological arguments had their domestic counterparts or consequences. But probably the most striking part of the Reformation for many contemporaries was to see their clergy married.

The Clergy's Big Step

Getting married was a big step and it took some urging to get the clergy — even Protestant clergy who had lived in concubinage — actually to tie the knot publicly.

In the Roman Catholic Church, marriage had been quite secondary to virginity and to celibacy. It served the Catholic Church to have clergy who would not marry, not have families, and not want to live in the suburbs, or be away from their mission. The argument was always that a celibate cleric had more time to spend on his pastoral duties than did the married cleric. It was against that argument that the Reformers took care, when commenting on their wives, always to praise them as helpmates, insisting that they never gave them any trouble. Sometimes that is read to be a kind of condescending comment about their wives. Actually it was an answer to the medieval clerical criticism of wives as burdens. Even Catholic clergy living in concubinage could agree that those who were married had certain concerns, worries, and tensions taken away from them that made them better at their mission. Not only could it be argued that they were more stable human beings, but in many ways marriage gave them a connection with their parishioners who were married and knew what marriage was. Clergy in this kind of situation probably had an easier time relating to their parishioners.

With the Reformation, not only did Reformers marry, they conveyed the notion that there was something not quite right about a pastor who did not marry. Very interestingly, Luther was the slowest to come around to that point. He finally did marry in 1525. There were lots of people urging him to do so given his position of leadership.

Clerics had desires, but they also had qualms. Obviously, clergy living in concubinage thought it was a pretty good situation. They paid fines to live under those conditions. There was such a thing as a cradle tax that the Church charged clergy in concubinage who had children. Living in concubinage and paying a fine kept one's celibate status together to a certain extent. Having to surrender that status — that is, to say that marriage is a secular matter and not a sacrament, and to agree to being married fully like the burgher and the lay brothers — was a big, frightening step for clergy trained for celibacy.

The Reformation was very eager to make marriage easier by both removing many of the Church's impediments to it and by making it a public social estate. The most striking thing about the Reformation in terms of its marriage practices, by comparison with the Catholic Church, was its permitting full divorce and remarriage after divorce.

A Kind of Golden Age for Women

One of the things that we're discovering today is that the lives of women in this late medieval period — maybe because so many of the women were not married — had quite a lot of opportunities. A number of gender studies argue that the period between 1200 and 1500 was a kind of golden age for women. It was such because of the development

and growth of the merchant society in the twelfth and into the thirteenth century and the great demographic crisis caused by the Black
Death in the middle of the fourteenth century. Those two things
opened up possibilities for working women that they had not known
before.

Women moved into guilds and into trade industries in very sizable
numbers. In some of the cities you had an enormous number of trade
guilds that accommodated women. There were guilds only of women,
and guilds mixed with men and women. Women felt at home there and
were respected there. The new appreciation of this situation has led to
a reinterpretation of the tone of the period. Gender historians are beginning to see that these things that were not totally negative; the Black
Death and a century when everything seemed to be a dark age also
opened doors to women that had not been opened before.

Another aspect of women's situation in this late medieval period
that I think has been surprising to some is the degree to which women
were not just drudges. There were many helping hands in the family at
this time and in society. The ability to hire servants was great. Even
poor people could have a servant. So women were working and could
afford to pay for services from the outside. A brighter picture of
women's status in the late medieval period generally is beginning to appear.

A Lot Going On in Marriage and the Family

Most scholars today would say that the Reformation contributed to a
demeaning of women's status. By the sixteenth century, opportunities
for women to work were beginning to close. Males in the artisan guilds
were behind that. To conteract competition from the countryside, they
wanted to control their profession within the cities, and there was a desire to squeeze women out as positions shrank. Women apprentices began to decrease in guilds, where they formerly had a secure and respected place, and were pushed back into the home.

The Reformation is today popularly portrayed as sanctioning this
development. This was not something the Reformation was itself actually doing. Economics was doing this, but because the Reformation
went along with this and sanctioned pretty much the relationship that
developed through the economic stresses, the Reformation has been

tarred and blamed for much of this development — quite unfairly so. The Reformation was always interested in gaining acceptance within established society. It wanted to co-op established institutions, not revolutionize them. To the extent that it was not contradictory to their own biblical beliefs or their own reform projects, they always embraced, supported, and went hand-in-hand with established society.

There are those who argue that divorce, the ability of a man and a woman to enter into a new marriage after separating from each other, was dignifying for women. The Protestant home also has, I think quite fairly, been praised for an informal sharing of authority within the home. *He Is the Sun, She Is the Moon* was the title of a popular marriage manual in the second half of the sixteenth century. In the manual, the hierarchical relationship between the husband and wife is displaced by one in which both husband and wife have their own space and time. Each is recognized, and the two work together as a team with a certain pragmatic equality. They're not in some kind of hierarchical, degrading relationship.

There was a lot going on in marriage and family in this late medieval/ early modern period that was not directly connected with the Reformation, but to which the Reformation gave its approval and sanction. The Reformation was eager to present itself as supporting model marriages, so much so that it communicated the notion that the reproductive or parent-child unit, what we would call the nuclear family, was the very core of society and marriage the farthest thing from an unnatural or oppressive institution.

Luther's wife Katharina von Bora, for example, was a woman who in many ways seems to have had it all in the sixteenth century. Not only did she bear the great Reformer six children, but she also ran her own businesses and was greatly praised by Luther. Luther praised her ability to speak German better than he could — this from the man who may be said to have created the modern German language! He would call her "Mr. Kathy" to express his respect for her authority. In his will, he left absolutely everything to her. He did not write a will that gave other men the authority to oversee what she did. He said she could do it herself, and his will was initially written in that way.

In this connection, there's a very interesting statement made by Eileen Power, who wrote a little book called *Medieval Women*. She said if you look at theology and law, you may get the impression that women are inferior and that patriarchy and hierarchy stands out everywhere.

But when you study actual relationships and family life through family archives of the period, you see the high degree to which men and women shared authority within households. The Reformation didn't create that. It was happening in the society. The Reformation embraced it in a positive way and tried to exemplify it in its own lifestyle through clerical marriage and the model of the Lutheran or Protestant family. This worked to the good. I don't think it's accidental today that women easily move into the priesthood or receive church orders in Protestant churches. That is rooted in changes that were going on in the sixteenth century. The contrast with Catholic tradition in this regard is obvious.

Marriage As a Sacrament

When marriage is seen as a sacrament, it comes under the authority of the Church as much as the sacraments of penance or confession, or that of the Eucharist — that is, it is a sign of grace; it is an article of revelation and a matter of the soul. Before the Church came along, marriage was in the sphere of the state, or what there was of the state or political authority, and it remained that way through much of the Middle Ages. In the process of injecting itself into marriage, the Church did enhance the institution and increased morality. There are scholars who even argue that contraception, which was widely practiced in the late Middle Ages, was used out of an ethic of love that the Church, certainly unintentionally, brought into the family through its sacramental view of marriage, as it sensitized married couples to be aware of the needs of one another, including too many burdensome pregnancies for wives.

When the Reformers studied marriage — the conditions of marriage, the rather difficult history of marriage, the plight of the clergy who were living in concubinage, and those who were sexually active in one form or another — the Reformation concluded that this was not a sacrament. There's nothing one can derive from the Bible, except metaphorically, that marriage was a special revelation or sacrament from God given over to the Church to administer and to govern within the Church's laws, which often encumbered marriage in nonbiblical ways. So, when the Reformation came along, marriage disputes and the moral problems related with marriage were shifted to civil courts or to lay clerical courts.

Luther Understood

There's never been a movement that has done a better job, at least initially, of recognizing what was historically possible in its times. To succeed as a historical movement, to win in history in such a way that your beliefs and values become laws that shape institutions and shape the people that come into the institutions, you have to be rather perceptive about the course of history. Luther understood this.

The Bedrock

As far as the inner life of the family is concerned, it's very hard to study that before 1400. It's only really in the fifteenth century that we begin to get the sources that let us go into the family circle and see what marriage was and how it existed from the inside out. Prior to that time, we are largely dependent on sources that historians would call oblique and rather fuzzy.

What one discovers in family archives, where contemporaries speak for themselves and are not the victims of modern theories and prejudices, is a vibrant relationship between spouses and even more vibrant relationships between parents and children. If we had the right sources — family archives of the quantity and quality that we have by the fifteenth century, say — going back to the third and fourth and fifth and sixth centuries, I'm not sure but what we would find something similar. I personally subscribe to the view that the so-called "sentimental" marriage and family existed as far back as there are sources to document them.

I think a great distortion has occurred in portraying marriage before the pre-modern or modern times as having been a highly challenged and very stressed institution, often without a clue and certainly without modern love and affection. We just don't know enough to make that kind of judgment on marriage. Certainly, when Reformers and even humanists speak about marriage, they speak of it as a very wonderful thing.

Catholic Reformers, as well as Protestant Reformers, had no trouble understanding and interrelating to the nuclear family, that parent-child relationship, that center from which all life comes and around which all social forms of life necessarily revolve. It is the eternal nucleus of the social world. The Reformation understood that. People long before the Reformation understood that. Two people get married or two people find themselves with child. This in itself has a force that sets things moving in such a way as to make parents out of spouses and a family out of virtually nothing. The Reformation understood that. I think people long before the Reformation, since there were families, have understood the uniqueness of this parent-child unit as the origin of us all.

A family of course is also a household. There are workers, people who are unrelated by blood or by marriage who together also make up part of what is a family. There are wet nurses, cooks, etcetera, who are embraced as family. It's not unusual in the past to see a burgher or a patrician husband and wife standing as godparents to their wet nurse's child, or standing in as parents to a maid or servant whose parents are dead, sending them gifts and maintaining contact with them long after their service. People have always understood this.

The other concept of family that has always been obvious is that of descent lines, matrilineal and patrilineal. People have understood that they have kin by marriage and by blood and that these kin are very helpful to their progress in the world and real family.

Many historians have said that kinship was more important than the parent-child unit or nuclear family for people up until the eighteenth or nineteenth century, again because of the prejudicial notion that people in the past couldn't think of two things at the same time. The home was basically a workplace, so, it is argued, they were so geared up to run the home as a workplace that the nuclear family couldn't cocoon and develop affectionate relationships until there was major structural change, namely the separation of home and workplace. As far back as we can go, the records indicate that people understood they had kin relationships and a household that was virtual family. But they also understood every bit as clearly that there was a nuclear family — father, mother, child — that made all of these other worlds possible and held them together.

The history from the latest research on family is really good news for a society that's facing a crisis of marriage. There's a lot to be learned there about the situation we find ourselves in today and many cautionary tales about societies that neglect the family unit.

Thoughts

When we look at history, we need to look at what is really happening between people, try to hear them in their own words, on their own terms, and within their own space. For example, one finds an account book where a father is just listing the money he spends on servants and taxes and the like. All of a sudden he'll list buying a new bed for his child, and he'll draw a little box around it with flowers, or call attention to it by fluffing it up with extra ink scribbles. This is going on in the fifteenth and sixteenth centuries. It's obvious that all of a sudden one sees what's really important to this man. In the midst of his everyday life, he treasures and values his family and his children. I find in such sources not only the awareness of the stages of childhood but of the special needs of children as well.

Family has been there in history. It has been the basic thing. This idea that the family did not really exist until modern times reflects a great lack of knowledge. It's also a great exercise in hubris. What are we saying to the past when we say that it did not know until probably the seventeenth or eighteenth centuries what a child was, when we say that parents did not know how to enter a child's world or properly relate to their children? Is there anything more damning of a civilization than saying its people could not recognize, love, and care for their children? There simply is no greater insult to the past. It is also a commentary on how historical ignorance is preventing us from accessing information about human behavior that is the only deep, reliable, clinical information we have about human behavior over centuries.

John Witte Jr.

John Witte Jr. is the Jonas Robitscher Professor of Law and Ethics and the director of the Law and Religion Program at Emory University. He traces the changes in the institution of marriage from the Reformation through the Enlightenment and on to the present day.

Marriage Was a Mess

Marriage in the eleventh and twelfth centuries, right before the papal revolution inaugurated by Gregory the VII, was a mess. It was a mess in part because there was no authority, there was no law, there was no academic tradition, there was no consistent theological education. This was a time long after the Roman Empire dissolved. The Carolingian Empire of Charlemagne was over. The rivalry among his sons and successors had broken down. Tribal warfare was increasingly on the rise. The Church was feudalized in the sense that feudal lords controlled the Church, controlled bishops' appointments, including the Bishop of Rome. As a consequence, one finds in the ample anecdotal evidence that we have widespread concubinage, widespread prostitution, coerced marriages, cohabitation, absent marriage, very difficult patterns of intergenerational wealth transmission. The coerced marriages were often for the sake of diplomacy, for the sake of commercial convenience. There was lack of control on the part of parents vis-à-vis their children, especially fathers. Marriage was a mess.

Marriage was prohibited to clergy. The ordination of a cleric or of a monastic had among its obligations foregoing marriage and foregoing sexual contact. The problem with that institution was that in practice there was an ample expression of sexual contact through concubinage. Keeping of a concubine played the role of a surrogate wife. Sometimes multiple concubines played the role of multiple wives. You had de facto polygamy in place. This was contrary to Roman law, contrary to canon law, and contrary to local bishops' regulations, but there was no mechanism whereby it could be aptly policed.

Illegitimacy was always a difficult problem in the Western tradition before the papal revolution of the eleventh and twelfth centuries and until the reforms in the late 1930s. A child basically bore the scorn and the stigma of his or her parent's extramarital dalliances. A child born out of prostitution, out of concubinage, out of an extramarital affair, out of fornication, had to bear the stigma of being illegitimate. An illegitimate child by his or her very nature was formally precluded from a number of different professions, from property rights, civil rights, social rights, as we would call them today.

There were a lot of arranged marriages. There was a difficulty of having no clear rules for marital formation. As a consequence, there were formal relationships of incest that were allowed, especially in small communities. There was a difficulty of coerced marriages, where it was convenient for a father to marry off his daughter, possibly long before she was of age.

There were no rules requiring consent on the part of the woman or the man which could be enforced. As a consequence, children were pushed into relationships they didn't necessarily want. Women were traded. Women were put on the marriage market. Women were held out for the best dollar payment. Women were used as pawns in diplomatic relationships. Women were put in context of basically being commercial consideration for contracts. These were some of the problems that the Church confronted and that the state confronted in the vacuum of authority that confronted Western tradition around 1050-1100.

Consent: An Invention but Certainly Not a Solution

The notion that marriages had to be formed by the consent of the man and the woman antedates the eleventh and twelfth centuries by more than a millennium. It's inherent in Jewish law, it's inherent especially in Christianized Roman law, and it's very much in place in some of the early canonical law that the Church inherited in the eleventh and twelfth centuries. The notion was, consent was important. But it meant something quite different in its Roman and Judaic context than it began to mean after the twelfth and thirteenth centuries.

What the canonists and theologians of the twelfth and thirteenth centuries put in place was that what makes marriage in its essence is the voluntary consent of a fit man and a fit woman who come together in a marital union. The consent alone made it a social obligation that was permanent and indissoluble. It made it a set of expectations with respect to responsibilities for each other and for children that might come from their union. That was the thirteenth-century invention.

The consent could be manifested in a variety of ways. Increasingly in the canon law in the fourteenth through sixteenth centuries there was an expectation of some oral or written form of agreement. There was a formal betrothal process whereby parties would agree to get married and then upon a certain period of time would get married. But all of these were considered to be prudential recommendations rather than essential requirements. Marriages that were simply a private agreement between a man and a woman were marriages, even if there was no parental consent, even if there were no witnesses, even if there was no Church consecration, and even though there was no civil registration.

Invariably, the marriage litigation docket is full of instances where the woman thought she was married and the man thought he was not married. There were instances of spurious kinds of consent that were given simply for seductive purposes. All these kinds of things begin to pour into the Church courts in part as an inevitable consequence of having that thin, formal requirement for marriage.

Marriages without Witnesses

You could be married by just saying it if the parties themselves did not dispute it. If Jack and Jill, who came together holding hands or one being pregnant, said, "We were married," they were married in the eyes of the Church. If they were fit adults, not related by blood, without a godfather or godmother relation between them, and no prior vow of chastity or celibacy, they were married in the eyes of the Church and their marriage was indissoluble.

Sure, the Church got a lot of complaints about the system. There was no registration process. Jack and Jill get married in one town. Jack goes on a business trip and meets Jennifer. Jennifer and Jack get married in the next town. Jack goes to the following town. You have a form of polygamy that takes place. There is no responsibility that can be assigned to the man or the woman when it's not known whether they're married. There's difficulty with the expectations of the parents, especially for inheritance. All these kinds of things have property implications, and they have criminal implications that get drawn out in subsequent decades and centuries.

Those are some of the problems that the Church responded to by thickening the marital formation requirements. It's response was designed so that the community, which invariably bears both the costs and the benefits of this husband and wife coming together, could participate in the decision that they make to enter into their union. That's what the Council of Trent and other reform movements in the sixteenth century began.

Catholics and Protestants Take On Marriage

The Council of Trent was the religious Super Bowl of the mid sixteenth century. It was convened by the greatest leader of Western Christendom, the pope. It involved the intellectual elite of the Catholic community: the best theologians, the best philosophers, the best canonists, the best church leaders and administrators were there. It was a meeting of the greatest minds of Western Europe and the Catholic world in the sixteenth century. It gave rise to a powerful set of documents, which by reason of their power guided the Church for the next four centuries.

The Council of Trent was formed in part in response to the difficulty of these kind of private marriages or secret marriages, and the difficulties that ensue from both seduction and spurious claims and inarticulated expectations that both sides would have. The notion that marriage depends in its essence upon the consent of both the man and the woman was an enormous reform in the Western tradition. It effectively nullified a long tradition of arranged marriages; some were made for diplomatic convenience with absolute anonymity on the part of the husband and the wife. Marriage based on consent gave women more than any other time in the Western tradition an opportunity to participate actively, voluntarily, and fully in a decision about the rest of their lives. If the marriages occurred by coercion, by trickery, by fraud, by collusion, or any other means, these are impediments that break the betrothal and break the marriage and both parties can march into a Church court and seek dissolution on the basis of that. That's an enormous reform. Neither Roman law nor Germanic law had put this into place.

The immediate cause of the Council of Trent's convocation was the reformist energies within the Catholic Church. But it also occurred in response to the outbreak of the Protestant Reformation in its Lutheran, Calvinist, Anabaptist, and Anglican varieties.

Sacrament, Celibacy, Secret Marriages, and Kidnappings

The kinds of critique that these reformist traditions within and without the Church were making were specifically with respect to marriage. The Reformations in their various forms took on three main features of the theological tradition that the Catholic Church had been teaching since the twelfth century.

First was that marriage was a sacrament. The Protestant Reformists denied the sacramental quality of marriage and thereby denied its indissolubility. It also denied the notion that the Church has exclusive and formal jurisdiction and lawmaking power over marriage.

The second thing that the Protestant Reformations did was attack the notion of clerical celibacy, monastic vows, and a whole series of other rules that were in place in the life of the Church, especially surrounding the sacrament of holy orders. The Reformation put in place clerical marriage. Oftentimes, one of the badges of honor in the first generation of the Reformation was for clerics to leave their holy orders, or for monks to leave their cloisters, and to marry a former nun or a woman in the community. This was a way the Reformation signaled itself symbolically before the surrounding community. The Council of Trent had to respond to that forcefully and it did.

The third problem that Trent confronted dealt less with the Reformation and more with the accumulation of problems in the canon law action from the thirteenth century forward. These, as we have seen, dealt with clandestine or secret marriages, difficulties of seduction, difficulties of abuse, and difficulties of lack of mutual consent. There was the problem of coerced marriages and the problem of kidnapping where a woman was taken away from her parents with the promise of marriage and then despoiled. There was a very great difficulty with impediment practices that had run awry. Impediment practice meant that even though the marriage was considered indissoluble and a right to remarry was not available, there was a rife practice of annulment. The parties could state an impediment, some legitimate and some increasingly tangential, as the ground by which an already consummated marriage, sometimes with many children in place, could be revoked retroactively.

To all of those accumulated problems, the Council of Trent responded forcefully by saying that marriage is a sacrament. Marriage became a sacrament of the Church that represents the union between Christ and his Church. Trent invoked the famous passage in Ephesians 5:32 about the sacramental qualities of Christ's marriage; it talked about the union between Christ and his Church being symbolic of the union between a husband and a wife. It also invoked some of the passages in Ezekiel, Hosea, and Malachi that speak about the relationship between God and his elect people of Israel as a relationship as if between husband and wife.

The Council of Trent also stated forcefully that marriage belonged within the jurisdiction and the lawmaking power of the Church. The Church courts could speak to marriage questions and resolve marriage issues that came before them and local councils and the conciliar apparatus in Rome could pass legislation for marriage questions.

The Protestants, the State, and the Ten Commandments

The Protestant Reformers have a political theology and a sacramental theology, both of which result in marriage no longer being a matter of Church jurisdiction but rather state jurisdiction. This political theology is that Protestants of all sorts — Anglicans most pronouncedly, Lutherans less so, Calvinists less so — emphasize that the magistrate, the emperor, the duke, the lord, the mayor, or whatever, is God's viceregent, God's representative, who participates in the governance of God's earthly kingdom. And the magistrate therefore has power directly from God without Church supervision, and ultimately holds the power under God's supervision.

The way some of the Reformers began to talk about it is that this power is to appropriate and to apply the natural law. Where is the natural law most easily summarized? In the Ten Commandments. What do the Ten Commandments talk about? Well, the relationships between God and his people: "Honor God, don't take the Lord's name in vain, observe the Sabbath," and so forth. Then, on the second tablet, "Don't kill, don't commit adultery, don't steal, honor your parents," and so forth. The notion is that the magistrate is responsible as God's vice-regent to apply the norms set out in the Ten Commandments, which is a summary of the natural law, and then put in place a whole series of specific civil laws to implement. There are three commandments that touch on the questions of marriage, sex, and family life. As a consequence, the magistrate, in that new political theology, had a critical role to play in the governance of marriage questions.

The other side of the Protestant apparatus is that it removes jurisdiction of marriage from the Church to the state. It is the notion that marriage isn't a sacrament. The Protestant tradition from the start — and Luther was especially important in articulating this — does not recognize the sacramental quality of marriage. In the Reformers' view, the creation of the sacrament of marriage, formalized by Peter Lombard and by Thomas Aquinas in the twelfth and thirteenth centuries and canonized in the Council of Trent, was simply a power grab. That was a way, in Luther and Calvin's view, by which the Church claimed power that properly belonged to the state and claimed control over the population. They thought that the Church is there to preach, administer the sacraments, care for the poor, and catechize the young. Administrating the sacraments meant baptism and the Eucharist and nothing more. That reduced the role of the Church. The Protestants viewed marriage as being an earthly institution, a social estate, a local covenant, a little commonwealth, a little seminary, something that ultimately has to be left to local jurisdiction; and local jurisdiction lies first and foremost in the state.

Celibacy and Divorce

The Reformation began, in part, with a shrill critique of clerical celibacy. The Protestant Reformers said there is an important role that celibate folk play, and God sometimes calls parties to a celibate life, and it's perfectly appropriate if that calling is discharged by the party. But the

Reformers said to make celibacy a requirement of the Church, rather than a calling of the divine, is ultimately fruitless. You cannot make celibacy a condition for holy orders. You cannot make celibacy a monastic ideal that is considered to be superior in virtue. Why? Because that ultimately is to act against nature, said the Reformers, first and foremost, and it is to act against Scripture as well. What's the problem with celibacy? It acts against nature because, by virtue of its requirement, it forces parties into all manner of unnatural conduct that is unbecoming of a Christian and unbecoming of a person.And marriage is God's remedy. Marriage is the opportunity that God gives to channel one's natural passion to the service of one's self, one's spouse, one's child, and one's broader community. The Reformers said that to hold that the priesthood is the highest and most lofty calling of the Christian was ultimately to act in a way that's self-defeating.

The Protestant Reformation reintroduced the concept of divorce. Remarriage was permitted, at least after a period of healing and at least for the innocent party. The basis for that was, in part, the denial of the sacramental nature of marriage. Marriage was not a sacrament; marriage was a social estate, a covenant, a little commonwealth, and marriage had basic earthly and social goods that it was trying to achieve. And if they can't be achieved, and attempts at reconciliation don't allow them to be achieved, the marriage can be broken. The Catholic sacramental tradition taught that marriage is indissoluble. Parties could separate from bed and board, but there was no opportunity for remarriage, even though the parties were permanently separated until death.

Marriage exists for three things, according to the classic formula going back to St. Isidore in the sixth century and resurrected strongly in the sixteenth century. It exists for the mutual love and companionship of a husband and a wife, the mutual protection of husband and wife from sexual sin and temptation, and, if God is willing, the procreation and nurture of children. If any of those three goods or goals of marriage is frustrated, the Reformers taught the marriage could be broken.

The Jewish Heritage

Both the Catholic and the Protestant traditions recognize the Jews as God's chosen people. They recognize that God chose, in his providence, to reveal himself and to reveal his law first and foremost to them, before the time of Christ. We have an enormous testimony to that revelation in what is the Hebrew Bible and what Christians call the Old Testament. A whole range of things that seem to be modern questions are, in fact, pre-Christian questions. There are three millennia of Jewish reflection in place by the time Christ rolls on to the scene, and there are two millennia of reflection thereafter, which are useful and informative for the Christian tradition from the start.

Most informative of all are the great texts. The texts in Genesis 1 and Genesis 2 speak about the creation order of marriage — "Be fruitful and multiply," "it's not good for man and woman to be alone." These texts show men and women as naturally inclined to each other. Those kinds of passages, which are organic for the Jewish tradition, are also organic for the Christian tradition. The exposition of that in the Torah, and some of the provision in Leviticus and in Deuteronomy, are essential for Christian understandings of what's appropriate and inappropriate in a relationship between a man and a woman. And they have been interpreted in every generation of the Christian Church from the first century forward. Those texts are critical, and the Hebrew tradition is critical for its formative and constant reformative energies on the Christian tradition.

The Enlightenment

Another great watershed after the Reformation is the Enlightenment. Let's take John Stuart Mill. John Stuart Mill is a brilliant, iconoclastic, caustic, gifted writer in the nineteenth century. He happened to enjoy a long life and wrote formal publications like monographs, books, and anthologies, but also was a journalist. His stuff is pithy and, as a consequence, has an enormous influence on public opinion of the day and especially on public opinion in decades that follow.

There was a lot of agitation for reform in England and on the Continent beginning already in the late seventeenth century. Mill formed his critique of a variety of institutions and ideas of the tradition, including institutions of marriage. He had a number of different worries.

His first concern was what happened to the Achilles' heel of the Reformation. This was the notion that the father was God's vice-regent within the home and controlled, unstinted, what goes on within his household: his wife, his children, his servants, and other members of the household. The man being lord of his castle is a wonderful property concept. But it is not a very good pastoral concept, says Mill, because ultimately it gave no recourse to the abused woman, the abused wife, the abused child, or the abused servant. There was no recourse for that party. The state's not interested in participating because the state participated in the formation and the dissolution of marriage but nothing in between.

The second concern was the common-law doctrine of coverture, which was a species of this first critique. The doctrine of coverture is the notion that upon marriage the property of the husband and the wife are merged and they all become the husband's. The woman sacrifices her property rights, the woman sacrifices her personal rights and comes within the sovereignty of her husband. It's wonderful if it works. It's not so wonderful if it doesn't work. The notion of headship again informs that institution. But here it had a particularly cynical expression, says Mill. The woman basically is a slave to the husband. She is to work within the home; she has no opportunity in commerce, and she has no opportunity outside the home unless she's independently wealthy. She basically has one profession, which is to be a housewife and mother.

His third real concern was children. Children and social welfare had no greater prophet in the twentieth century than John Stuart Mill. Mill took a variety of familial practices and institutions of the day and exposed them. Number one was what we've already talked about: The child in the home, basically, was at the whim of his or her parents and had no recourse in the instance of abuse. There was the condonation, if not the encouragement, of corporal discipline as a means of upbringing. Secondly, Mill was concerned about the control that parents had through the Reformation's emphasis on parental consent over the marital decisions of children, especially for young women. Although it was supposed to apply mainly to the very young, it often worked to bring back coercion into marriages. Daughters basically became commodities on the marriage market, which the enterprising father could sell to the highest bidder. The notion that there is consent to the marriage on the part of the woman may exist there figuratively and formally at law, but in reality in the household, says Mill, it doesn't occur so often. The woman basically goes to the husband that the father picks for her and that's abusive. Mill put all those things very, very pungently in his critique of the tradition.

Marriage Is a Contract and Only a Contract

The notion that marriage is a contract is ancient and goes back to ancient Jewish, Greek, and Roman constructions and to the very early understanding of marriage within the Church. Marriage has always been
understood to be a contract. What constituted the contract were the
contractual requirements. What allowed for contractual revision has
always been a subject of change and diversity among the different communities that have used contract as a basis for describing what marriage is.

What drives the Enlightenment project, which Mill adumbrates as
much as anybody, is the notion that marriage is a contract and only a
contract. Marriage is no longer a sacrament, marriage is no longer a
covenant, marriage is no longer a social estate in which the broader
community participates. Marriage is simply a privately negotiated relationship between two parties. Marriage is reduced to that. No other
party should participate in its formation. No other party should participate in its dissolution. It's the parties themselves who are the decision-
makers about what the contract entails. It is that contractual notion
that the Enlightenment begins to adumbrate in the eighteenth and
nineteenth century and that increasingly drives the reformation and
revolution of marriage in the twentieth century.

The Enlightenment began to hold up liberty as an ideal that had
not been sufficiently recognized and institutionally expressed in the
prior traditions and needed to become an end in its own right. That
Enlightenment ideal, which had a variety of political, cultural, and religious implications, also spoke to questions of marriage and family because it effectively had, as one of its consequences and one of its causes,
a contractual view of society and a contractual view of marriage. Whatever the rationale, marriage is a contract, and marriage is formed as a
bilateral exchange. That notion becomes increasingly sterile. That notion becomes increasingly abstracted in nineteenth- and early twenti-
eth-century discourse about marriage and the family. Ultimately, marriage is not a sacrament. Marriage is not a covenant. Marriage is not a
social estate. Marriage doesn't involve anybody public. Marriage is simply a private, bilateral exchange between the man and the woman, who
are contractually capable of coming together. That's all it is, and nothing more. The state should not participate in it except minimally, to set
the contractual requirements. The Church has no role to play whatso-

ever. The broader community has no role to play, because this is a private relationship between those two parties.

We're in a Watershed Moment

I think we have begun a moment which is on par with the moments of Christianization, the papal revolution, the Reformation movements, and the Enlightened revolutions of the later nineteenth and early twentieth centuries. I think that at the end of the twentieth century and the beginning of the twenty-first century we are in such a revolutionary moment with respect to the future of the institution called marriage.

The period from roughly the mid 1960s to the mid 1990s was the Jacobean phase of this broader revolution. This was a period of enormous sexual liberty, enormous respect for sexual privacy, enormous respect for the contract of marriage and the will of the parties themselves. The state itself abdicated its responsibility for the union. Parties could voluntarily enroll themselves in whatever religious or legal system was in place to govern questions of sex, marriage, and family life, but parties had no obligation to do so.

This was a revolutionary phase. It was scornful of the tradition. It oftentimes deprecated and distorted the tradition. It oftentimes left the tradition outside of its curriculum so that the next generation of kids having been brought up in the 1970s, 80s, and 90s knew nothing about the tradition. The churches and religious communities themselves participated rather actively in this growing amnesia and have participated rather actively in acquiescing to the expressions of sexual liberty and privacy that have been part of this phase.

I think the pathos that has emerged from that experiment — the cost to women, the cost to kids, the social fallout, the kinds of juvenile delinquency, the kinds of grave cultural costs borne of that experiment — have begun to come home.

Is There a New Inequality?

There are thirty million children in this nation that are now owed fifty billion dollars in unpaid child support. It's a tremendous problem.

GERALDINE JENSEN

As soon as I said I was pregnant, he told me that he hated me, that I was a whore, that he wasn't sure he was the father.

SADIE

"Single mother" is a popular term. But it's important to realize that it's not a uniform group.

JUDITH STACEY

Your kids have to be fed and clothed whether the child-support check comes or not. You can't just say, "Sorry kids, no food today."

AMY

Non-support is a crime. It's the only crime in the country that causes poverty.

GERALDINE JENSEN

M arriage didn't just materialize out of thin air. It took centuries to establish marriage as a freely chosen union of two people based on mutual love and supported by the church, state, and community. But in a very short time, much of that work has come undone. The shift from marriage to low-commitment relationships has contributed to a new source of inequality for women and children.

In the 1960s and '70s many people believed that freedom from the bonds of marriage would liberate both men and women. But as it turned out, freedom from marriage liberated men more successfully than it liberated women. Men are able to reduce their commitments to the minimum legal requirements, while women most often have to take on greater responsibility for both breadwinning and caring for children in the household.

More and more young women are supporting and raising children on their own, a baby-sitter and a paycheck away from the streets. Sadie is one of these. A model of independence and what politicians like to call "personal responsibility," Sadie works full-time. She also shops, cleans, cooks, does laundry, and cares for her son Isaiah. She doesn't expect a handout or even a hand up from anyone. One of Sadie's biggest problems is money; she can't count on regular child-support payments. Her situation is all too common. As recently as the early 1990s, half of unwed mothers received no child support at all and of the half that did receive some support, less than a quarter got the full amount they were due.

Sadie

Sadie is a single mother whose boyfriend broke up with her when she became pregnant. Her son, Isaiah, is now a year old.

What Happened with Your Boyfriend?

I don't know. Things didn't work out. He had other things going on, another girlfriend. He didn't want the baby. He was trying to manipulate me into having an abortion by lying to me and stuff like that. I just wanted to have a baby. I didn't want to have an abortion, so I went through with it. About six months into my pregnancy, he sort of became a peripheral part of it. Now he's pretty active in my son Isaiah's life.

At first he was saying to me, "Oh yeah, I'll give you all this money, and I'll buy diapers and clothes in addition to paying you child support." No. That never really came to fruition. It was just constant arguments about money. Up until a few months ago, he wasn't really taking the responsibility.

For a while I didn't have a good job. I was making $10.75 an hour, and I couldn't work forty hours because I didn't have a baby-sitter. I was struggling to pay the rent, and I was hungry. It was pretty bad. It was hard at first. It was pretty bad. And he was just .... I can't get inside his head. I have no concept. I have no idea who he is anymore. He's the father of my son, and now that's the only conversation we have. It's like, "Are you going to come pick him up? Are you going to give me some money?" That's it. There's no friendship.

Did He Ever Talk about Marriage?

Well, we talked about marriage, but that was before the word *pregnant* ever came up. As soon as I said I was pregnant, he told me that he hated me, that I was a whore, that he wasn't sure he was the father. He told me a huge lie that he had this other girlfriend and that she was also pregnant and that he was marrying her. Well, anyway, that turned out to be a lie. That was just to manipulate me into having an abortion. He never talked about marrying me after I was pregnant. Never.

But I don't feel like I got the raw end of the deal. I feel like he's got the raw end of the deal, because I get to spend all of this time with this wonderful little boy. That's so amazing.

I think he's the one who is missing out. He's the one who missed Isaiah's first birthday. He missed out. He never came for any ultrasound. Never came to listen to the baby's heartbeat while I was pregnant. Wasn't there during the delivery. Wasn't really around much in the first couple of months. Didn't feel like it was important to be there. Felt like it was more important to advance his musical career than to spend time with his son. In his words, he's building a nest egg for Isaiah. Unfortunately, the price of that nest egg is a relationship with his son. I kept trying to beat that into his head. He just never, you know, understood, or never cared.

What's a Day Like?

I don't even want to talk about it. Right now, I'm working at an ad agency. So, I get up at 6 A.M., take a shower, start cooking breakfast for the baby. He gets up around 6:30. He eats breakfast. I get ready for work. I have to be out of here by 7:15. I strap him to me, and I walk to the train. I take him to the baby-sitter, which is on Chicago Avenue. Then I walk back to the train, take the train downtown, go to work for eight and a half hours, and then I do the whole thing over again in reverse. It's a lot, but I stay in good shape because I get a lot of exercise.

The thing is that I don't get to spend as much time with him as I like. I was just lazy about getting another waitress job, and that's why I went back to temping, cause I don't feel like looking for a job. I wasn't expecting to lose the other job, which was a really good job for me.

It's hard, because I only get to spend a couple of hours a day with him. On the weekends, now, his dad wants to take him every Saturday, so I get half a day on Saturday and half a day on Sunday and a couple hours a day during the week. Usually he's pretty crabby during those times. So, the fun times are sort of gone for a little while. But I don't plan to work these hours, or be as far away from him, as long. Hopefully I'll get a car soon, too. That'll help. But, you know, I just do it every day.

Isaiah

Isaiah seems crabbier now. I was spending so much time with him, because I took some time off after I lost my job. I didn't do much for like three weeks. We just sort of hung out together. I thought it would be a good time for us to hang out. Then, the first day I had to drag him off to the baby-sitter, he freaked out.

I don't know. He's just been sort of crabby lately. When he got home from his dad's on the weekend, he's real clingy to me. After I get home, he wants me to hold him. He's adjusting, but it's hard for him. I don't know. I just hate to have to sacrifice my relationship with him because I have to go to work to make money, which really isn't much money anyway.

Is it difficult? Definitely. It is. It is difficult. It's not so difficult having him. It's difficult being away from him. That's the part I don't like. I wish I could be independently wealthy and not have to worry about going to work.

On his own accord, Isaiah's father called me on Monday and said, "I'm going to bring over some money." I was like, cool. Like, all right. He brought over $200, and he gave me $150 at the beginning of the month, so he gave me $350 this month, which is pretty good. That's the most I think he's given me so far. He's been good lately about it. I'm happy about that, 'cause it helps.

I'm going to go back to school. What I'd really like to do is be able to work while the baby sleeps. I'd like to get a bartending gig or something like that. But it's hard for me to find a nighttime sitter. The only reason I work days is because I have a really inexpensive baby-sitter, which I was really lucky to find. I want to work part-time and go to school full-time. Finish school, so that I can have a career and don't have to think about struggling any more.

I want to be a teacher. I've always wanted to be a teacher. It's little kids. I like helping kids. But a good perk about being a teacher is that I could get a job in a private school and Isaiah could go to school there, which is what I want. I want him to go to private school. I definitely don't want him in the Chicago public school system. I don't know. Maybe I'll win the lottery, and I won't have to worry about any of this.

The Sounds of the City Never Seemed So Loud

Being pregnant was the hardest time. It was the hardest thing, I think, I've gone through, because I was completely alone. I didn't really have support from anyone except a couple of friends. I thought about everything.

I didn't want to have an abortion. I knew that. I knew that I was going to be okay. I always land on my feet. I've been on my own since I was seventeen and I never looked back. So I knew that I could do it. I also knew that Isaiah's father was not going to be a total loser, because I knew him. I knew him for five years. I knew that he wasn't this jerk that he was behaving like. I knew that underneath he was a good guy.

Bringing Isaiah home the first day was scary. I think the scariest part was when I left the hospital. I had him, and I was all tight with him. I didn't want anyone to look at him. I didn't want anyone to even see him. I was standing there with him, and I never felt so scared. The sounds in the city never seemed so loud. Chicago never seemed as scary as it did that day. I was so scared. I knew that when I left the hospital, I was going to be alone. There wasn't going to be anybody at home to help me. It was just going to be me. It was like the scariest day of my whole life. Then I brought him home, and my mom had my apartment all fixed up. She brought me flowers and some stuff for the baby, and so she helped me. Then she left. Then I was alone with him. It was really, really, really hard, and really scary. The first six weeks were really hard.

When I was pregnant, I was afraid to tell my parents, even though I was twenty-three. I always knew that I would never ask them for money. I was just afraid to tell them that I was pregnant. Believe me, it took me a long time before I told them. I wanted them to know that I was going to have this baby, too. It took them a while to get used to this. It definitely took my mom a while to get used to it. So I told myself and I told them that I would never, never ask them for anything. So I really don't.

What to Tell Isaiah?

I will always be open with Isaiah about what was going on. Maybe it's different from the other kids in school or whatever, but I'll never lie to my son. I'll never be ashamed of who I am, and I'll never let him be ashamed of who he is or who his family is. I don't live my life based on what outside people think I should be doing. What other people think is none of my business. You know what I mean? What other people think of me is none of my business. I don't live my life according to values set by society or whatever. If I feel like I want to live with a guy, then I'll live with him. I lived with Isaiah's father for a long time.

Friends

One friend has the same sort of struggles that I do. My other friend, who has a baby, is not married but is living with her son's father, her boyfriend, fiancé, whatever. I don't want to go into my friend's problems, but I don't think that some of my friends are handling it. One of them is doing great. She's got her life. She's single, but she's living with a guy and he's taking care of them. She's working. She's a nurse. My other friend is not so good. Her boyfriend is abusive. She keeps going back to him. He doesn't give her any money. She can't find a place to live. She's homeless this time with a ten-month-old baby. She's not doing well at all. So we're not really friends. I can't deal with that kind of drama. She has to have drama all the time. I'd rather just not have drama, if possible. You know what I mean? Being homeless because of your psycho boyfriend is another thing altogether. Thank God I'm not her.

I think I'm doing pretty well. Everyone is always saying things like, "Oh man, I give you a lot of credit. I pat you on the back for what you are doing." I made my bed. I have to lie in it. I'm the one who got pregnant. I can't just be like, "Ooh, I got pregnant. Someone else should have to pay, and I should go on welfare." No. So I went and got a job. My friends, they have so much ambition. They're like, "Go on welfare. Go on welfare. You can get money and food." Yeah, great. Go on welfare. No. That's not me.

I'm not saying that there's anything wrong with being on welfare. I'm just saying, I didn't want to be on it, for myself. I always feel like I should be doing something, making myself smarter and taking care of my life, like you are supposed to. I never felt because I got pregnant that anybody owed me anything. I don't feel like I'm doing such a great thing by raising this baby. I mean, I got pregnant. That's what I'm supposed to do now is raise the baby.

Dating

I don't have a boyfriend. I could get sex if I wanted it, no problem. I just choose not to because I told myself after that whole fiasco with the baby and getting pregnant and all that, I was going to wait before I got back involved with somebody that way. So, I am.

Most of the guys I meet are just kind of boring. I don't know. I'm not even looking for a boyfriend. I don't even care. If I meet somebody I like, well, then, great. But I haven't. Dating, it's hard.

Having a child makes it really hard to meet men. I mean, I have no problem meeting men. But as soon as they find out I have a baby, the story changes a little bit. I've dated a couple of guys since Isaiah. They think they are ready for it. They have to understand that Isaiah has to come first. That's that.

What's Up with Guys?

I don't know. They're cowards, some of them. What do I think they are afraid of? Responsibility. Life. Reality. Women. Themselves. Each other. I don't know.

Being a Single Mother

I'd like to get married some day, I think. If I met a really great guy and he wanted to get married or we thought we wanted to get married, I think that would be cool. I think marriage is a good idea when you have children. Yeah, definitely. I think that there should be a mother and a father. When I first got pregnant, I thought everything would be fine. Everything was not okay. My boyfriend didn't want anything to do with it. I don't know I just sort of stopped caring. I was just like, "Oh well." It breaks my heart when Isaiah's father didn't come over on his son's first birthday. That broke my heart.

I don't want it to be like that all the time, where Isaiah's counting on his dad. I know Isaiah is not aware now, because he's only thirteen months old. But I don't want him to be three years old and four years old and expecting his daddy to show up, and he just doesn't show up. That's my big worry.

If Isaiah's father and I were married, obviously it would be different. I think the woman has to take the brunt of taking care of the baby, but it's nice to have somebody there at night to help you with the dishes and feeding the baby and cleaning up and changing diapers and doing laundry and all that kind of thing.

So, I think that being married would be ideal if you're going to be having babies. I don't recommend being a single mom. It's hard work. I don't like being away from Isaiah all the time. I don't like dropping him off at a baby-sitter, although he has fun there. I just wish I could stay home at least four days a week, instead of just two. And on those two days a week I have tons of stuff to do, so I don't get to really spend too much quality time. I try to spend as much quality time with him as I can, but it's hard. Being a single mom is a lot of work. It's an unbelievable amount of work.

The Hardest Part?

Getting up in the morning and doing it all over again. I don't know. I don't know. I guess being alone is hard, too. You always want to have somebody there. It's hard. I have Isaiah, but it's not the same.

Judith Stacey

Judith Stacey makes the point that single mothers are a diverse group, and argues that the vast majority of children with single mothers are just like the vast majority of children with other kinds of parenting relationships.

Single Parents

Single moms, of course, are a complicated group. It includes women who have had children outside of marriage, women who have lost their husbands to death, and women who have divorced. Women who are in cohabiting relationships and lesbians in two-parent families are listed as single, but in fact are not. So you see how difficult it is in sociology to use a category. "Single mother" has become a popular term. But it's important to realize that it's not a uniform group.

They say that single motherhood is bad for children. They say that children with single mothers are two to five times as likely to wind up in prison, or two to five times as likely to attempt suicide — you name it, to be drug addicts, etc. Well, what I would tell you is that that is certainly not true. It's true only in a misguided sense. The vast majority of children with single mothers are just like the vast majority of children with other kinds of parenting relationships. When you say that twice as many, you sometimes are talking about 4 percent rather than 2 percent.

Yes, that is a lot of kids, but you haven't shown that the single-parent family was the cause of that. You haven't shown that those children would be better off in two-parent families. I'm not saying that none of them would be better off, or that all of them wouldn't be better off. I say that it is always a much trickier issue.

What we do know is that impoverished children, even with two parents, are worse off than affluent children with one parent are. That is absolutely clear in the data. Now I'm not going to tell you that money in and of itself will produce a successful child, because it will not. But we certainly know that a secure income and a working parent are, on average, better for children than the opposite. That is a much more secure finding than the finding about a single-parent versus two-parent family.

Amy

Amy has been married twice and is now a divorced mother of three sons. She has trouble collecting child-support payments and says that that is a major hardship on the family.

Sorry Kids, No Food Today

People who don't receive child support don't know what it's like when you count on it every week, and what it's like to go four, five, or six weeks without child support. It's very frustrating. Your kids have to be fed and clothed whether the child-support check comes or not. You can't just say, "Sorry, kids, no food today. I didn't get the check." So other bills have to go unpaid: power, phone bills, mortgages, and whatever. You have to more or less, I guess, rob Peter to pay Paul. It's really frustrating, and it's really stressful not knowing if you're going to get a child-support check or when it's going to come or how much it's going to be. It's very, very scary not knowing whether next month, will I have enough money to pay my mortgage?

I don't really talk to the boys much about child support because I don't like to make it an issue whether they can or can't have something. If it's something they really need for school, it has to come from somewhere else. So, it's just the little extras: "No, you can't go do that this weekend, because we don't have the money." "No, you can't do that."

It's hard. Anytime you go through a divorce, it's hard. It's hard on the boys, too. I think it's hard on everybody. So, yes, it was hard on them. What do I try to teach the boys? I've tried to talk to them about it, which right now they don't really want to talk to Mom about it. But I say just don't have children until you're completely ready to have children and you can afford to have them. If you're still in school that's not going to work. I'd tell people to just make sure that they can afford to have the family. And if they ever do get a divorce, I hope that they would pay their child support on their own and not have to have it taken out of their check. That's the whole problem. If my ex-husband would pay it on his own, we would never have to have an order of withholding. It wouldn't have to come out of his check. So I tell the boys that if they do have children and they end up getting divorced at some point, just be responsible and take care of your obligations.

I'd like to see my boys treat their girlfriend or significant other or wife as an equal, and not, "I'm the man of the house and you do what I say." Not that kind of thing. Just treat each other equally is really a big thing, especially nowadays.

Want to Get Married Again?

Not really. I sort of do. I like the family. I like being settled down. I like just having stabilization, and, of course, the extra income doesn't hurt either, having two incomes. But I don't know. I probably will at some point. Right now, I don't see it at all in the near future.

Mom and I joke about this, but a future husband has to have a job, a driver's license, and probably hair and teeth, although the hair is optional depending on how much money he makes, and the teeth, well, if he's got a good job, false teeth are always okay. He'd have to be basically just responsible, and somebody who would treat my kids like his own. That's really important. If he didn't act like he wanted to be around them or anything like that, it just wouldn't work from the get-go. That's real important.

Yes, I think relationships are very hard. I think it's so easy for people now to get a divorce after they've gotten married that people get divorced and get married within a matter of months. It's so easy to get divorced. People don't realize how much of a commitment getting married is. It takes work on both parts, and it takes work all of the time. I think people enter into it sometimes maybe too lightly and don't realize how much work it is. Then they just give up instead of trying to work on it.

The most important thing is probably communication. Communicating with each other and just being able to talk about anything. If there's a problem, talk about it. I think communication is really a big thing with any couple whether they're married or not married.

Deadbeat Spouses

If you're going to father children then you need to be responsible for them financially and emotionally. If you're able to father them, then, yes, you should have to help pay for them. It should not be the mother's total responsibility at all. I think it's good that they are finally getting a little more aggressive in collecting child support.

To deadbeat spouses, I say, just be responsible. If you've got a child, help pay for them. They're not cheap nowadays. Kids want and need a lot of things, so just help pay for them. Also, child support does not cover everything and once in a while if your kids want something extra, it doesn't hurt to give them something here and there for something extra.

Single Parenting: A Tough Job

People should know that it's just really tough being a single parent, whether it's a woman or a man. Having to work two jobs just to make ends meet, two or three jobs is sometimes a necessity. But it still doesn't work sometimes. You don't see the kids as much. People should try to make their marriages work and not give up quite so easily. And if you do have to go through a divorce, just be responsible.

I think the financial aspect is really the hardest, especially with teenagers. Teenagers require a lot. If they play in sports, that takes a lot. You have to really put out a lot of money for that. Second on the list would probably be just no support as far as, if the kids are sick then there's nobody to stay at home with them but me. So then you're missing a day's work. Just having an extra person in the house, so if you have to work late somebody else is there that can get them from the sitter or just be there with them to supervise. That's really hard, and that's one thing that I miss a lot too.

Geraldine Jensen

Geraldine Jensen is the founder and president of the Association for Children for Enforcement of Support in Cleveland, Ohio. A divorced mother of two children, she founded the group because her ex-husband would not pay child support and the government was not effective at collecting it.

Kind of "Hidden Homeless in America"

I'm an American statistic. I'm part of that 50 percent that ends up divorced. I had two children. My husband and I were supposed to live happily ever after, and instead we were divorced after seven years of marriage. My sons were two and four years of age at the time. Their father participated in their life, and he spent time with them. But he made his child-support payments, as ordered to by the court, for only about six months after the divorce.

Once the child-support payments stopped, I didn't earn enough money at my job as a nurse's aid to be able to take care of my sons alone, and pretty soon the bank was foreclosing on the house. Suddenly, we were homeless. We were kind of "hidden homeless in America," because we were lucky enough to be able to move in with relatives rather than go to a shelter.

I got a second job to try to support the kids on my own, but I just couldn't keep up with taking care of the kids and reestablishing a household and working so much. Eventually, I ended up on welfare. In fact, 87 percent of the families on welfare aren't receiving child-support payments.

I'm really kind of a lucky American statistic in the sense that I was able to go back to school, become a nurse, get off of welfare, and try to reestablish my life. But I never really earned enough money to make sure my kids really had the things they needed. I couldn't afford health insurance, so when my son had ear infections I couldn't afford the prescriptions. My other son wanted to be on the little league team and I couldn't afford the baseball mitt.

Finally I got so fed up with the fact that the government, which was supposed to go after the boy's dad to make him meet his child-support obligations, did nothing. I began to organize parents to become advocates for their children to make sure that our kids receive these much needed child-support payments.

I put an ad in the newspaper. I'd gone into the child-support agency for about the fifteenth time, and I had said, "You know, I am really desperate. I have twelve dollars. I have two hungry children." It was very frustrating, and it took me a long time to get angry enough to really take action. One day I went into the child-support government agency, and I said to my caseworker, "It's been seven years. He owes twelve thousand dollars. We're desperate. I don't have enough money to feed my children. Please do something to collect the child support. You know where he works. He works for the railroad. You know where he lives. I really need your help." The man working there said, "I am so tired of you women coming in here and whining and complaining. If you think you can do a better job go do it."

That was it. That just made me so angry. I knew I had to do something to help my children and other children not go through this anymore. So I put an ad in my local newspaper and I began to get phone calls. The ad said, "Not receiving your child support? Call me." It was mainly people just like me who called: Moms who were divorced, who had court orders and had gone to the government for help and had not received any help. It was moms that were never married to the dad and needed to establish paternity. I even had dads call me who had custody of their children and the moms hadn't paid support in years. So we banded together and we formed this group called ACES, Association for Children and for Enforcement of Support. We've been busy ever since, fighting for laws to help our children and then fighting to get those laws enforced adequately.

The Scope of the Problem

Well, there are thirty million children in this nation that are now owed fifty billion dollars in unpaid child support. It's a tremendous problem. Over 50 percent of these kids grow up in poverty because the child-support payments are not received and the custodial parent is unable to provide for all of their needs alone.

This sends a message that they're not important and they're not valued and they're not loved, especially in this nation that is so materialistic. The ability to be able to have things that other children have, to be able to go to activities with your friends, participate in sports — every aspect of their life is impacted. In fact, over 30 percent of the moms report that within a year of the father leaving the home the children experience hunger. Forty-five percent have a housing crisis and have to move and the kids are totally uprooted. Thirty percent report that they're unable to take their kids to the doctor when they're sick. They're devastated in every way. Their whole life is turned upside down.

What Should the Government Do?

Since it's obvious that after twenty years of the government having a child-support enforcement program in which the best that state government is able to do is collect from 20 percent of the parents, it's time for change. It's time to reform the system. We believe that we need to move collection support into a government institution that is good at collecting money.

We would like to see child support be collected by the Internal Revenue Service just like taxes. It would be payroll deducted like federal income taxes. It would be collected from self-employed through social security tax withholding system. We would be able to collect from most Americans the child-support payments they've been ordered to pay by the court. We get taxes from 83 percent of Americans. We get child support from 23 percent of those who owe it.

It seems to us that the IRS collecting child support is a very basic responsibility of Americans, just as basic as to take care of your children. So, it's not just another bill. These are your children. This is a legal and moral responsibility. If you are not going to do this voluntarily, which has been proven time and time again that most people do not voluntarily pay, we should make kids as important as our taxes.

Anything to Say to Deadbeat Parents?

We ask deadbeat parents, "Why don't you pay your child support?" The answer that we got from about 20 percent of them was that they really believed that their car payment was more important, because their car would be repossessed if they didn't make the payment or their lights would get shut off. So they prioritize their bills above their children. About 20 percent said, "Well, I don't have any money." Other parents said things like, "Well nobody really made me." About 10 percent reported that they were very angry at their ex-spouse and that they were holding the support payments to get something from their ex-spouse. They may believe that their ex ripped them off in the divorce, and so this is how they were fighting back. They are literally using their children, holding them hostage.

I'd like to shake them and empty their pockets and make sure the kids got the money, so that not one more child in this country goes to bed hungry tonight because their parent didn't send a check that week.

Non-support is a crime. It's the only crime in the country that causes poverty. It's not a crime that occurs just once. It's day after day, week after week, month after month. Those who have an ability to pay and turn their back on their kids are abusing their children. They are criminals, and they should be prosecuted.

It's amazing that the collection rate can be so bad. Part of the problem is that some parents don't have orders, because if you don't have a divorce yet or if you're low-income you can't afford to go through the system. You're reliant upon the government child-support agency to get you an order. Thirty percent of the children now are born to parents who never got married, often who just lived together. Those children need to have paternity established and get an order. But even with the typical divorced families, only half of those parents make regular payments. So if you just have the typical divorce, where you both use a private attorney and you're middle class, you only have a 50 percent chance of getting support payments to help make sure your kids have food and clothing, shelter, education.

The Most Difficult Part Is the Guilt

When we talk to the ACES members — about half of us were divorced and about half were not married to the father — we all say, "Well, what happened? How did you get here?" People didn't plan to get here. They thought they would live happily ever after and never get divorced. So, they're pretty surprised and shocked.

They're even more shocked that after the divorce and after you go to court and you have this child-support order that this person just vanishes from the life of the child. Those that weren't married really thought that they would live together, and that maybe someday they would get married or that they would stay together. They didn't look at their situation as temporary, and yet we've all found that in this changing, fast-paced world it seems like nothing is permanent.

I think the most difficult part about being a single parent is the guilt of not being able to take care of your kids, to not have enough money to buy food. When you have to move for the third time because you just couldn't come up with the rent money, and the kids have to change schools again, you just feel so inadequate and so awful inside that you've really let your kids down. You might work two or three jobs to try to make up for that, but when you do that then you're not there for the kids. So you're not there to help them with homework or to make sure that they're hanging around with the right crowd. So you lose the ability to really protect and nurture your kids if you go out and make it economically. If you don't go out and make it economically, you sit there and you watch your kids suffer and go without and you worry.

It's a total nonwinning situation, and a lot of people just give in. They become very depressed, and that just even further harms the kids. We need to fix the child-support enforcement system. Families need to know that they're going to receive those payments and they can count on them to have at least enough money to meet basic needs.

What about Fathers?

The fact that 40 percent of the children in America are going to sleep on any given night without a father in the house says powerfully that men in America today have abdicated their responsibilities.

U.S. SENATOR JOSEPH LIEBERMAN

There's the old saying, "Why buy the cow when you can get the milk for free?"

KEITH

I think fatherhood is a little bit more fun. Isaiah's father gets nothing but fun times with him. Instead, I carry a twenty-two pound baby on my back three miles a day.

SADIE

Seventy percent of all African-American children are born out of wedlock. That data haunts me every day.

RONALD MINCY

So now you have a whole generation of young men not wanting to be men, but wanting to be players, wanting to be ballers. Nobody is growing up now.

KEITH

If you go back two hundred years, most of the parenting advice was directed toward fathers, not toward mothers.

WADE HORN

The crisis in marriage is also a crisis in fatherhood. Men who walk away from pregnant girlfriends very often walk away from their responsibilities as fathers. The crisis in fatherhood has reached such epidemic proportions that in some areas children grow up not only with their own father absent, but in a climate of fatherlessness, where there are few if any male role models available to them.

This crisis is perhaps a symptom of deeper changes in men's and women's family roles and relationships. The breadwinner role is no longer exclusively the man's role. Women bring home the bread too. Men still earn more than women but that's changing rapidly. In a quarter of marriages today, wives earn more than their husbands. In fact, except for the very well educated, male wages have declined in the past twenty-five years. Women are also going on to college in higher numbers than men; in the African-American community, twice as many women graduate from college as do men.

But women's greater independence creates tremendous confusion and uncertainty about men and their roles. This problem cuts across class, community, and ethnicity, but it is especially acute in the African-American community. There, a generation of young boys is growing up on the streets or in the foster care system, a living legacy of decades of urban poverty and discrimination and of the longer and darker history of slavery and racism. Talk to these young African-American men about what troubles them, and the conversation inevitably comes around to their own fathers.

Ron Johnson and Young African-American Men

Raised in New York City and a former gang member, Ron Johnson earned a Bachelor of Science degree from Columbia University and now leads the National Family, Life, and Education Center in Culver City, California. As part of his work there, he presents workshops on self-esteem and cultural sensitivity for African-American youths, some of whom are interviewed with him here.

What Does It Mean to Be a Man Today?

Ron Johnson: My program addresses the need to teach boys about manhood, to make them understand that manhood is not an extension of your anatomy, but, rather, it's a social function, or, spiritually, it's an earthly response to a heavenly mandate.

To teach boys about manhood we have ten rites of passage. For example, the personal rite of passage talks about the fact that life is hard. How to get through a rough life? You need a sense of self-esteem, you need a sense of self-respect, you need a positive self-image, and you need a vision that speaks to what you want out of life, and what contribution you'll make to our people. Then you need a plan. After you establish your plan for life, then you need discipline. That requires four things: that is, accepting responsibility, that you must live in reality, that you must forestall immediate self-satisfaction, and you have to have balance in your life. You have to understand that boys play before they work, and men work before they play. So you have to have this balance in your life, where you can't play all the time and expect results, but you can't work all the time and be happy and healthy. That's just a first.

Then there's the spiritual: that God is on your side, won't forsake you, won't let you down, won't let you go. There's the economics: how to manage your money long before you make money. The emotional: to understand that your emotions or feelings are designed to feed you information, they are not designed to direct your behavior. So, as you become a man, you've got to master your emotions. That does not mean suppress them, but rather to express them in an appropriate fashion.

The mental rite is how to study, how to take tests, and how to make a decision. Never find yourself without a book. The social rite of passage is the family, the block, the neighborhood, the county, the state, the region of the nation, the nation, the continent, the hemisphere in which you live. It's the world in which you live, the universe and the galaxy in which you live. It should not suffer because of your presence, but rather should be placed at a distinct advantage simply because you're there. That's the word out to all men to organize boys.

The problem right now in America is black, red, brown, and yellow. The most organized boys are in gangs, and that's because we've failed to organize our boys to do something to help their neighborhoods as opposed to hurt their neighborhoods. So there's the cultural, to find out who you are, who your people are. The historical is to find out your history, because history is not just a list of dates, times, and places, but rather it contains the springs and motors for action today.

So I know as a black man that part of my manhood is vested in that I'm a soldier on behalf of my people who fights for freedom, justice, and equality; and not just for my people, but for all people. So, there are ten rites of passage, but, in a nutshell, that's it: to train boys about manhood, that manhood is something that must be learned, earned, attested, and trusted at some point.

I Just Wanted to Run the Streets

Omar: How did I get into the program? I was sort of forced. It was mandatory for the group home. If you wanted to do anything, get out of the house, you had to go on the weekends. If you wanted any freedom, you went to "Rites of Passage." Other than that, there wasn't nothing else. I didn't want to be there, but now I like it. I was a hard head; I wanted to run the streets or whatever, or find me a female or something.

Robbie: Omar was probably in a unique group because it was a collaboration between Ron's program, which is the "Rites of Passage," and the Department of Children and Family Services here in Los Angeles. He was servicing high-risk children in the inner city, so the department provided case management and Ron's program provided the curriculum. The kids, the teenagers, were in long-term foster care and were not going home. Omar was one of that initial group of children.

Ron Johnson: Omar's response is appropriate. There's not much in a boy's life today that mandates that he become a man. In fact, for African-American boys, it's a struggle to accept adulthood, because here we are now in a nation where we want to prosecute kids who are twelve and fourteen years old as adults. So why would anybody want to become a man?

So we began to work with that population that we saw as the most severely at risk, because they were in foster care, permanent placement, their families had been destroyed by alcohol and drugs for the most part, and we knew that they would need these lessons. Initially, they were resistant, but we found out through an audit from the county that we were successful.

Seventy percent of the inmates in the United States have spent some time in foster care. So we had a severely at-risk group of young students, but we did well. Although they were between sixteen and eighteen and read between the second- and fourth-grade level, we found out that 43 percent of them went to college and 75 percent of them were emancipated from the system successfully.

Why So Many Absent Fathers?

Ron Johnson: Why are there absent fathers? We need to teach them. My dad was an alcoholic, my stepfather was a heroin addict, and it's easy for somebody to think or to say, "Well, he's absent because he's an alcoholic, he's absent because he's a heroin addict."

When I began to reestablish my life and leave the street I had to find out — because I was angry, because I was in pain — why was my father not there? I went back and I began to ask my father's friends, "What happened?" and they told me. They said "You know, Ron, your dad was a great man, and he worked hard, and they unionized his shop, and they pushed the black man out, and he began to drink and gamble, and he didn't drink well, and he gambled worse, and he lost it."

So part of it is the supports are not there for us to be fathers. But, at the same time, we have to accept the responsibility, if those supports are not there, to build those supports in our lives. It comes down to a basic decision: you gotta teach boys not to make babies before they get married. That's the bottom line. We have to reestablish families.

Kevin: Is marriage important for having babies? I believe so. I'm in a situation now where I have two kids. Well, I have three kids, one I have from a previous relationship that I was in. Y'know, when you're young, you really don't think about, "Well, do I want to get married?" All you just think about is I want to hit this girl and this girl. But as you grow older, you realize you've got to start thinking about when you do have kids. You want to provide a stable home for the kids that you do have, and not just go back and forth, go here with you on weekends and then go back with the mother. My two youngest kids stay with me, and I am with the mother, and we do plan on getting married soon.

What am I waiting for? Trying to settle down. I just want to be able to provide for my family. I want to be able to provide for my wife a nice wedding, just be able to give her what she didn't have when she was growing up. I just want to be able to provide things. I don't know.

Keith: I think we have a lot of absentee fathers because we have stopped valuing the family. It's not a role model anymore; it's not something that young men look up to. My grandfather, who raised me from the time I was twelve, role modeled the behavior for me, so I knew that when I became an adult I wanted to follow his pattern. Unfortunately, we don't have that model anymore. Something happened with the value of the family; the traditional family broke down. So now you have a whole generation of young men not wanting to be men, but wanting to be players, wanting to be ballers. Nobody is growing up now.

What is a player or a baller? To do what Kevin did when he was young. To get as many as you can possibly get as often as you can possibly get it without having the responsibilities. It used to be that young men grew up seeking out someone that could be their mate. Now we grow up seeking out whomever we can to make us feel good.

So we don't value the institution of families anymore. That's not our goal anymore, unfortunately. And the reason why we don't is because we don't have the examples anymore.

Family: What Is It?

Charles L.: I think that's difficult to try and capture one definition. Trying to speak for all black people I think we do a big mistake, because different people have their own understanding of what family is. For some people family can be just mother and child, because of the death of the father. Family takes on many different dimensions. Historically, in our community, family has been not only just mother, father, and offspring, but also grandmother, auntie, and uncle. It's an extended family complex, and I think pretty much everybody's aware of that. That's usually how we function. Now a lot of that has been destroyed; I consider it destroyed.

Robbie: I think family, like you said, is a lot more than just, "Okay, this is my blood mother, my blood father." I found out, I guess about a year and a half ago, after talking to my grandmother, that a lot of my uncles and aunts and cousins were not really related. They were people who came from Texas with my grandfather. He came out here and he brought like a slew of members with him and they became family. To us that's blood.

We always had a more generalized concept or picture of what family was. It's not just, "Oh, this is blood, this is blood." We have lifelong relationships that are not related, but in my heart, in my mind, the way I think, they are family. I think that's different in black culture from the larger society. We don't have this sort of definition of family; we don't, like, put it in a box. We sort of say community.

What about Marriage?

Jerome: I can speak personally with a situation in my family with my nephew. My sister got married; they had a child. A month after the child was born, the father decided he didn't want to be married anymore. So he divorces my sister. Now all my nephew sees is my mother and his mother. His father never comes around. I think it's just the pressure of the responsibility that sways a lot of young people, not just black people, but just the pressures and responsibility of being married: "I don't want to be married and tied down to one woman. I want to still hang out with my boys. I still want to be able to do what I want to do, when I want to do it. I don't want to have to come home and do this and do that, and I don't want to have to work forty hours a week and pay this note on this apartment. Ah, she wants a house; she wants a car." All those responsibilities weigh hard on a young person. I think that that deters a lot of them from being married in the true sense of the word.

Charles L.: It's come back to me. I've been married for two years now. I got married at twenty-two shortly after my wife was pregnant. It was automatic for me that, "Okay, yeah, hey, we're going to get married," because my personal belief is to have a happy baby, you have to have a happy mother. So I married my wife.

But marriage is tough. I mean, from the beginning, from when I was trying to get health insurance for my son, I'm talking to the social worker, and she's trying to tell me, "don't include yourself on the application." She said, "I want you to act like you're not a part of this house." She was splitting my family. That's how I felt. Everything that I've tried to do that's public, it's like I'm always excluded. It's always, "don't put him on the application, don't include him, act like he's not in the house."

The fact is that this is my house. I live here. We're married, and that's how it should be. But I think in many facets of society you're locked out and you're excluded. You're put down, and that's how I feel. It's extremely tough, especially when you are supposed to be a provider. It gets tough being the provider when everyone's looking at you like you ain't providing. It gets real tough.

I think that's why a lot of men run from marriage — being scared, that fear of not being able to provide. I know a lot of men who have been scared to get married just for that reason, the fear of not being able to provide, of having to look at faces like there's nothing I can do.

Omar: Do I have that fear? Yeah, I mean, it's part of not taking care of myself. I can't really worry about someone else. If I was capable of doing it, I probably would, but right now, the last thing on my mind is marriage. I'm only twenty-two. I don't even like the word.

Charles B.: I think Charles makes an excellent point with regard to the primary purpose and function of the man in the home or in the marriage. It is to be a provider and a protector. I think we may have a too narrowly defined description of absentee fatherhood. I think everyone has a visual image of a man who has a child who is just not in the home. Absentee fatherhood also might include the father who is in the home, but, because he can not provide or protect his family, he emotionally kind of cops out and is not there as a support for his children.

My father is an example. I think my father had very, very clear aspirations as to who he wanted to be as a man, as a father. I read some of his writings from while he was in college, for instance. At nineteen years of age, he dropped out of school and joined the military and served two terms in the Korean War. He came home and married my Mom, who he had dated since he was thirteen or fourteen years old. He wanted to pursue a career in civil service. He took the Civil Service exam in Westchester County in the mid 1950s. Although he scored number one on the Civil Service exam, he could not get in the police or the fire department. He had an expert background in demolitions, but he could not get a job while they were building the New England thruway.

So he chose other options. He became a burglar and was very good at it. The police in Westchester County could not catch him. They framed him and planted burglar tools in the back of his car. He served three years in prison. He came out when I was in the sixth grade, and it was just a continual cycle of criminal activity based on the people he had connected with in prison.

I think my father was probably an exemplary individual who had all of the aspirations for a family, but because he could not provide for us on a consistent basis, he was not there emotionally. I struggle with this now, with my children. I find myself not being equipped with the necessary skills to lead them into manhood and adulthood. So just being involved in this kind of setting, being connected with those that are skilled in the "Rites of Passage" program is certainly a blessing to me, and I try to learn as much as I can while I'm here. It's a daily struggle.

Does my wife earn more than I do? No, she doesn't. I've been pretty blessed with regard to earning potential. But I think that what I hear now in our community, and I say "our" as being the African-American community, is that many black women are now vocally saying that they are not going to put up with the things that they saw their mothers put up with. A lot of times women stayed in marriages that were dysfunctional because the men were the primary breadwinners. I think women today are basically saying that this institution of marriage doesn't work for me. I'm earning just as much or more than my husband and I don't need it.

Why Even Get Married?

Donnel: Why bother with marriage? It's love. I'm married and my wife makes more than me, and it doesn't bother me a bit. I mean, marriage is teamwork. You know what I'm saying? My wife is older than me. I'm thirty-three years old. My wife is thirty-five. A lot of times I look to her for all the wisdom and the knowledge that she can give me.

She's helping me; she's picking me up when I fall. She's there for me mostly. We have respect for each other, we communicate, and we talk. I had a problem with that at first, because I didn't like to communicate. I didn't like to go to people and share. I wanted to solve my problems myself, because that is what I had to do: I was on my own since I was twelve years old. I did what I had to do to get by and I had sense enough to stay in school. I made some mistakes and I paid for them, whatever, but, I don't know, I enjoy my marriage to the fullest.

Keith: I need to say something. I'm a young man, but again I was raised the old-school way. I think part of the problem is twofold. First of all, I still think as a culture, we've stopped valuing marriage. Why should I marry her when I can live with her? There used to be a time when that wasn't acceptable. You didn't live with her unless she was willing to marry you. As a matter of fact, you really shouldn't even lay down with her unless you are ready to commit yourself to her. We've gotten away from that, you know. There's the old saying, "Why buy the cow when you can get the milk for free?" So, because society and because our culture and because our values have changed, we just shack up, we don't marry anymore. That's a problem.

Why is it a problem? Because when I don't have a commitment to her, I can leave anytime I want. I have not fully committed myself. If I love you and I want to make you a part of my life, if I believe that you are indeed my helpmate, then we're committed. If I'm just simply living with you for sexual reasons, or convenience, or simply economics, then when my situation gets better or I find somebody else who can satisfy me more sexually, or if problems arise, then I can just walk out the door, because I have not fully committed myself to you.

What about the high divorce rates? That's my second point. Those of us who are marrying don't fully understand what marriage is all about. We get married with this ideal and with this dream that we are automatically going to have the big house, we will automatically have the fine car, we will automatically have the expensive things, and we don't understand that the first two or three years of marriage is a struggle. We don't understand that when we initially get together we should start with nothing and build up to something. A lot of us get married simply because we just know, "I love you, baby," but I never really learned you. I never knew anything about you.

I do marital counseling all the time, and I would say about half of the couples that I bring in don't get married right away because there are some things you need to learn about each other. That love will blind you. Then once you get married, you start seeing the person for who he or she really is. So, that's a problem. We don't take the time to learn each other anymore.

Donnel: A lot of the reason why people live together before they get married is 'cause it is a totally different situation when you live with someone. You know what I'm saying? If you get to that marriage point without having been lived together, it's going to be a totally different story. You going to know a lot more about a person in the morning than in the evening. When you're there all the time around each other, you see so much more about the person than you did when she was living over here and he was living over here. It's just a totally different situation.

Keith: But while you were getting to know yours, you're still having sex with her. And while you are in the process of getting to know her, you're probably having babies by her, and then once you realize that she's not really who you really are, then you're gone. She's stuck with the child, and here we go again.

Sex — People Don't Wait

Robbie: I think from a reality standpoint, people are having premarital sex. For the most part, they always were having premarital sex. They may have acted as though they weren't, but they were. We definitely should try to go back to teaching more conservative values. But in the face of that, when you talk about the people who don't have the values, what do you tell them? You don't tell them, "Oh, you should go back." That's not reality. I think we need to devise a way, a lesson, that deals with the reality of people's lives. People don't wait. People don't wait to have sex until the marriage. Let me ask you a question. How many people here did not have premarital sex? So it's okay to say it.

Ron Johnson: Okay. Just because we did something, it does not mean it's right. Here's the thing, man. See, I'm not liberal or conservative. It's about nation building. If you don't have strong families, you don't have a strong nation. It is butt out of control. We're talking forty years ago, 85 percent of black families had men in the household. Today, we're talking about anywhere from 60 to 80 percent of black births are from unwed mothers.

When we look at the research, it points to what happens to children that come from single-parent families. When we look at it, we don't have families. When we look at what happens to our children, it's time to stop and reconsider; maybe we've gone too far down this road, and it's time to go back and do things traditionally the way our people did things.

Robbie: How do you reach the other people out there who don't have the wisdom, the history, that you have, who do not have your life experiences? I mean, what would have made you say, "Oh, you know what, let me not have premarital sex." It is easy to go back and say, "Oh, man, you shouldn't have done it."

What Are We Teaching?

Ron Johnson: What I can tell you is that one of the problems that we have in the black church — the white church too, but I'm talking about the black church — we have failed to teach Christianity as a lifestyle. It's something that we do now on Sunday morning, and Wednesday evening, and choir rehearsal. It needs to be taught as a lifestyle. It's real important.

Yes, I think marriage is important. I think family is important. I think children need both their mother and their father, and I think they need them there in their lives, actively. I think that you can maybe parent away from your child, but, yes, I think the ideal thing is for a man and a woman to be married before they have babies.

All the things you talked about in terms of why guys don't do it, I think that's real. I don't want to have to work all this hard for my job, and bring all this cash home to this woman. I don't want to have to work this hard in this relationship or the responsibilities.

That speaks to the boys' need to be trained to be men. When you hear young men talk about that, and he was honest, and I'm with him, I hear it all the time. Manhood is not about *want to*; it's about what you have to do. You have to train them to be prepared for this. It's not easy. I mean, without commitment, I would not be in my marriage today.

Babies and Second Thoughts

Ron Johnson: How many of us have children out of wedlock? Everyone. Although I know you love your kids, if you could go back and do it all over again, would you have them in wedlock? Everyone. How many of you would not have had them, if you could go back? No, I don't mean abortion, no, no, no, no. What I'm saying, if you could do it over, if you had a choice? Everyone.

Robbie: If I had a chance to go back, it wouldn't have been that I would have gotten married, and it would have been that I wouldn't have had children.

Donnel: What's the problem? For one, having children at a young age, without the financial responsibility, you are not Mr. Ready. You know what I'm saying? This is a fight; this is an uphill battle raising kids. When I had mine, I didn't know how to communicate with them, because I didn't have it. My father didn't talk to me. My mother didn't even talk to me. I was always fighting, fussing, and arguing. That's how I was raised. Basically, I was left to fend for myself. When you have your own kids, you look at them and you wonder, how you supposed to do this? You are always down on yourself because you don't know if you are doing the right thing.

Keith: But the reality of it was, when you were having that relationship with your girl, I don't think you were actually trying to have a baby. That was just a byproduct of not using protection.

Donnel: Exactly.

Keith: But, once the baby came, I congratulate you on the fact that you said, "I'm going to father this child." I don't think that most of the young men that have babies out of wedlock were actually trying to have a baby. They were just trying, as the street says, to get their groove on.

Omar: I was trying to have a baby. I think I was stupid enough, just because I felt that it would make me feel like a man or something. I was always searching, you know, going to get you some booty, and you a man. If you don't, something wrong with you. I was trying to get a baby and get some booty.

Why was I trying to get a baby? For the simple fact that I was missing my family. I felt that if I had a child by somebody, it would make up for what I was missing. I was. I was trying to have kids, trying to get all of that. I was trying to have all of it up and get something.

What kind of a father am I? I'm not a father at all. I don't do nothing. I don't attend to none of my responsibilities. Nothing. I would like to be a father. I still want to learn what it is to be a father, because I never had a father who taught me anything. Where are you going to learn the skills? Groups like this and the people that's in this group, pretty much.

Keith: I don't think we should miss his point, however. He said he wanted a kid. He wanted that. But now that he has it, he doesn't know what to do. I think in all of us we have a desire to be good fathers. We all have a desire to be good men. Many of us just don't know what to do. And it's because we have no one, and no one has taught us. No one is teaching anymore. The guide is not there anymore. The teacher is not there anymore. The desire is there.

Do You Need to Be Married to Be a Good Father?

Robbie: I think everybody will agree marriage is important, but you don't have to be. Case in point: I'm not, but I have my daughter every other day. My schedule is Monday, Wednesday, Friday, and Saturday until like 5 P.M. I didn't want to be "weekend dad." When she said, "Okay, I'm having the baby," then I had to make the choice for me. Do I want to be involved, or do I not want to be involved? So I said, "Okay, I want to be involved."

This is what I want to be; I don't want to be a weekend dad, and I don't want to be a good-time father. I want the days — the day-in, day-out, you know, role of being a father. I want to be a part of her life; I don't want to just be a weekend ride. From the time my daughter was born, even though me and her mother weren't together, I was there. When she was sick, every other day her mother would stay up with her, and the next day I stay up with her. I wanted those experiences of being a father.

I was raised by my mother, and I know what it is to be a mother. I know what it is to spend time. But my father wasn't there, so I didn't know what it was to be a father. All I could do was to rely on what it was my mother did. She was there, through thick and thin. So that's the example I had. When I had my daughter, I don't have women over. I don't have nobody over. I don't get on the phone until she goes to bed at 8. It takes work. It's just like if we were together. It takes absolute work.

Ron Johnson: Robbie does put in a lot of time with his daughter. But what I think you are also hearing in this group, particularly from those of us that come from households where our fathers were not there, is that as little boys we promised ourselves that if we ever had a child, we would not do to our children what was done to us. That is, to abandon our children. What you're hearing is that we have grown and matured and understand for most of us, that if we had to go back and do this all over again, we would have preferred to have done this in the confines of a marriage. We need that. It's not just for us; it's for our kids.

How does a girl learn how to take care of a man if she doesn't see her mother in a positive relationship with a man who she takes care of? I don't mean take care of him in terms of, you know, work for him and that kind of thing, but I mean how to be a partner. How to be a partner in a relationship.

How will a boy find out how to treat a woman if he does not see his father or some positive, real role model in a relationship with a woman? The best way that is done, traditionally, historically, the way that it's been done is to build family. As a people, that's how we got through with our spiritual base and with our families in this country. That's how we got through. The plight now of our children is so dire and so severe because we've let slip from our hands the grip we had on family.

Men, Women, and No Respect

Akili: Men don't respect women, and women do not respect men. No, there is no respect. It's for the same reasons. Like Ron was saying. Like me. How I get the way I am with women, I can't lie; it's from my father. My father had women. I grew up with my father; I went from father's house to mother's house, back and forth, back and forth, so I had both my parents, never in the same household, but I had them. So when I see him doing the things that he did, and I look at myself now, I'm like, "dude, you just like your father." I always said I never wanted to be like my father. I said that though pertaining to a child like my daughter. But it's the overall, general thing that I do have my father in me.

Keith: We as men who are not married or men who are married, have children or don't have children, just need to set positive examples. Let them know this is how it should be and needs to be. This is what has to be done. Those of us who are married, who are happily married, need to talk up the joys of marriage. You hear so many people say, "Oh man, I would want to be married, but the ball and chain." It's work being married, but it's wonderful being married. We don't talk about the good side of marriage anymore, so now everybody's afraid. I have a wonderful relationship with my wife. We need to talk more about that. When you find that special person, she does become your joy, your peace, and your happiness, and we need to talk about that instead of being cool about it.

Ron Johnson: We've got to teach the boy what it means to be a man. He's got to go inside, 'cause if you look outside, you'll find somebody with the hips that you want, the legs, the breasts, the lips that you want, but you won't know anything about yourself internally. One of the ways to straighten it out is to train both the boy and girl what it means to be a man and woman, to go inside and look at themselves and find out what is it that you need. That's why Keith talked about his wife as his joy, or my wife as my joy, because I knew what I needed, and I was blessed and I got it.

Charles L.: There's a lot of healing that has to take place, a lot of healing. There's a lot of people who are just hurt; lotta guys who are hurt by what they saw their mothers do or what their mothers are still doing, what their fathers did not do or are doing. It's people who are hurt, and that's where the disrespect comes from.

Money, Money, Money

Charles B.: Clearly, we cannot escape the fact that this is an extremely materialistic society. I think everyday people feel the pressures more and more. This is probably the single biggest cause of breakups that I hear about. Usually it starts in with some money issues. There's tension in the home. Responsibilities are not being met. People start opting for the easy way out.

Charles L.: It seems to be economic because a black married couple still makes less than the average single white man. That's the bottom line. Even with two breadwinners in the black house, both of them working, they still don't equal up to one person in the average white American family.

Charles B.: I think it is unfortunate that it is that, but I think what I'm saying is that everybody's responding to increasing pressures around money. In other words, it's a change in the values. In the 1940s, if a family made six thousand dollars, whatever their lifestyle afforded at six thousand dollars, they came together and loved each other with a six-thousand-dollar income. But now if you are chasing the Lexus and the larger home, and the better neighborhood, the private schools, the demands are increasingly putting stresses on families.

Omar's Story

Robbie: Omar's not an active man yet. Could I say something about Omar? — because it's a unique situation. I was Omar's social worker.

Charles L.: Fine job you did.

Robbie: Well, I think you have to talk about the reality of his life. The reality of his life is that his father was on drugs. I hope you don't mind me telling it. His mother was on drugs. Omar spent a great portion of his life in a foster home, which meant no connection with people. You've got to understand that's what Omar's reality was.

In his twelfth-grade year, I tried to keep Omar in the group home to graduate. Omar was like, "I want to go home." His mother got out of jail. He wanted to go home to be with his mother. He wanted to take care of his mother, and he spent time taking care of his mother. He didn't finish school, by the way, but he was taking care of his mother. Even to the point of where he was the parent. It became a struggle that way.

So to say that he's not a father is not fair. He's got a whole lot of more shit to ship off, and I hate to say it that way, than the normal person. He has the kind of scars that he has to take out, look at, and deal with. I think just the fact that he was taking care of his mother and his sisters said a whole lot. He didn't want his sisters going into foster care. So we got to get beyond just looking at snippets, one snapshot or one situation, and look at the man's total life. Omar has come a long way. He's working for independent living. He's got a job now. (He was homeless.) And he took the GED. We said you're not doing anything until you take the GED. He didn't study; he passed it the first time around without studying.

Ron Johnson: We certainly all have stories, but Omar's story is probably one of the most severe in this circle and in Los Angeles County. Unfortunately, his story is not that untypical. I mean, there are eighty-two thousand kids in foster care here in Los Angeles.

But what hurts me is not Omar. It is the guys that we didn't reach who are like Omar. Omar is tremendously gifted and bright and has tremendous potential, and we've all circled around him to help. Not only have we helped Omar, but Omar's presence in our lives has helped us to understand how serious our work is with young people. But what pains me are the young men out there that we haven't touched, the young men that Charles has talked about whose father is in the house but is emotionally and spiritually absent. We work with them every day, and we see the pain of them not having family.

See, Robbie's not the guy that we're talking about. Robbie's the father who is not married but who is there. He's with his daughter almost every day, at least in contact every day and sees her every other day. I'm talking about fathers that haven't seen their children in five or six years, living on the same block. I'm talking about the father of a boy that was in my house for every weekend for six months. His father didn't even know he was there. His father made him sleep in the living room on a mattress on the floor while he brought ladies in the house to sleep in the bed. See, I don't respect that. That's not a man and that's not a father. I'm talking about the father who is the one that understands that when the rubber hits the road, don't even take a number, you're last. Your children, your wife, are first; you're last. They are first with the food, the resources, they are first with your time, and they are first in your heart. That kind of thing. Men have to learn. It's God, my family, and then my work. Most men think, God, my work, and my family, and sometimes God even ain't on the list, just my work, my money, my other women, and that kind of thing. We have to teach them.

The Men of the Village

Charles L.: The future is that it is going to change. You have a lot of young couples now who were getting married better. It's on the rise. You have a lot of people who are setting examples. I try and to be more vocal when I see people who aren't doing the right thing. I try and speak on it. I tell people that if your girl's pregnant, go to appointments, 'cause I did the same thing. Make sure you in the labor room, 'cause I was there. It's through that constant pushing that I think we are going to reach them.

Keith: The future is that the older men of the community must become more vocal. Whether you are his biological father or not, you have to begin to tell young men in the community the same thing that was told to me. If you are going to get married, there are three things that my father told me: Love your wife, pay your bills, and take care of your children. That was the advice that my father gave to me.

Now, he summed it all up in a nutshell, but the bottom line is, we have to counter the negative information that our kids are receiving.

We have to be willing to talk and say things even if we think they are not listening, because the bottom line is they are listening.

We need to become more vocal. The men that's watching this TV that's sitting in his living room and has a wonderful family, you need to begin to talk to that boy next door and tell him exactly what you did to make it. That's what it is going to take. It's going to take the men of the village to begin to teach the boys in the village how to be the next generation of men. If we don't teach them, no one's going to teach them, and it's going to repeat.

Keith: I want to stress the point that it has got to be the men, because right now we have rappers who are boys and teenagers, we have our sports figures who are boys and teenagers, dictating how a man looks and how a man acts. We need the men in academia, our men in the community, to step up and say "this is what a man does." Because I can tell you, most of the superstars haven't even worked out their issues, dealt with their scars in terms of being a man yet. We need to sit down and take back control of our community.

Does society need to begin to honor men? Society needs to begin to lift up men. Who gets all the pork now? TV shows are not about men handling their responsibilities. TV shows are about men not handling their responsibilities. We need to value that working father. We don't do that anymore. They need to become the new role models. They need to become the new centerpiece, they need to be the ones doing the Pepsi commercials and the 7-UP commercials and the Coke commercials — not these fly-by-night guys that are not handling their responsibilities. We need to lift up men who are just working as garbagemen, but they are taking care of their family. Men who are cutting grass, but taking care of their family.

U.S. Senator Joseph Lieberman

Joseph Lieberman is a United States Senator (D–Conn) and is a co-sponsor of the Responsible Fatherhood Act of 2001. He says that fatherlessness is a great crisis of our time and that men in America have abdicated their responsibilities.

A Great Crisis of Our Time

Fatherlessness is one of the great social crises of our time, not just as a matter of anecdote or philosophy but as a matter of evidence. Children who come out of homes without a father have a much higher probability of ending up in poverty, in trouble with the law, and giving birth to children themselves while they're unmarried teenagers. Unfortunately, fatherlessness produces greater difficulty for children in becoming self-sufficient, productive citizens.

How did we get to this stage of fatherlessness? It is a very perplexing and puzzling question and it's affected obviously by many factors. Some of it had to do with the sexual revolution that went through the country in the '60s, '70s, and '80s. Some of it was a kind of "anything goes" mentality. Some of it had to do with a popular culture which increasingly celebrated sexual involvement at any age without ever really portraying the consequences of various forms of sexual involvement. Some of it had to do with the decline of respect for authority generally in the country.

Of course, one of the ways in which children become fatherless is that either marriages don't happen in the first place — the children are born to a mother outside of marriage without a father in the house — or the marriage breaks up. The rate of divorce has increased enormously. We have the lowest marriage rate today that we've ever had in our history. Of the marriages that are actually occurring, half of them are still ending in divorce. So you end up with a situation where on an average day in America four out of every ten children are living in a home without a father. That hurts.

The fact that 40 percent of the children in America are going to sleep on any night without a father in the house says powerfully that men in America today have abdicated their responsibilities. They are doing something that we used to think was so unnatural that it would happen only in the most aberrant cases, which is a father leaving his children. They are not only not taking care of them, but in a lot of cases not even being in touch with them.

Government: Helped or Hurt?

My own sense of this is that there are ways in which government policy has strengthened this very corrosive trend in our society toward families without fathers, but it really has not created it.

Now, what are the ways in which government policy has encouraged fatherlessness? Well, the welfare system certainly seemed to do it. For poor families there was a pretty clear message, certainly before welfare reform, that you'd get less money if the father stayed in the house. So there was an economic incentive provided for the father to move out of the house.

There are other areas in which government has committed not so much a sin of commission, but a sin of omission. One of those is in child-support collection. Fathers leave their homes almost always after divorce or a cohabitation separation. The mother is in worse economic condition and therefore the children are in worse economic condition. For a long time, the government — federal and state — did a very bad job of collecting child support. When it did collect it, it didn't pass it through, and certainly not in a sufficient sum, to the mother and the children. Now we've begun to change that, changed it to provide for tougher child-support enforcement, and more of the money being collected goes to the family and goes to the children. There seems to be evidence that a father is more likely to pay child support when he knows that the money goes to his children. When he knows it goes to his children, he may even be more involved in the life of the children.

But ultimately I think the causes of father absence have come from within the culture, within the communities, within individual families. It's been a remarkable and revolutionary and very rapid change. It's not so long ago that to live without a father, except in the case of death of the father, was pretty rare in this country. To live together with somebody who wasn't your spouse, to have a child out of wedlock, was very rare. When I grew up — and I don't consider myself antiquated yet — there was an expression we don't hear anymore: They got married. Why did they get married? "They had to." Of course, why did they have to? Because the woman became pregnant. Today, of course, it's very rare that anybody has to get married. In fact, there's no sense of responsibility; either the mother has the baby out of wedlock and the child grows up fatherless, or she gets an abortion.

I'm afraid that the mass-entertainment media have been a contributing factor to the painful increase in the number of kids growing up in America without fathers in the home. Now, why do I say that? I want to underline that the media have contributed to the problem, they haven't caused it. It's caused by a lot of other social and cultural phenomena. But we've gone a long way from the media that I saw when I was growing up — *Ozzie and Harriet, I Love Lucy,* then into *Father Knows Best,* and all the rest. They were stories of parental responsibility and, generally, a father and a mother in a home together. They were role models. I know one can satirize them and say they were unreal. In fact, they did reflect the general condition of families in America in the '40s, '50s, and at least at the beginning of the '60s. Mom and dad and kids growing up. I grew up that way. I consider myself blessed, fortunate, to have grown up that way. You go from *Ozzie and Harriet* to *Friends,* or any number of the other popular shows today, which tend to be not about family units but about basically unconnected people living together. We've gone from *The Cosby Show,* which was another great model of an intact family, to people living together not married, involved mostly in sexual behavior, again without any portrayal of the consequences of the sexual behavior.

When you set up a role model which not only does not encourage the standard, traditional, two-parent family, but it encourages the kind of early premarital sexual activity that results in a million babies being born every year to teenagers out of wedlock . . . . Evidence shows the traditional two-parent family is still the best way to raise children. Therefore, I'd say that the media is very popular and directly connected to kids in ways that the culture didn't use to be. It is a major contributing factor to this problem of father absence.

Fatherlessness in Our Poorest Areas

This problem of fatherlessness in the poorest areas of our country is probably the most difficult problem we have to deal with and it's one that has awful results for the people involved. Part of what we have to begin to do with the children who are there now is to give them mentors, to give them big brothers, and to have the schools effectively be in loco parentis. They need to be in the position of fathers to try to give the children the confidence, sense of self-worth, to try to do better at school and then reward them when they do.

Beyond that, we have to really begin to work at the next generation with a whole host of programs that should cover the spectrum. Programs that talk early on about the importance of abstinence and not letting yourself be taken advantage of or sexually abused, especially if you're a young woman. For young men, try to create role models that will talk quite directly about sexual behavior, quite directly about the immorality and also the self-damage done when you father a child and walk away.

None of this is going be easy. You have to also be practical. It gets into ideology and controversy. You have to be very aggressive after you preach abstinence with the provision of birth-control information and materials. You just have to do whatever you can to stop the cycle of children being born to children in poverty. It's a disaster for the mothers, for the children, and, of course, for society.

What Exactly Is the Responsible Fatherhood Act?

The Responsible Fatherhood Act is, first, a way for Congress to recognize that the absence of a father in twenty-five million American families is consequential. It's a real problem. It's a real problem because it affects and contributes to some of the other problems that we do things about legislatively all the time — poor educational achievement, criminal violations, anti-social behavior of every imaginable kind, including drug abuse. So this is a way, first, to say there's not an enormous amount that Congress can do to encourage fathers to stay with their children, except to remove the disincentives as we did in welfare reform and child-support enforcement. But we recognize in this proposal that fatherlessness is a problem in America. It's a crisis.

Secondly, we begin to provide some money to do a couple of things. In the modern age, what do you do when you have a problem? You create a public-service advertising campaign to send the message that something bad is happening. I say it lightly, but it can have an effect. What people see on television affects their behavior. So we are creating a fund to leverage broadcast industry and nonprofit interest in a series of advertisements similar to ones that the National Fatherhood Initiative has already carried out to urge fathers to stay with their kids, to do what we used to think was natural. How could a father walk away from his children? They're doing it in the millions today.

In addition, there's a kind of counterrevolution going on now, a pro-father counterrevolution going on started by religious groups, by community groups around the country. Our legislation would provide a pot of money for grants to these local initiatives to encourage fatherhood, to encourage fathers to be with their children. It would also encourage young people, as they begin to think about becoming fathers, to do so seriously and with a sense of responsibility; in other words, to stay married and stay with their children.

How Do You Produce Good Citizens?

Part of turning this around is to use whatever methods we can to restore some sense of responsibility to men who are fathering children and walking away from them. It is probably the most outrageously immoral and irresponsible and destructive act that any class of people can perform in our society today, because of the extraordinary ramifications of it.

Some of this can be done by religion. Some of it can be done by culture, setting up better standards for responsible fatherhood. Some of this can be done by the government, sending the right messages, giving the right incentives, giving the correct punishments. Some of these, I suppose, can be done in a school as children grow up, talking to them about character issues like responsible fatherhood.

What role the state should have in its relationship with the family and children is a very complicated question. All societies struggle with it, particularly a society like ours which is a free society. We don't want government involved in every aspect of life, certainly not a private life. Marriage is private, and yet marriage has profound societal implications, which is why we decided a long time ago to license marriage and to essentially draw some ground rules. We changed some of that in the last generation by the way in which we allowed people easily to break the license, to break the contract of marriage, to get divorced.

Let me step back and say the reason the state has an interest in marriage, though limited, is because we have reached a judgment which is in part based on morality but also, I think now (sadly because of the experience we've had with broken families), about the best way for a society to raise its children. One of the great responsibilities of a society is how do you produce the next generation that will continue and be good citizens, and be self-sufficient? The best way to do that is in a two-parent, mother-father family. So we want to do whatever we can to encourage that. We can't mandate it. We shouldn't mandate it. That's a choice that people will make.

Just briefly to go back to something I said before: the state is interested in promoting marriage, while of course respecting people's privacy, because broken marriages have a higher probability of children growing up without fathers in the home, have a higher probability of ending up in trouble, and that's not good for the rest of us in society. Right now, for instance, different states are experimenting with waiting periods before marriage or courses before marriage to instruct people about marriage. Louisiana has the Covenant of Marriage, where couples take on a higher set of contractual obligations to one another than in a standard no-fault marriage. There are laws making it harder in some places to get divorced, because divorce has consequences on the children.

We're feeling our way, but we're at a point now where we've seen enough families break up, enough children be raised either out of wedlock or in families without fathers, that we know that that's not good for the kids and not good for the country. We're trying, while respecting privacy, to use the law to encourage more families to stay together.

This is one of those cases where I fear that the culture is more powerful and influential than either the traditional sources of values like religion, which tends to uphold the strong family, or government, which in different ways tries to uphold it. I have the feeling that the writer and producer of the next family sitcom or serious show about a family will probably have as much or more effect on children's attitudes toward parenthood and fatherhood as a senator or as their minister.

But accepting that, and also accepting the inherent limited role of government in something as private as relations between people, we've got to make sure that we in government are not doing anything to encourage father absence. That we're doing everything we can do to encourage families to stay together and particularly to encourage fathers to be responsible to their children.

Then we need to support, encourage, and enable this great uprising of religious groups, community groups, and neighborhood groups that are trying to support strong, sound families and responsible fatherhood. We need to give them money and give them the wherewithal to do what used to seem natural, which was to be a good father and to teach people how to be good fathers.

It's Not a Liberal or a Conservative Issue

In some ways you have to give credit to what is either called the "religious right" or, whatever, social conservatives. They first began to focus on this problem of broken families and teenage mothers giving birth to children out of wedlock. But this is not a liberal or conservative issue. This is a people issue. This is an American issue. Every category of public official and social thinker has to be and generally is deeply concerned about father absence in families in America.

Probably ten years ago, I sat with a child psychiatrist who was very active in this field, and I said to him, "If you could change one thing in America, what would it be?" This was somebody who had broad concerns about social pathology and culture in our country. He didn't hesitate a moment. He said, "I would try to deal with the problem of teenage pregnancy, of babies being born to teenage girls out of wedlock." That remains the challenge. That still happens about a million times a year.

Wade Horn

Wade Horn is the founder of the National Fatherhood Initiative.
He discusses the effects on children of absent fathers, and says
that divorce is worse for a child than the death of a parent.

What's the Big Deal about Dads?

We know that when kids grow up without a dad involved, a committed and responsible father in their lives, they're at greater risk for a whole host of negative outcomes. We know they are more likely to fail at school, to have emotional behavioral problems, to drop out of school, and to get involved in drugs and alcohol abuse. If they are boys, they're more likely to engage in criminal activity as juveniles. If they are girls, they're more likely to engage in early and promiscuous sexual activity. For both boys and girls, as adolescents they're more likely to commit suicide. It seems that in almost any measure you can imagine, kids who grow up without a positive, actively involved father in their lives are at greater risk of poor outcomes.

Moms and dads do things differently. We think that moms and dads ought to be interchangeable. We know, for example, that fathers are much more likely to be physical with their kids. They're more likely to get on the floor and wrestle with them. Moms are more likely to verbally stimulate their kids, to spend more time talking with them. We also know that fathers are more likely to encourage risk-taking and moms are more likely to encourage caution. Just go to any playground in America and watch the way that moms and dads interact with their kids on the jungle bar. What you'll see is a dad who will say, "Keep going. Keep going. You're almost at the top." You'll see a mom saying, "Hey, be careful. Be careful."

Now, it's not that one is doing it right and the other one's doing it wrong. Kids need both. They need somebody to wrestle with them on the floor, because that helps teach self-control. They also need a mom who stimulates them with language, because that helps them with language development. We don't want a nation of foolish risk-takers. We want a nation of cautious risk-takers. So, lucky is the child who has both a mom and a dad, because of the complementary attributes that they bring to the parenting equation.

The news is not good when large numbers of children are growing up disconnected from their fathers. It's not that every child who grows up in a fatherless household is going to have these kinds of difficulties. But it is true that there's an increased risk of these negative outcomes when kids grow up without fathers.

When you only have a few fatherless children in the community, they have lots of other role models to understand what fatherhood is all about and what good manhood is all about. They also have good men around to teach them the kinds of skills that keep them out of trouble. The problem in today's world is that it's not just that a few kids are growing up fatherless. We have always had some kids who were fatherless. The problem today is that there are so many children in so many communities growing up without fathers. In some communities there are very, very few good role models of what a good father is and does. That's the problem today. That's why today's problem of fatherlessness is so much different than what we've seen before. The scope is so much greater than it has been in the past.

When the Idea of Dad Dies

For a number of years, I was the director of outpatient psychological services in an inner-city children's hospital. Half of my clientele were in the inner city and half of my clientele were in the much more affluent suburbs. What I found was a lot of kids who are very rageful and depressed. And they were rageful and depressed about the same reason. They're rageful and depressed because they had no connection with their fathers. For kids in the inner city, it might have been because they were born out of wedlock and the father abandoned the family. For children in the more affluent suburbs, it might have been because of divorce or workaholism on the part of the father. But the effect on the child seemed to be the same. These children had a genuine hunger for a father. It was having a profound impact on them.

There is one category of absent father that doesn't seem to have those negative impacts. That's a dead father. If you think about it, we can hardly imagine a worse situation for a child than to have the parent die. And yet, what we find is that children whose fathers died do better than kids who fathers are not there because of abandonment or divorce or even workaholism. The reason is because when most fathers die, the moms keep the memory of the father alive in the home. Their pictures stay up on the wall. The memory of the father is often invoked in positive ways like, "If your dad were here today, he'd be so proud of you." Or, the mom might even invoke the father as a punishment, saying, "If your dad were here today, he'd be so disappointed."

The issue is that when a father dies, the idea of the father is not dead. The father idea in that household is still very rich. The problem with divorce and abandonment is that the idea of the father has died because the pictures are off the wall. The mom speaks very disparagingly, far too often, of the father. If the kid brings up the father's name, the mom might say, "Oh, don't bring up his name. He's a bum. We're better off without him. Don't bring him up anymore." It seems that children can survive the physical death of the father better than they can survive the death of the idea of the father.

Divorce and Dads

Unfortunately, when men experience divorce, as fathers they tend to become disconnected both psychologically and financially from their children. Forty percent of all children who don't live with their fathers have not seen their fathers for even one second in over a year. Half of children who don't live with their fathers have never — not once in their life — stepped foot in their father's home.

Now, that doesn't mean that there aren't some divorced and unwed fathers who are terrific dads; but it is harder. We need to be honest about that. It is a more difficult experience to be a father if you do not live with your children. One of the reasons for that is because you are less accessible to your children. If you come around and you see your child once every other weekend, that's nice. You know that certainly is helpful.

The fact of the matter is that kids are not light switches that can be turned on when we want, when it's on our schedule to be with them. What children really need are parents who are accessible to them so that when they need us, we are there for them. That's the problem with not living with your children. It's just less possible for you to have that kind of accessibility. So when you're not with your kids, you're less accessible to them.

Fathers pay a price for this. We know, for example, that divorced fathers are much more likely to be depressed. They're more likely to have alcohol or drug problems. They're more likely to have difficulty on the job. It seems that fatherhood is good for children, but fatherhood is also good for men.

Fatherhood and Marriage

The National Fatherhood Initiative was founded in 1994 with a very clear mission: to improve the well-being of children by increasing the number of kids growing up with involved, committed, and responsible fathers in their lives. You see, fatherlessness is not a small problem. It's a big problem. Four out of ten kids today will go to sleep in a home without their father present — *four out of ten.* That's twenty-five million children. Big problems demand big solutions. We think the only way we're going to successfully turn this trend around is by helping to stimulate a social movement, a society-wide movement on behalf of the institution of fatherhood, not just for the benefit of fathers but for the benefit, primarily, of children.

Well, we've made a lot of progress since 1994. Before that, if you asked a lot of people, "Gee, do fathers matter?" their answer would have been, "Well, not necessarily." Today, increasingly, we understand the consequences of fatherlessness, particularly the cost to children. That's a very important advance.

We've made advances in terms of attitudes. We know from a recent Gallup Poll, for example, that 80 percent of Americans now say the absence of the father from the home is the single most important social problem facing America today — 80 percent. The bad news is four out of ten kids are still going to sleep in homes without their fathers. The even worse news is that Americans don't seem to accept the idea that somehow marriage is important to the institution of fatherhood. That seems to be the next big challenge for the fatherhood movement. Certainly there are a lot of married fathers who aren't so good, but we need to convince the American public that married fatherhood, as an ideal, is something we ought to be pursuing.

Historically, fatherhood and marriage were in fact tied together. But, even more than that, fatherhood and children were tied together in very intimate ways. Many people are surprised to hear that if you go back two hundred years, most of the parenting advice was actually directed toward fathers, not toward mothers. Fathers were the ones who were seen, after the child was weaned, as being primarily responsible for whether that child grew up to be a good person or a not so good person.

What changed all of that was industrialization. For the first time in human history, large numbers of men were going away from the home to work in a distant factory, often for eight to ten hours a day, often for six days a week. By default, child rearing had to fall to the one person who remained in the home, the mom. So the mother became the person primarily responsible for rearing the children.

This was very different from most of human history. As we proceed into the nineteenth century and particularly the latter part of the twentieth century, with the advent of birth control, we see a disconnect between sex and marriage. We also see increasing numbers of women entering the paid labor force, which meant that they were less dependent upon marriage. All of these social forces have combined to reduce fatherhood to a thin shell of what it once was.

Peanut Butter and Jelly and the Bedtime Story

I think that marriage and fatherhood go together like peanut butter and jelly. Marriage and fatherhood are important for us to understand. They are intertwined. That doesn't mean divorced fathers or unwed fathers can't be terrific dads. Of course they can. But we have to be honest: It's harder. It's more difficult precisely because that father cannot be as accessible to his children as the father who comes home every day and eats dinner with his kids or reads a bedtime story.

We need to be supportive and encourage divorced fathers and unwed fathers. But there are consequences for children dependent upon the different category of father — a married father, divorced father, or an unwed father. So, yes, be supportive of those other categories, but let's be clear, the ideal is married fatherhood.

There are some who are very queasy when the word *marriage* is brought up. So much so that some people refer to it as the "M" word, the word that shouldn't be spoken in polite company. I think that for some the concern comes from a concern about domestic violence. Certainly domestic violence is a terrible thing and we should have no tolerance for it. But the myth that has arisen around domestic violence is that the most dangerous person for a woman is her husband. It's not so. Research is very clear that the greatest risk of domestic violence occurs when a man is cohabiting with a woman, and particularly when that man is not the biological father of that woman's children.

What we need to do is to dispel some of the myths about marriage that it's a bad deal for women. It's not a bad deal for women. Both men and women are happier if they're married than if they're not married. Both men and women are wealthier if they're married than if they're not married. And they enjoy better sex. Men are more likely to advance in terms of the workplace and so are women. It seems that marriage is good for women as well as men, but some people find it difficult to promote the idea of marriage because of the domestic violence issue.

Sadie

Sadie explains why she wants Isaiah's father to be part of his life.

Does Isaiah Need a Father?

Yes, Isaiah needs a father. That's why I forgave my ex-boyfriend. That's why he is in Isaiah's life. I could have moved. When I was pregnant, I could have gone back to California. I didn't because I didn't want to take Isaiah from his father. That's the reason why I fight with him, why I fought with him while I was pregnant. It was like, "Look! This is your baby here."

In the beginning, financially, he was giving me basically nothing for five, six months. Until finally he said, "Okay, well, I guess this is my kid." Whatever. So, no, I don't need a man. I could take care of myself, and I will and I do. Isaiah's father helps me out financially, and if he didn't I might struggle a little more, but I would find a way to make it work.

I think Isaiah needs a father in order for him to be secure as a person. He has to know where he came from. I can't keep him away from his father. That would be selfish on my part. I want him to know his father. I want him to know that side of his family, especially since he's biracial. His father is black. I can't give him that culture. I'm white. So I want him to have that part of himself. I want him to know himself. He's part of his father. He's his son.

He deserves to know his father and he deserves to have a father in his life. I could go on for two hours about the value of fatherhood, I guess. But I think the most important thing is a father should be a role model, and a father should be there for his son or his daughter. You know, to talk to him, to listen to him, chuck the football around, or whatever. Give him things I can't.

Fatherhood vs. Motherhood

I think fatherhood is a little bit more fun. For Isaiah's father it is, anyway. He gets nothing but fun times with Isaiah. Instead, I carry a twenty-two-pound baby on my back three miles a day. He gets to come and pick him up in his girlfriend's van. He gets to take Isaiah to breakfast while I'm eating eggs and toast, here. Which is okay; but I just don't have it as good as he does. Which, you know, it goes either way. I mean, he loses time with the baby. I have time with the baby, or did before I got this stupid work situation. I don't know . . . I think fatherhood is different in that mothers work harder. Mothers' lives change more — or, at least, mine did, especially because I'm a single mother.

William J. Doherty

William J. Doherty says the most important thing that can be done to promote the presence of fathers in their children's lives is to promote high-quality marriages.

Good Fatherhood Depends on a
Good Relationship with the Mother

I got into fatherhood research before really getting into the marriage area. What I saw as I began to look at the research on father involvement with children and father absence in the lives of children is that we cannot separate a father absence and father presence from marriage.

The research is very clear. As a society or a culture, if a woman has a child, she's to be obsessed with that kid until that kid leaves home and then psychologically forever. Whatever happens to her relationship with the father, this is her kid.

We have culturally defined fatherhood as a triangle, as a three-way relationship, as more dependent on what happens to the relationship between the mother and the father. The clearest example would be a nonmarried woman and man having a relationship. She gets pregnant, has a child, and then they break up. If they break up, there is a high likelihood over time that the father will be less and less involved in that child's life — particularly if her mother doesn't like him and if the mother gets into a new relationship. But she's to be the mother forever.

What I'm really saying is that the father's relationship with his child tends to be very dependent on his relationship with the mother. If that's going well and, say, the mother and the father are not married, then he's probably going to be involved with this child's life. If they break up, he tends to not be that involved and not be expected to be that much involved.

What I really came to see is that the single most important thing we can do to promote presence of fathers in their kids lives and high-quality involvement while they are in their children's lives is to promote high-quality marriages. Inside a marriage, children have the best fathering that probably any generation in the history of the world has ever had. Fathers are more nurturing, they're more involved, they're more hands on, they're less distant and patriarchal — inside a marriage. Not that we can't do a whole lot better, but it's the best fathering kids have ever gotten in the history of the world. Outside of marriage it's a whole other story. You have father absence. You have less involvement. You have fights between the parents. And those kids get lousy fathering in general. What that says to me is that one of the things that we need to do to promote active, involved, and responsible fathers is to promote high-quality marriages.

Stacy

*Stacy reflects on the positive qualities her father brought to
her upbringing.*

What about Children?

If I was very, very successful financially, I could and would have kids
outside of marriage. I can go and call a good male friend of mine to do
it. I can go to a sperm bank. I told myself that I would adopt. Do I want
to go through the process of pregnancy? Yes, I do. I don't want to go
through it alone, though. I don't think it's worth it to go through it
alone just for the experience of saying I carried a child for nine months
and now I'm a parent. I've parented a lot of kids. I've mothered a lot of
kids that aren't mine.

What about Fathers?

I think two parents are necessary, but I don't think that one parent is
not a good role model. Good role models come from extended family,
uncles, brothers, and grandparents. Grandparents in the black community have really become parents all over again to another generation.
Maybe other extended places like community centers and church fathers and so forth. A lot of different social and civic organizations are
starting to become that extended or surrogate father. I think that's a
good thing. There's a lot of work that needs to be done. It's been a long
time coming, and I hope they can really make some serious differences.

    What did my father bring to me? He brought me trust and respect.
He brought me honesty. He brought me love and compassion and sup-

port. I think that's what a good parent brings to their child. The fact that it's from a male, a father — my father had all girls, too. He raised us not to consider the fact that we were girls as far as, you can play football and you can run track. He said, "I'm not going to raise any little sissy girls." I think that's very important.

I don't necessarily want my father's equal. My father is still my parent. I don't want my mate to be my parent, but do I want my mate to give me the things that my father did? Yeah. I think my mate is out there. It's just a matter of meeting him.

Ronald Mincy

Ronald Mincy is the Maurice V. Russell Professor of Social Policy and Social Work Practice at the Columbia University School of Social Work. He sees the decline in male wages as a key factor affecting men's capacity to provide for their families.

The Underlying Dynamics Have Changed

To understand the government's role in the problem of father absence we have to understand why our welfare and child-support systems were created in the first place. We reformed our child support and welfare systems in the early 1970s because, at the time, most child poverty was caused by the divorce or separation of a middle-income couple. When a divorce occurred, the guy left and took his money with him. So we created a welfare system designed to help single women recover from a divorce or separation, and we created a child-support enforcement system to make sure that the guys continued to pay for their children. That was a smart plan, a strategic plan, in the '70s, but the whole demography of child poverty has changed.

Today about two-thirds of all children who enter our welfare and child-support system come from an unmarried birth. Roughly 23 percent of the fathers who should be paying child support are poor themselves. It is not clear that all the relationships between the moms and dads are over. It is not clear that the only issue is money. There is still a child who has been born out of wedlock. In some instances there is no hope of recovering a relationship between the mother and the father, but in many instances there is.

So the underlying dynamic of child poverty has changed. The question is, has government policy caught up with the changes? The couple having the child is usually a lot younger. They don't have the work experience or the secure relationships that used to exist. But many of these couples are together. Our data indicates that about 24 percent of all children who are poor are born into what I call "fragile families." These are young, low-income mothers and fathers who are either living together or the father is visiting the child at least once a week. We have another 38 percent of poor children who are born to married-couple families.

Again, the underlying dynamic of child poverty has changed. The question is, when will our government policies catch up with the change? They need to not only ensure that fathers have the money to support their children, but also to secure relationships between mothers and fathers so that both of them can weigh in there for their children.

Realities of Child Support

There are a lot of ways in which men can contribute to their children's well-being: They can read to them. They can help supervise their activities. They can help mom manage the challenges that she experiences with a young child, and especially with adolescent children. But, in the case of poor men, all of that has to be mediated by child support. I don't care what you try to do to engage a low-income man in the life of his child; if he's not living with the mother of his child, he has to pay child support. And, if he doesn't have a job, he can't pay child support.

Often, low-income men who want to be involved in the lives of their children but are behind in their child-support payments have to look over their shoulders. They are looking to see whether the child-support agency is after them. Often they don't want to surface to visit their children and be in a relationship with their children because they are afraid of what's going to happen with child support.

My own strategy is about helping men establish paternity for their children as close to the birth of their child as we possibly can; help them negotiate child-support orders that are manageable in the first place, so the likelihood that they get behind does not occur. If we can work with the child-support agency so it doesn't feel that it has to chase these guys around, then we can work to develop parenting skills and work with the fathers' hearts.

I'm Haunted Every Day

Let's get to the real set of issues. Seventy percent of all African-American children are born out of wedlock. That data haunts me every day. But 30 percent of all children in the United States are born out of wedlock. For these children, the discussion of marriage is off the table. They are born already. The question under these circumstances is, how will we give these children the benefit of both of their parents?

I think the fatherhood movement increasingly has begun to recognize the difference between prevention and intervention. For young people who have not had their children, it is appropriate for us to talk to them about waiting to have children, waiting until you can afford them. But for 70 percent of African-American children and for 30 percent of all children, those conversations are off the table. Now that the children are here, the question is, "how are we going to help those parents give those children what they need, which is the support of both parents?" Questions of helping parents negotiate their relationship, after the fact, are germane. But questions about child support, unfortunately, are paramount because of the absence of a marriage.

I think the question of marriageability is not only important for black men, but it's important for most men of marrying age. Since the early 1970s, the wages of most men have declined. The only men to experience double-digit increases in their wages are men who have gone to graduate school. So, most men have experienced declines in wages; that has a lot to do with delays in marriage, increases in divorce rates, and the like.

Since black men's wages have declined the most, and since black men's employment prospects have worsened the most, the marriageability issue is most severe among African-American men. Marriageability is important. It increases the likelihood that black men work in the first place, and increases the likelihood that their wages will increase once they work. African-American women can be poor all by themselves. Until we enable most men to sustain their families, the whole question of their marriage prospects is sheer foolishness.

Marriage is important because we know that children raised in married households that never divorce do better than children in any other household arrangement except widows. But we have a long way until we can get there for most young people in the United States.

Learning from the Black Community

I think the white community, unfortunately, has a lot to learn from the black community about this whole question of family formation and family stability. If you continue to pay no attention to the needs of men, you will unfortunately inherit a situation that the African-American community has now. Many of our men are disconnected from their families and disconnected from their children. Their gender relationships are experiencing serious stress. Black women and black men have a very difficult time maintaining relationships with one another.

I think there have been a variety of reasons for this over time. We have not focused on the notion that many men have needs. They have emotional needs that are neglected when they're children, and they surface when they're adults. Unfortunately, men are perpetrators of a whole lot of bad things that happen to women. They're perpetrators of domestic violence and child violence, and because they're always on the perpetrating end, we end up pursuing punitive strategies and never get under the *why*. Why are they doing what they're doing? Are there ways of helping them?

I think the legacy of slavery has a lot to do with it. The relationships between black men and black women began to undergo lots of stress during slavery. After all, men could not protect women from sexual assault during slavery. The meaning and relevance of marriage was ridiculous under slavery. The basic conditions of marriage were undermined during slavery.

I think the migration patterns of African Americans after slavery further undermined the nature of their relationships. Men and women had to move from the South to the North in order to maintain a living. Employment discrimination in the North, especially among men, undermined their positions as fathers and husbands. They couldn't maintain a living. They couldn't maintain a household. It complicated their gender relationships.

I think that if white Americans continue to not pay attention to the nature of gender relationships among young people and the decline in the earnings of young white men today, their family situations will deteriorate. They're already deteriorating, and I think they will continue to do so.

Unfortunately, people talk about the fatherhood problem as if it's something that's germane to the black community but not germane to the white community. I think that's simply ridiculous. If you look in our society today, grandparents and especially white grandparents are inheriting their grandchildren. They don't know how to deal with it.

We, unfortunately, in the black community do know how to deal with it. It's, "Honey, I'm going to help you raise this child, and we don't have to deal with that knucklehead." I think that was the wrong answer then; it is the wrong answer now. We as a society just need to revisit the whole question of how do we reengage men in the lives of their children.

Patrick Murphy

Patrick Murphy's work with the juvenile court system has given him a valuable perspective on the importance of fathers. He says that in all the years he represented delinquent kids, he only represented one that had a father involved with him.

Fathers: Very, Very Important

My mother got married at sixteen. She had her first child at nineteen. But it wasn't unusual back in 1930 for a kid to drop out of high school and get married. But my father married her and lived with her until he died. It was a different time. My Dad never went beyond seventh grade, for instance. He lived in an orphanage and went to work in seventh grade. He could go to work in the stockyards as he did, and then he drove a streetcar. Those were jobs where he could raise eight kids. You can't do that anymore.

In the first place, jobs which would let you support a family are not there for high-school dropouts. So getting married young and making it financially doesn't make it anymore. The simple fact is if you delay having a child at fifteen or sixteen, then maybe you'll delay it at seventeen or eighteen, and suddenly you'll be nineteen or twenty or twenty-one or twenty-two and maybe the man will be there.

When people say the man is unimportant, these people are living in a different world. They're smoking too much smelly stuff. For adolescent boys, I'm telling you, it is so very, very important. I'm not a statistician, but I can tell you that from hanging around juvenile courts since 1968. In all the years I represented delinquent kids, I represented *one* that had a father involved with him. Over 90 percent have no involved dad. If there's a father involved, chances are they don't get involved in delinquent behavior. That is a given.

There is something — whatever it is, whether it's magical or whatever — a teenage boy suddenly looks for a male figure. When the fathers walk out on their kids, the pressure comes down to the moms, and those are the people we see in court. But it's the fathers who are the real villains here.

Forget the money. I would get the father involved not for the nickels and dimes, but it's so very, very important for those kids to know that there's a man involved in their life. I can't tell you any other way than just being involved for thirty-two years and seeing it. It's just important; I just can't emphasize that enough.

U.S. Senator Sam Brownback

Sam Brownback is a United States Senator (R–Kans.). He is a supporter of family and fatherhood legislation and says that if we have strong families our societal problems are dramatically reduced.

Core of a Strong Country

Why do we want the Senate to focus attention on the state of marriage today? We need to have strong family values. We need to have moral and cohesive family units. What's at the center of the family? We normally thought it's a two-parent married couple — that's the center around which you build a strong family. And yet, as you look at the numbers in the United States, the institution of marriage, around which you build family, has been in substantial decline over the past thirty years. So I think you've got to start looking at the issue of marriage and the decline in the significance of the institution of marriage in a number of people's minds. If you have strong families, our governmental problems fall in half. If you have weak families or dysfunctional families or children raising themselves, our problems significantly increase. It's at the very core of a strong country.

I'm talking about divorce, single parenting, and children born outside marriage, but mostly I'm talking about attitudes — cultural attitudes toward marriage and toward that institution. It used to be people generally just went with the notion that I'll become an adult, get married for life, have a couple of children, and that's the order of things. It's a way we can build a strong family. As policy-maker, you look at it, and it's a way you can build a strong, vibrant nation of character.

What's increasingly happening is a decline in the value of people's attitudes toward the institution of marriage. Instead of it being focused on "we're going to raise strong children, and this is a lifelong unit," it's been more, "I want to get married, but I'm not as sure it's going to last for a lifetime." It is about children, but it's also about my personal happiness. Those are competing issues at times. If I'm not sure which one I would put more value on, then at the end of the day the children suffer.

The children are the ones that are being nurtured and raised by this strong unit. If that unit falls apart, the children will frequently look around and say, "Do I side with Dad, do I side with Mom? Am I to blame?" Increasingly, the children have to shoulder the parents instead of the parents shouldering the children. There's a personal stress on the child.

We've had enormous and increasing problems for children in America. We now have survey numbers that show half of the teenagers in America have either contemplated suicide or know somebody who has contemplated or attempted or completed suicide. Suicide is one of the top three causes of teenage death in America. I meet with a lot of teens and I say, "Why?" You've got chances galore. You've got great educational opportunities ahead of you. And yet, you go into the schools and there's this great feeling of hopelessness, helplessness. They know exactly what you're talking about when you ask, "Why are people thinking about suicide?" It's a very real issue to them. Frequently, they'll cite problems at home, problems in the family, and they feel somehow responsible for the problems.

Fatherlessness: What Does It Mean to Kids?

I can't answer that from a professional standpoint. I know what some young men, teenage boys in a fatherless situation, have said to me, and it's just that there's this hole for them. They want to know how to be a man from their dad, and it's not being filled.

They get it from somewhere else. They get another idea. They watch something on television. But they know that it's more than fathering children. It's about character. It's about heroism. It's about chivalry, in a sense. It's about honor. It's about equality and treating people of the other sex with equality. It's about justice. It's about character.

I think more is taken up by what is seen than what is taught. The term that some people use is they get more from what is caught than what is taught from their parents. How do Mom and Dad interact?

How does Dad deal with somebody he doesn't necessarily get along with? What happens when somebody cuts in front of Dad on the road? What happens when we're struggling within our own family with a wayward child having a problem? More is caught than taught. They feel that.

Family: The Original Social Service Agency

The marriage unit is the core unit. It's the union of the two people around which we build strong families. That unit has been under such pressure and so much strain. It needs legislative support. Fathers have more frequently pulled themselves out of the family unit or been left out of the family unit. We need to get dads to turn their faces home. It will be one of the most positive things that can happen to us legislatively, and as a country, if dads do turn their face back home.

If these bonds of marriage stay strong and build strong family units, it's the best thing by far that we could do. Some people use the example that the family is the original Department of Health, Education, and Welfare. The family is the original social services agency, and by far the best. It's certainly the place where, as a country, we trust the inculcation of character and values. We have this great national debate about values, and should we be setting those in Washington or should we be taking the values of Hollywood. You wouldn't have anybody disputing the fact that families should instill values. If you don't have that strong marriage, that father there as well, you're going to have difficulty in many cases — not all — creating and sharing those values. I want to emphasize the "not all."

There are some marriages that are just in great difficulty, and these people cannot stay together. There are circumstances where that happens. I don't think anybody is saying that we've got to end divorce in America. There are certain situations when it just doesn't work for one or many reasons. Nobody is talking about that. But when you look at a country where nearly 50 percent of our children at some time before they reach the age of eighteen will live in a single-parent household, you have got to think not quite all of those marriages were ones that we just couldn't work. We haven't valued the institution of marriage enough, and that brings a lot of problems for us as a nation.

Should the Government Reward Marriage?

I think there are things that we can and should do, and I think there are a lot of things that would be very problematic if we tried to do, and shouldn't do.

For instance, to me, perhaps the most ridiculous tax there is is the tax on marriage that we currently have in the United States. If you are a two-wage earner family and you make a combined income between $21,000 and $72,000, you actually pay a tax on being married. If you just live together, you pay on average $1400 a year less. That's the most wrongheaded tax that we've ever had. It directly affects family units right in the middle income categories, where typically people are struggling. That's clearly a bad signal.

The second thing we need to do is provide more statistical information. When the United States got into economic data, it really helped change a lot of situations. When we started putting forward unemployment numbers on a state and a major metro area, it focused attention. If in Chicago the unemployment rate gets up to 8 percent, people would say, "We've got a problem with unemployment. Now what are we going to do in Chicago to get this rate on down?" It's a very powerful tool. Yet at the very time that we know that statistical information has an impact, we are actually reducing cultural data. We no longer ask on a short form of the U.S. Census about marital status. We are reducing our amount of actual social and cultural data when we ought to be expanding it. We ought to be making it available on states and major metro areas. We ought to know the levels of teen pregnancy, teen suicide, and divorce rates, and be able to track that over a period of time. If they're going up, people can start saying, "Why?" It should be reported like we do economic data on a quarterly basis. We put out those numbers and people react, governments react.

To me those are positive things that the federal government could do. Now, if the federal government came in and took over divorce laws and put in a federal policy that you have to go back to the system of fault divorce, that would be a completely wrong way to go. So to me there are some good things that we can do and there are some wrong things that, if we even started discussing, the people in the country would react very negatively.

Government Intrusion?

You have had this increased push of the government chasing fathers to be economically responsible, even if they may not be responsible in some other ways. That's been an unfortunate result of what's taking place in the decline in marriage. You've had more government intrusion. I'm one that believes in less government. I'm also one that believes what Lincoln said about how you change things in America. He would say that America moves by a common thought. The most powerful thing that we can do culturally is move to a common thought that marriage is important and it is for life. We need to move toward those norms. It's about children, too. It's not just about my happiness. It's also about these beautiful, young, fragile, wonderful creatures that are entrusted to us called children.

A single parent may struggle heroically to raise this child and do a good job, and some have and some do; but broad numbers say that single parents have some difficulty because they just don't have as much time as two parents do in a committed family. And there is an impact.

I think one of the unfortunate side effects of some of the cultural breakdowns is that you are seeing more governmental intrusion into something that has typically been private. What I'd like to see us do is move back to more of a cultural norm that is far more supportive, so we wouldn't have the governmental intrusion.

Where Are We Going?

Tell me the worth of a society where it is easier to get out
of a marriage contract with children than it is to get out of
a Tupperware contract.

OKLAHOMA GOVERNOR FRANK KEATING

The number one reason given for divorce in this country
is irreconcilable differences. The research finds that every
couple — every happily, sexily married couple — has
approximately *ten* irreconcilable differences.

DIANE SOLLEE

I don't think it's good enough just to become neutral
about marriage. Public policy is about making choices
and providing incentives for things that we believe are
social goods.

WADE HORN

I'm quitting. I'm quitting premarital sex.

NISSA

It's not like gay people are going to come in and use up all
the licenses and then there won't be any licenses left for non-
gay people.

EVAN WOLFSON

Sociologists have spent a century describing the decline in
marriage but tend to be fatalistic about whether anything can
be done about it. I believe we have a responsibility to do
something about the decline of marriage. And I think we can.

WILLIAM J. DOHERTY

Today, almost everybody would agree that something's gone wrong with marriage. About four in ten marriages will fall apart. Millions of other couples will never get married, even if they have children together. These concerns have sparked a marriage movement, a controversial and diverse new effort to support marriage. It is made up of liberals and conservatives, people of faith and people from the secular world. Some people advocate marriage education. Others say that government has to get involved, including state governments, since the states are where marriage and divorce laws are made. Others think businesses and corporations have a role in helping. Still others think faith communities should do more.

Religion has always supported marriage, and seven out of ten weddings are still religious ceremonies. But leaders in the marriage movement believe more needs to be done. Mentoring initiatives and controversial convenant marriage programs are only two of the many ways churches and religious leaders are addressing the issue.

The marriage movement has gained confidence from new research showing that married people live longer and amass bigger savings accounts. But that doesn't make all the questions surrounding the institution of marriage easy to solve. Ever since the Middle Ages, when lawyers of the Roman Catholic Church proclaimed that marriage should be based on mutual consent between the couple rather than political arrangements between families, love has been central to our marriage tradition in the West. But if love is so important, how do we make it last? Is there one model of married love or several? And nobody, yet, has a definitive answer to the most contentious question of all — who should have the right to marry? If marriage is good for everybody, should gays and lesbians be permitted to wed?

Despite these lingering questions, if the past is any guide to what lies ahead we can be hopeful about the future of marriage. History teaches us that the story of marriage is not one of relentless progress or inevitable decline. It is a story of crisis and renewal, achievements and failures, things done and things left undone. It is a story whose next chapter all of us, from the very oldest to the very youngest, will help to write.

William Galston

William Galston is a professor in the School of Public Affairs at the University of Maryland and director of the Institute for Philosophy and Public Policy, and was formerly deputy assistant to President Clinton for domestic policy. He believes that marriages must be based on mutual respect and economic interdependence if they are to be successful in the twenty-first century.

A Broad Consensus

The debate over the American family in the early 1990s was sharply polarized, as indeed it had been since the late 1960s. It was polarized between liberals and conservatives, between people who celebrated the cultural changes that began in the late 1960s and those who deplored them. It was caught between those who focused on economic factors and those who focused on moral issues, between those who believed that family structure was an important element of family functioning and those who denied that.

There are lots of dissenters all around. But there is a broad middle of the political spectrum in the United States today, which I think is at the level of mass public opinion as well as political elites in public policy and activists. That consensus is that family structure is important for family functioning and child outcomes; that, for example, teen pregnancy, out-of-wedlock births, millions of kids being raised by young, single mothers is not a good idea either for the kids or for the young mothers or for the absent fathers or for society as a whole. There is an increased disposition to believe that keeping families together is a good idea whenever possible, whenever the costs are not too high.

There is a very interesting turn in opinion among the youngest

Americans, teenagers and young adults, people who are dispropor-
tionately the children of divorce. As you examine the public opinion
surveys focused on that generation, Generation X and Generation Y,
you'll see that they are much more conservative than their parents
were on questions of family integrity and marital stability. In fact,
many of them vociferously blame their parents for breaking up marriages that in the judgment of the children, although that's necessarily
a one-sided judgment, could have been maintained and should have
been preserved.

We Don't Have a Good Handle, But . . .

Let me be perfectly frank. I don't think we have a very good or reliable
handle on the sorts of public policies that would be highly effective in
strengthening marriages and in keeping families together. But there are
some things that we can do that I'm convinced would be helpful.

First of all, the tax code and economic policy in general should encourage marriage and reward marriage rather than discouraging it. We
can have an elaborate debate as to the best way of curing it, but that
would certainly help.

I think it would also help if the sorts of resources that families
need to carry out their essential functions were made more available.
We ought to be evenhanded between families where one parent stays at
home and works at home and families where both parents are in the
paid workforce. They both have special economic and social needs.

In addition, I think there is a role for public policy — not necessarily national or federal policy but at the state level and perhaps even at
the local level — in thinking about ways of making would-be married
couples more thoughtful about the very important commitment into
which they're about to enter. I think that there ought to be better marriage counseling prior to marriage, not during a time of marital troubles alone. I think that faith communities have a very important role to
play, though they shouldn't be the exclusive players in that.

There's also a role for increased reflection when parties to troubled marriages are thinking about leaving. I also believe, and here I'm
venturing into more turbulent waters, that there is a rising body of empirical evidence suggesting that the no-fault divorce laws, which were
adopted between 1970 and 1975, are not just a reflection of cultural and

economic change but are themselves contributing to the high levels of divorce that we have experienced.

One of the most important things that we can do to improve outcomes for kids is to intensify the efforts that have been made during the 1990s to reduce the incidence of teenage pregnancy and out-of-wedlock birth. I've been a longstanding warrior in this particular battle. Since 1995, early sexual experimentation by teens has been declining significantly. It is a trend that no one would have predicted in the late 1980s or early 1990s. To the extent that fewer children are born to young people — who are clearly unprepared economically, educationally, and emotionally to take care of them — the country will be much better off.

Here is what I have sometimes called my favorite statistic: Take two groups of children. In the first group, the parents are high school graduates who got married before they had their first child and they waited until they were out of their teens to have that child. In that group, about 8 percent of the children are living in poverty. That is a rate of child poverty less than half of the national average. Now take a second group, where the parents did none of those three things. They didn't graduate from high school, they didn't get married, and they didn't wait until they were out of their teens to have a child. In that second group, 79 percent of the children are living in poverty. That is a rate about four times the national child poverty average.

So there are three simple things that young people can do to give their kids a better chance: they can stay in school until they're at least high school graduates, they can get married before they have their first child, and they can wait until they're out of their teens to have that child. That would be a social revolution if it happened. It would also be the best thing that's happened for children in many years.

We Can't Pretend

I think we have to begin by acknowledging that economic changes, changes in technology (including the technology in the medicine of reproduction), and other sorts of social and cultural changes have created a new context for marriage and families. We are not free to pretend that those changes have not occurred, and we are not free to disregard their consequences.

I think we are going to need a twenty-first-century family, which is different in some important respects from the family that existed through much of the twentieth century, at least in the United States. Many people have jumped — and, in my view, jumped hastily — from the obvious need for change inside families, a different division of labor between husband and wife, to the conclusion that families don't matter anymore, that their essential role in creating a nurturing and supportive atmosphere for child development can somehow be parceled out to public institutions or to single adults. I don't think that there is any evidence to support the proposition that strong families are dispensable for children. They may be more dispensable for some adults than they used to be, but they are not more dispensable for children.

To the extent that the public as a whole has a stake in how children grow up — whether they grow up able to contribute economically, whether they know how to relate in appropriate ways to others in society, whether they are good citizens in basic and not so basic ways — to the extent that there is a continuing public interest in these matters, there's a continuing public and state interest in the structure and functioning of families.

A Fascinating Turnaround

The very first no-fault divorce law in the United States was enthusiastically signed into law in the state of California by then-governor Ronald Reagan, himself a divorced man. The conventional wisdom at the time was that divorce is very much a matter between two adults. Kids were not worse off because of it. Indeed, on balance they were probably better off and therefore there would be no particular public interest in maintaining restrictive divorce laws.

One of the fascinating things that's happened in the past ten years is that the research community of sociologists and social scientists, including many people who were strong supporters of the view that divorce didn't have negative consequences for kids, have now turned around. They turned around because of evidence both in the United States and from a very important study in Britain, which is now more than thirty years old.

We can now distinguish pretty clearly between high-conflict marriages and low-conflict marriages. In high-conflict marriages there is evidence that kids are not worse off when divorce occurs. They may actually be better off in some respects. But when low-conflict marriages end in divorce, because one party gets bored or something better comes along, then the kids are much worse off.

You might say that most marriages that end in divorce are high-intensity conflict marriages. But that is not true. Recent studies indicate that about 50 percent of all divorces occur in families that can be categorized as low-conflict rather than high-conflict. So, in at least 50 percent of the cases, one can demonstrate harm to kids.

One of the striking things about the law of marriage and divorce in the United States is that we jumped very rapidly from a very restrictive system to an almost entirely unrestricted system. There were points in the middle where divorce reform could have stopped. But in characteristic American fashion we figured that if some change is good, more is better. And here we are.

Money, Money — the Argument Is Backward

The irony of our current situation is that at this beginning of the twenty-first century, marriage is not less of an economic necessity or less of an economic benefit than it used to be. One of the best ways of escaping poverty and of helping one's children escape poverty is to get married and stay married. It's not just because two can live more cheaply than one. It's also because partners to a marriage can be mutually supportive for economic as well as other purposes. For example, problems of childcare become much more manageable. If you have a husband and wife who can make their schedules fit together, they can cover a substantial portion of the childcare themselves, as opposed to purchasing it in the market. There are many, many other economic advantages, too. If a young man or a young woman needs to go back to school for education or advanced skills training, the other party to the marriage can produce a stable income stream while the first is retooling. That is much more difficult if you're not dealing with stable, intact marriages.

So I do believe that there is a misunderstanding, and it is not a misunderstanding that's confined to the African-American community. The argument that, "Well, we need more money in order to get married" I think has it about backward. If you want more money, then get married; creating a mutually supportive and reinforcing economic unit is one of the best moves you can make.

Having said that, I would go on to say that especially in the African-American community there are some difficulties that have to be acknowledged frankly. Our country, for good and for ill — and we can have a long debate about this — has embarked on a high prison incarceration strategy as its principal approach to crime control in the past twenty years. That has had the effect of stripping the African-American community of many young men. These facts are well known. This greatly complicates the task of restoring marriage as a norm rather than a rare exception in the African-American community. I don't have any blithe answer for this. But I do think as a society we have to think harder and more systemically about the consequences of one social policy on the full range of the other things we care about.

Flux, Tension, and Choice

I think the attitude of today's young about marriage is in a state of flux. They are torn between the desire for commitment and the fear of commitment. That tension is the fundamental fact of their emotional lives. On the one hand, they say they don't want to go through what they saw their parents go through. They don't want to go through that for themselves and they don't want to inflict it on their children. On the other hand, precisely because many of them have not had good models of stable, committed marriages, they are very, very skittish about entering into those relationships. In part as a result of this skittishness, the average age of marriage for both men and women has risen by fully four years during the past generation. When I got married, young men and young women typically got married at the age of twenty-one or twenty-two. Now it's more like twenty-six or twenty-seven, even twenty-eight.

In case you've been wondering why all the sitcoms feature young unmarried people in cities in their twenties and early thirties, it's because that is a demographically exploding group, and it is expanding so rapidly because of this tendency to postpone marriage. The fundamental tension in American society today is a tension between the desire for choice on the one hand, individual choice, and, on the other hand, the desire for strong interpersonal and communal bonds. The problem is that those two desires don't go together very well. To have untrammeled choice you have to be willing to walk away from a wide variety of interpersonal and communal bonds. Similarly, in order to have bonds that endure over time, you have to be willing to accept restrictions on individual choice. You have to be willing for the sake of the relationship to refrain from exercising choices that otherwise you would claim a right to make.

Americans across the board, not just young people, are wrestling with this tension. If I wanted to be fancy, I would call it a conundrum. They are searching for a new balance between choice and bonds. We haven't found it as a society. We haven't found it, but we're looking for it.

Strong Marriages in the Twenty-First Century

In thinking about the family, I think it's very important to take into account the profound economic, social, and cultural changes that have occurred in the past thirty years. There's no question that the relations between men and women inside marriage and, for that matter, outside of marriage have been transformed.

Strong marriages cannot be maintained on the basis of the same cultural assumptions or the same economic relationships that existed thirty years ago. There's no question about the fact that women are more economically independent than they were thirty years ago. That's a fine thing. I don't think anybody would want to turn the clock back. Therefore, relationships that existed only because of the economic dependence of women on men are going to be much weaker and much less prevalent than they were thirty years ago. Let's acknowledge that. Let's also acknowledge that cultural norms of relationships between men and women have changed and that forms of female subordination to men that were widely accepted thirty years ago are now totally unacceptable.

If you're going to have strong marriages today in the twenty-first century, they are marriages that have to be built on the fact of economic interdependence rather than economic dependence. They also have to be built on the premise of equality between men and women rather than inequality. Equality doesn't mean the same in all respects, at all points in the lifecycle, and for all purposes of parenting. The roles of men and women, even when they're equal roles, will be different and will shift over time. But I am confident that strong twenty-first-century marriages can be created on the twin pillars of economic interdependence (as opposed to dependence) and gender equality (as opposed to inequality).

In order for marriages to be strong in those circumstances, marriage will have to change. The division of labor inside the family will have to change. Women's economic contribution to the family will have to be acknowledged in the use of funds and the authority over funds within the families. I disagree with those who say that economic and cultural change has rendered the family obsolete or unnecessary. But I do agree that the changes of the last thirty years necessitate profound changes in strong families in order for them to remain strong.

Judith

Judith discusses her plans for the future and reflects on the past.

My One Regret

Do I date? No. Oh, I would love to be married again. I would love to. If not married, I would love to be in a relationship, particularly because I've learned so much and I would never go about a subsequent relationship the way I went about the first one. I don't date. I don't think that men my age are particularly interested in women my age.

Also, I work in an environment where, though it's large, it's very young people. They are mostly in their thirties. I don't really know even where to go to meet people that would be my age. I really don't. I mean, I am clueless. So I don't date at all. But, interestingly, the men that have really been attracted to me and that have shown interest in me have been incredibly young. I mean they're thirty-five, thirty-six, thirty-seven, and I'm just not interested. I think that's a lot more acceptable in Europe or if you're a movie star, but for someone like myself, I'm very uncomfortable going out with somebody that's that much younger than myself. But that's kind of a surprise to me.

I feel that I'm a better person today. I feel that I'm more the person that I was meant to be today than I was all those years when I was in that marriage. So, I'm pretty comfortable. I do sometimes think that I always knew deep in my heart that it might come to an end, and I did nothing about it. I really didn't do anything about it.

If I would make a recommendation to anyone, it is if you're feeling in your heart that it doesn't feel right, you should really take action and not wait until you're fifty-seven years old to make the jump off the high dive. That is my one regret. I think I waited too long. Yes, I did — way too long. But you know, better late than never, I think.

Wade Horn

Wade Horn says he doesn't care if you're a Republican, a Democrat, a vegetarian, or a Communist — if you care about fathers because you care about children, then you're on his team.

Can't Think of Something That's Crazier

If we wanted to construct a society that punished couples for getting married, we couldn't have constructed a better society than what we have right now. We have a welfare system that for over sixty years has said the one thing you can't do if you want to get cash welfare is marry an employed man. We have a tax code that punishes two people who decide to get married as opposed to cohabiting.

The problem is that cohabitation is a very weak family form. It's a lot easier to break up a cohabiting relationship than it is a marriage. People are psychologically more committed to marriage than they are to cohabiting. When you cohabit, you simply take your toothbrush and go someplace else. If you're married, it's a little bit more complicated. What we do with public policy is we punish couples who decide to get married as opposed to cohabit. I can't think of something that is crazier than that.

So, What Can We Do?

Public policy includes incentives for all sorts of things that we think are social goods. We think home ownership is a social good, so we provide a home mortgage interest deduction. We think charitable giving is a social good, so we allow you to deduct that from your taxes. If marriage is

332

good for children, if it's good for adults, and if it's good for communities, why in the world would we shy away from providing at least some incentives for marriage?

What we do is we punish marriage. We have to reverse those policies. I don't think it's good enough just to become neutral about marriage. We're not neutral about home ownership. We're not neutral about charitable giving. We're not neutral about a lot of things. Public policy is about making choices and providing incentives for things that we believe are social goods. Marriage is a social good. We ought not to shy away from providing incentives for it.

There are some who argue that if we provide incentives for fathers and if we provide support for fathers that it's a zero-sum game and moms lose. The fact of the matter is most moms that I know want the guys who father their children to be good fathers. Most mothers I know don't think it would be a horrible idea if the guy who fathered their children was a good guy, a guy who was nurturing, loving, caring, and supportive, not only of the children but of them. This is not a zero-sum game. This is a game that says if we support men in their role as responsible fathers it's good for men but it's certainly good for children and, in fact, it's good for women as well.

Think More out of the Box

There are lots of things we can do to encourage responsible fatherhood, but the problem is — and I'm sure this is the first time you've heard it — men have difficulty stopping and asking for directions. So you have to go where men are and help them where they're at. You have to think creatively. You have to think more out of the box than what we're currently doing in terms of working with parents in general, which generally translates into working with mothers. We can do fathering or father mentoring programs in maternity hospitals. We can work in the inner city, helping men who grew up without fathers learn the skills that are necessary to become responsible, involved fathers. We can help men understand the skills necessary to form and sustain healthy, equal-regard marriages.

There are lots of things that we can do, but the first hurdle is to call this problem by its correct name. The correct name is not poverty, as terrible as poverty is. The correct name is not simply high taxes, as bad as high taxes are. The correct name is fatherlessness. What we have to do is talk about it, recognize it for the problem it is. We also need to understand that marriage, as an institution, is not irrelevant to the discussion of how we deal with fatherlessness.

Resist Politics

The worst thing that could happen to the fatherhood movement is for it to be captured by either the political left or the political right. I do not believe that if you're a Republican it makes you a better father or if you are a Democrat it makes you a better father. I think there are good and bad fathers on all sides of the political equation. To be on my team you only have to really believe one thing and that's that fathers matter, that they provide something unique and irreplaceable in the lives of children. If you believe that, you can be on my team. I don't care if you're Republican, a Democrat, a Libertarian, a vegetarian, a conservative, a liberal, or a Communist. I don't care what you are. If you care about fathers because you care about children, you're on my team.

The really good news is that there is a growing consensus in this country about the importance of fathers that spans the political spectrum. We're seeing it in social workers. We're seeing it in politicians. We're seeing that in all corners of American society. There certainly are some holdouts. But if you speak to most Americans, and particularly if you speak to most children and ask them, "does it matter if the fathers are there," they'll say yes.

I am optimistic. I am optimistic because I think we can't survive without fathers and we can't survive without marriage. So I have to be optimistic, because the alternative is social destruction. I believe that in my soul, and I believe that for the well-being of my own two daughters.

The point of the fatherhood movement is to focus on what is good for children. It's not necessarily what's good for men, although fatherhood *is* good for men. It's not necessarily what's good for women, although responsible fatherhood *is* good for women. This is all about what is good for kids. If you ask most children, "Does it matter if your father is there for you? Does it matter if every night when you come home, your father is there to eat dinner with you, to read a bedtime story, to tuck you in and say a last prayer?" most kids will look you in the eye and say, "you bet."

Oklahoma Governor
Frank Keating

Frank Keating is governor of Oklahoma. After a state study showed that Oklahoma's high divorce rate was a major cause of poverty in the state, Governor Keating pledged to reduce the rate by one-third by 2010, and he created the Oklahoma Marriage Initiative to address the issue.

What Holds Oklahoma Back

Our state Chamber of Commerce did an analysis on what holds Oklahoma back. We hired the economic departments of Oklahoma University and Oklahoma State University to find out why our society is so poor and why we have a lot of lower-income people. The answer on the left hand of the ledger was tax policy or regulatory policy. But on the other hand, we have too many out-of-wedlock births, too much divorce, and too much drug abuse and violence. So we began an initiative in each one of those program areas to attempt to raise income levels and the prosperity level of the state, in part by attacking the very high divorce challenge, which is a serious challenge to the economy of Oklahoma.

The Oklahoma Marriage Initiative is funded with ten million dollars of the state's share of money from the federal Temporary Assistance to Needy Families program. The money is dedicated to such initiatives as community-based marriage, family-strengthening programs conducted in cooperation with religious leaders, statewide marriage conferences to train people to teach marriage-skills courses, a Marriage Resource Center to guide couples to information and mentoring programs, and the development of better statistics on divorce trends.

Attacking the Problem

The first thing and the most important thing is sensitizing the public to the fact that our high divorce rate is not healthy. Our high divorce rate results in a lot of impoverished children and a lot of impoverished families. There's a challenge to health care and there's a challenge to education. Obviously, there's a challenge to going to college if you come from an environment where you don't have a mother and father or a financial support base to go to college. So we need public awareness and public sensitivity.

We also brought in the church community. This is a state where 70 percent or more of the people go to church twice a month or more. Virtually every denomination, the Catholic church and the principal Protestant churches plus the Jewish and Moslem communities, signed a statement saying that the marriages they perform would require premarital counseling or training on conflict resolution, paying bills, fighting and arguing fairly, and those kinds of things. Again, with no force from the state, but a lot of voluntary persuasion from government and private sector working together to say that marriage is a good thing, marriage is a lifetime contract, marriage is a way out of a poverty trap. Stay married, work through your problems, and before you get married make sure you have a course in marriage.

One of the Highest Divorce Rates

As governor of Oklahoma, I'd like to say our divorce rate is fiftieth, but realistically we're probably in the top five someplace. The high divorce rate is a very serious challenge for a state like Oklahoma that has a Bible culture, a family-values culture, and it's a very serious challenge not only to the social fabric but to the religious fabric, and particularly to the economic fabric.

Why such a high divorce rate? I think there a number of reasons. I think probably first is the number of teen marriages. A lot of people get married when they graduate from high school. Many of those marriages simply don't work out. The good news is that people are getting married, the bad news is that many people are getting divorced. They just are not financially secure, emotionally secure, or educationally secure before they take that step into a lifetime commitment.

So the message is, "Hey, listen. Go to college. If you meet somebody, remember this is a lifetime commitment. If you want to get married, try to be financially and educationally prepared for marriage. Don't just jump into matrimony. Don't marry your high school sweetheart the day after you graduate from high school." I think that's a big part of it. I think part of it is a southern culture challenge. In the south, a lot of people get married at a very young age, frequently right out of high school, and, unfortunately, a lot of those marriages do not last.

Not a Religious Interest

I'm looking at all these things not as religious statements but as social statements and citizenship statements. It's a fact that most children who are raised in two-parent families have more of a chance of going to college and being financially secure, not being on drugs, and not being a school dropout than those who are from single-parent families. Single-parent families have a lot of the social pathologies that are destructive. That's not to suggest that every marriage is meant to last, it's not to suggest that divorce should be outlawed, and it's not to suggest that people who come from one-parent families can't make it. Many, many, many, many people do. But the reality is that for a strong society, it's important to have strong families, which means a mother and a father — a father being the disciplinary figure in the family, a mother being the nurturing figure in the family, the two of them providing the discipline and the love and the nurturing and the care children need.

We've drifted away from that. Maybe that's a result of the Hollywood culture. But today, I think, serious social scientists, serious business leaders, and serious political leaders are sitting down as we are and saying emphatically, "we have too much divorce, too much family breakup." I once said to my legislature, "Tell me the worth of a society where it is easier to get a marriage license than a fishing license. Tell me the sense of a society where it is easier to get out of a marriage contract with children than it is to get out of a Tupperware contract." I mean, this is nuts. But that's exactly what we've done over the last twenty years and we need to reverse that tide.

Our interest is not a religious interest. Our interest is a citizenship interest. A good, social contact interest that strong families are abuse free, have a disciplinary environment, and an educated environment.

Also that there's a mother and father pushing young people in the direction of being good, moral, and decent citizens. That's healthy for society.

As I indicated, in families that stay together the incidences of school dropout, of violence, of alcoholism, of drug use, are less than families that don't stay together. To the extent that we can have a young citizen who is secure because he's had a happy, secure, and stable home-life with a mother and a father, and who is a citizen who will be well-educated and financially stable, that's society at its very best.

Again, as I said, these are all voluntary initiatives. We're not suggesting that every marriage will survive. People change. Sometimes a husband takes up drugs or drinking, or a wife strays and goes to another person's side. Those things happen. But it is better to know this is a lifetime commitment. It is better to stay together, and it is healthier for us as a society to have intact families, educated families, and productive, tax-paying citizens. That is better for society at large.

Hoping to Cut the Divorce Rate

As I said, one of the reasons why we adopted this issue is because our state Chamber of Commerce and our economics departments at the University of Oklahoma and Oklahoma State University identified the divorce rate as one of the reasons why segments of our population live in a low-income environment.

We lowered the cost of a marriage license in Oklahoma if you've taken premarital counseling and training. But we think the best approach is a voluntary approach. Don't bribe people (not that there isn't probably some good in that), but don't bribe people. Simply say to the faith community, "Since you marry 75 percent of the people in your churches or synagogues or mosques, require a premarital course which includes counseling, dispute resolution, arguing fairly, and other issues that are most important in marriage breakup." So far, virtually every denomination in Oklahoma has signed on, and we think as a result of that you'll see in the years ahead much fewer divorces.

Our hope is within the next ten years, actually less than ten years, to reduce divorce by one third. Our hope is to raise up our people to the point where they are better educated because they are able to put the resources together to go to college, as they can be in many cases with two-parent families. As a result of being better educated they will make more money and turn our state, which has been a low per-capita income state, into a higher per-capita state.

Ronald Mincy

According to Ronald Mincy, we must find ways to reengage men in the lives of their children, both within married families and without.

The Best Teacher on the Planet

One-night stands are a lot more risky these days than they use to be. The Personal Responsibility Act required states to establish paternity for 90 percent of their out-of-wedlock births. As a consequence, it is nearly impossible today for young men to escape their responsibilities toward their children. Young men have to understand that. But the question is, who is the best person to convey that information? I think it's a young man who has already had a child, who thought the child would have no implications on his finances. All of a sudden he discovers that's different. I have an entire game plan for how to figure this out. A twenty-five-year-old man who has two children out of wedlock and earns $17,000 a year has to pay about $8,000 of that in child support — that's the best teacher on the planet to train a sixteen-year-old man who is just beginning to be sexually active not to go there. That sixteen year old is more likely to listen to that twenty-five year old than he is to me.

I think there is a lot of opportunity in working with young men to face up to their responsibilities of being a parent and to understand the emotional, developmental, and spiritual needs of their children. There is also an opportunity to help young men understand what their financial responsibilities are, because men respond to money in ways that they don't respond to other issues.

Team Parenting

In forty states throughout the United States we have a process for divorcing couples. Before they're granted a divorce, they're required to attend some kind of mediation process. The purpose of this is to help them learn how to communicate, so that the static between the parents does not adversely affect the child.

Thirty percent of all children in the United States are born out of wedlock, and there is no process like that for those parents. We need to create one. So we are inventing a strategy to work with unmarried couples to help them learn how to negotiate their relationship. This is the first time that such a strategy has been created for unwed couples. It's called team parenting.

In traditional programs, women sit with each other and talk about the challenges of employment, the fathers of their children, and the like. Men meet in all-male groups talking about their challenges with child support, employment, and a variety of other things. There is no way to have the father and the mother sit across the table from each other and talk about the challenges they are having jointly in providing for the needs of their child. Team parenting is going to do that.

Helping couples negotiate their relationships and communicate is something that as a matter of public policy we don't do. There is no place in family services in the United States today where that happens. This is simply unconscionable, because those children need the support of both parents.

The Cheapest Way

For 30 percent of the children in the United States it's a question of intervention, not prevention.

How do you intervene? I think you intervene in a number of ways. First, for many couples the conception of the child is the first time they seriously think about the nature of their relationship. We can bemoan that or we can take advantage of the opportunity. Both the mother and the father get all excited about the birth of their child. I've seen this happen. You get enormous changes in the demeanor of fathers, who they think they are. It forces men and women to rethink who they are, the kinds of behavior that they undertake, and the kinds of risks they can expose themselves. They understand they have this new life; there's this dependent child depending upon them.

When people are reflecting afresh on what their behavior means for this young child, we can begin to focus them on the needs of that child, not on their own needs. We can also focus them on the nature of the relationship with the other partner and help them think about whether or not it's time for them to get more education or more job training. This is true for both mothers and fathers. Since welfare has been anchored around women and children, we have an apparatus to get them the help and skills they need. But men have no apparatus to help them move from thoughts about reforming to doing anything about it.

Government should play a role in the interventions because we are going to pay for the needs of these children if their parents don't. It's a very simple idea. Recent research tells us that you can do more for human beings during the first three years of their lives than at any other point in their life. So, ask yourselves, do you want to wait until they're fifteen years old, or do you zero in on them when they're two? The research clearly indicates that you zero in on them when they're below three years of age. And who should be helping them but their parents? Even if we didn't care about the welfare of the child, the simple fact is it's cheapest to do interventions when children are young, and their natural parents are the most likely people to be interested in the children.

Welfare reform is increasingly requiring mothers to work, and we know that fathers are actively engaged already on behalf of children. They take their children to child-care centers. They take them to Headstart. We know that 27 percent of all poor children born in the United States are already either living with their fathers and their mothers, or the fathers are visiting them once a week. Intervention strategies are simply the cheapest way to promote the well-being of these children. If we don't allow their parents to do it, taxpayers will end up paying for it. It's as simple as that.

What we're asking is that government fund community-based organizations in order to deliver the services. If the child experiences problems associated with not knowing the child's father and gets in trouble, the government will pay to incarcerate that child. If the child is put in foster care because the mom has a drug problem, the government will pay for child welfare services. So I don't think this is a radical departure from what government is already doing.

If Not Now, Shame on Us

I think the future is quite exciting. We have the lowest welfare rolls in probably three decades. Federal and state coffers are booming with money in relation to the agenda around welfare reform. Fathers are part of the policy discussions at the federal level. We also have a very strong economy that can absorb lots of low-skilled workers. I speak of myself as an expert in this field and I say to myself everyday, if we can't get this done now, shame on us.

First of all, we have to solidify some of these community-based organizations and the national intermediaries who are experts in the field of fatherhood. That requires money, and I'm very clear about that. We've created institutions that have the capacity to deliver services at the community level and to do evaluations and studies of a whole variety of things. But those entities need money. That's why federal, state, and local resources are critical.

We also need to engage, as far as the African-American community is concerned, the church. We need to engage other faith-based institutions, too. Why? First of all, when men deal with their issues around fatherhood, there's a lot of guilt. There's no entity other than the church to help men and women resolve the issues of guilt. The other day we held a community forum and the lines were out of the doorway. The role of the church is critical. We have to get church leaders to understand that even though an out-of-wedlock birth is sin and an area that they don't want to enter, this is about redeeming young fathers and young mothers back to their children, back to their families, and back to their communities.

Another area where we have to go to is young people. I have to shut up and listen more. We have to understand how young people think about the process of family formation. We need to get young people to talk and think about how we can get a twenty-four-year-old young man who is not married to the mother of his child to begin thinking about marriage. I confess I don't know how to do that. No set of thoughts that I dream about in my office is going to help me figure that out. But if I sit down and listen to our young people talk about a child, the relationship with the mother, how things have changed for you and that child, then I can go back to my office and run that tape back in my mind. Then, I think, I can dream up a strategy. So, we are trying to create arenas to listen to young people. That's what the future is all about.

Larry Bumpass

Larry Bumpass believes there is no way to turn back the clock, and that we must look for ways to protect the stability of children's lives.

Turning Back the Clock?

There are many that think that by one social policy or another we can turn back the clock on these processes and strengthen the traditional family. That's a tough area. One of the reasons it gets so difficult has to do with the moving target of a definition of what a family is, and the ideological debates, sometimes quite heated, over what those boundaries should be. From my own perspective, we have a very strong interest in protecting the stability of children's family lives. That, I think, is a widely shared goal. But by children's family lives, I'm including children in families that aren't married, because that's just a part of the reality that we have to deal with.

Just one further point to illustrate what I'm talking about is that cohabitation rates with children are much, much higher following a divorce than they are before someone is married in the first place. So if we think of traditional stepfamilies as being a married couple with a child from one of the partners, and if you wish to limit your definition of families to such units, you're faced with some very difficult realities in the current world. Half of all married stepfamilies began as cohabiting stepfamilies. They were living together with the child or children of one of the partners and then they got married. One has to ask, did they become a family at the ceremony, and were they not a family before? If they were a family before, then it's clear we're going to have to think about families more broadly than defined only by marriage. If we began to think about that, then we're going to have to ask how our social policies impact children's family lives, whether or not their parents are married.

Let's say again, the traditional family-values emphasis would argue that if you extend benefits to unmarried couples, you are further eroding the stability of marriages. But those arguments run directly in the face of the fact that these children are already living in families, but they're not receiving the benefits that married families are. Again the argument is often made, "Well, if you keep it that way, you have a negative sanction for remaining unmarried." But you're doing so at the expense of the children, and it's obviously not producing the result that's wanted.

Absolutely No Effect

Indeed, there are a number of legislative initiatives that are being pushed throughout the country by those who believe that we can turn back the clock and restore a traditional family system based only on marriage. These include attempts to establish covenant marriages, where a couple agrees that only under the most extreme circumstances would they get divorced. Without going into the details with respect to that one, I would argue that such programs can have absolutely no effect. They may appear to have an effect in that those who sign up for a covenant marriage have lower levels of divorce; I would be amazed if it weren't so. But it's like the story we reviewed earlier with respect to cohabitation: the only ones who are going to sign up for a covenant marriage are those who are much more opposed to divorce in the first place.

Perhaps seemingly more plausible are the attempts to repeal no-fault divorce laws. There are initiatives in a very large number of states that are being pushed by these family-value think tanks, as again an attempt to reduce divorce and stabilize the traditional family. Such efforts may increase the income of lawyers; I think they will increase the hostility of the divorce process. If you've got to establish fault, then you're much more in an accusatory framework.

The evidence runs completely against the argument that the installation and implementation of no-fault laws caused our sharp increases in divorce. There was a sharp increase in divorce around this trend line that began in the early 1960s, but the interesting thing is that the increase began a good five years before no-fault laws were put in place and continued without any inflection in the increase when no-fault laws were implemented. In fact, as I've already said, of the last twenty years, there's been no increase in divorce despite the fact that no-fault laws are in place. So I can't believe that these changes would make any difference.

Similarly, attempts to require premarital counseling; now, surely some couples would benefit from that, but those kinds of emphases ignore the realities we've been discussing about cohabitation. If couples have been living together for a substantial length of time before they apply for a marriage license, what is it that's being stabilized even if it were to talk some of them out of marriage? You'll simply have a breakup of this family unit without being married. But if children are involved, the stability of children's family lives are simply not affected.

I Share the Premise of Family Values, But . . .

I should begin by saying that when it comes to the values themselves — an emphasis on the importance of marriage, an emphasis on the importance of stable family lives for children, on the value of commitment in a relationship — I share all of their premises. When it comes to whether that will have any effect on these trends that we've been discussing or achieve the policies that are being put forth by various marriage initiatives, that's where this discussion becomes highly relevant.

If the underlying forces behind these changes have deep historical roots and are tied to our economy, then the best that one can hope for, by my lights, are temporary changes at the margin. It's simply not in the cards to change the basic directions of these social changes. So if we care about the lives of children, if we care about the stability of intimate emotional relationships and what they offer for men and women, then we have to focus more broadly on preserving the stability of family units, whether married or not.

It's clear that many of these patterns that we're talking about like divorce, like unmarried childbearing, have clear relationships to economic well-being and are much more common amongst those who are less well-off. That, to my mind, brings us to social policies that are quite removed from trying to focus directly on marriage itself, but rather to try to improve the lives of many of the citizens in our society, such as the economic circumstances. I think we are truly able to do that. With the proper provision of health benefits and the like, we would, in fact, not reverse the trend, but at least moderate the levels of both instability experienced by children and the impacts of that instability on children's lives.

Can we teach people to build better relationships? I'm much more skeptical about the likelihood of making major gains in that regard. That's a pessimistic point of view. But the question is, once again, can we turn back the clock? If the underlying dynamic is somehow built into what's happening to our culture in ways I think are very closely tied to our economy, then that reduces the willingness to make long-term commitments and that pulls people away from the intense connectedness. Can we somehow turn back the clock with respect to that, and teach people how to live more connected, more committed lives? Can we re-instill in our youth a willingness to sacrifice their own self-interest by making long-term commitments that may in the future prove to be not in their best interest? If we could move in that direction, it would help. But I'm not optimistic that that is something we can successfully do in any large scale.

Is the Idea of Marriage Dying?

I don't think so. Marriage is being delayed. There are a lot of functions that used to be confined to marriage that no longer are, but the vast majority of both men and women say that they want to marry and most will. I think it's not a matter of rejection of marriage, as we often hear in the literature, but rather a delay of marriage and perhaps a declined significance of marriage in the mix of overall life opportunities. But it's not an antagonism to marriage.

Ultimately, the vast majority of people get married. What we don't understand well at all is why. Now, obviously, marriage serves as a symbol of one's commitment and love and the like, and that's very important from a sociological point of view, from a religious point of view, as a statement about commitment. But whether anything actually changes when people get married in terms of the dynamics of the relationship, we don't know. But marriage remains important. People value marriage, and they want to get married. It's just they don't have to do it right away.

Thoughts

I would re-emphasize the importance of family relationships, broadly defined, and the importance of commitment and stability in the family lives of children. At the same time, I would emphasize that we must understand that our current trends are part of our long-term historical evolution and are broadly shared with virtually every industrial society. The latter point simply means that we can't turn back the clock. So, recognizing the changes that are occurring, we have to ask what can we do to ameliorate the negative consequences for men, women, and children who are living in this kind of a modern world?

I wish I had an easy answer to what we can do. I can't claim to have professional expertise about what would ameliorate these problems for families. But my own biases are that we can make some headway by reducing the dramatic inequality in our society, an inequality that has increased over the last several decades, to provide those at the lower economic rungs greater opportunity to provide for their children. If such high proportions of children are spending part of their lives in poverty, that is clearly a part of what we have to address both for family lives and for the well-being of the children more generally.

I wish I could say more about what would increase the willingness of our citizens to make long-term commitments and to stand by the commitments they make. But one might take the argument back and say that children that grow up in such unstable, insecure environments may not find that conducive to developing attitudes and values that make the world seem a secure enough place that one can make a long-term commitment.

It seems to me that both sides of the political arguments have a vested interest in the well-being of children. This is, after all, the major productive element in our economy in the future. If we are not investing heavily in the well-being of children, we are engaging in very poor national economics, quite apart from the human dimensions involved.

Evan Wolfson

Evan Wolfson is the director of the Freedom to Marry Project.
He sees opposition to same-sex marriage as just another form
of discrimination.

What Is Marriage and Whose Business Is It?

Marriage in American constitutional life, in American social life, is the most important, most significant, most central social and legal institution in virtually every respect for almost all people. Marriage is primarily a committed relationship of two people, recognized and supported by the state, who undertake a commitment and who receive important protections and benefits and also obligations and responsibilities.

Anthropologists once catalogued human societies, and I forgot the numbers, but they found that out of the, whatever, 146 different human civilizations that they noted, all but 3 had some institution or another of marriage. Now what people called marriage in their society often varied widely and still does to this day. In some places, some people were allowed to marry and never terminated it. In some places, the women took the lead. In most places the men or the men's family controlled. For many, many, many centuries, families controlled marriage rather than individuals. For some part of our history, churches controlled marriage, but there were also parts of our history where churches had nothing to do with marriage.

So the institution of marriage is one of the most flexible, and yet one of the most enduring, human institutions. It's taken many, many forms. It's lasted, and it has vital significance. Today in this country it has extreme importance for many, many people. Many people consider the choice of whether and whom to marry one of the most important personal decisions they make. Some people think it's so important that they make that decision more than once.

What we're saying is that lesbians and gay men, like other human beings, have the same mix of reasons for wanting the freedom to marry and should be able to do so without discrimination by the government. The choice of whom to marry is so important and so personal that it belongs to the couple, not to the state.

Cough Up a Kid or Lose the License

Well, we all know that there are actually many meanings to the word *marriage.* First of all, in our society there's religious marriage and civil marriage. Even though people sometimes celebrate them on the same day, legally they're two different things. You can wear white and march down the aisle and have a lovely, very important day with your family and friends, and in the eyes of your church and your God you're married, but legally that doesn't mean anything. What counts legally is not marching down the aisle; it's the piece of paper that you sign in the vestibule, which says that you have a civil marriage license, which is the legal and economic institution.

Many people do get married, in part, because they have found somebody with whom they wish to have children. Their intention, and often what they do, is to have children within that structure of marriage. On the other hand, we all know that there are many people who choose to marry without being able to have kids, or without any intention of having kids, or when they're too old to have kids. Why did they get married? Not for children, but for the other reasons that marriage brings for people's lives: commitment, support, a statement of love, a structure in which to live your lives, the access to legal and economic protections and benefits, the spiritual significance that it has for many.

Although for many people one of the important things about marriage is it gives them a structure within which to raise kids, that's certainly not always true, and it's certainly not a requirement. The government does not issue marriage licenses with a sunset provision, which gives couples two years to cough up a child or lose the license. We recognize that people have many reasons for wanting to marry, and only some of them may have to do with children.

Those Children Exist

But the irony is that there are many lesbians and gay men in our country today who are raising children. They have kids and what they want as parents is to be able to raise their kids within the structure of protections that marriage brings. Unfortunately, people who claim they care about kids, and who claim they care about family values, are punishing those kids by refusing to allow their families to have the structure of marriage.

Even if it were true, as the right wing says, without a shred of evidence, that the best family were a man and a woman, not a gay couple or a lesbian couples with their kids, the fact of the matter is gay people are raising children. Those children exist. They are there. They're not some statistic. They're not just some theory. They exist. If you care about those kids, then what you want to do is bring them the protections and support that could come to their family through marriage, instead of punishing those kids for having "the wrong parents."

Also, gay people are not the people who invented alternative insemination. The vast majority of people who use alternative reproductive technologies in order to have the family that they want are heterosexual couples who have problems conceiving or have other medical or personal reasons for doing so.

Studies show that chosen families — in other words, where people really had to go out of their way, whether through alternative reproductive technology or adoption, as in the case of most lesbians and gay men and also non-gay people — those chosen families tend to do better. The kids actually tend to do better, because the parents have made a clear commitment in their mind to what they have to do as a parent.

Makes No Sense

I believe that in our society we should not condition all benefits and protections for families on the sole criterion of marriage. There ought to be ways that people can access important protections and benefits in their lives without having to get married. For example, I believe that we should have some kind of universal health care. Your access to health care as a human being should not depend on whom you're married to or where you work. You ought to have that.

But, on the other hand, lesbians and gay men who choose to marry are not just choosing to marry because of protections and benefits like that, although some are and many need those protections. They have the same mix of reasons for wanting to marry as non-gay people.

What's really funny is that the people who attack gay people wanting to get married are the same people who usually are running around the country saying everybody should get married. It's like marriage should be mandatory for everybody who doesn't want it, but forbidden to those who do. That policy makes no sense.

That Was Wrong and We Changed It

Not only has marriage as an institution changed dramatically over the thousands of years of human history and from continent to continent and culture to culture, but even with our own country we have seen many, many changes in the institution of marriage. Marriage has been a battleground as people have fought for equality and others have resisted.

For example, there was a time in our country's history when African Americans were not allowed to marry even each other. They were not allowed to marry at all. Marriage was used as a weapon to dehumanize them and to say that they were not worthy of the law's respect and that their love and their commitments and their families meant nothing under the law. Even though they developed personally important ceremonies — the famous jumping-the-broom that history talks about — the law did not respect it. Of course, they were treated as less than human beings. Well, that was wrong and we changed it. There also was a time in our country's history in some states where Asian Americans were not allowed to marry, particularly on the Western coast. That was wrong, and we changed it. Then we put in place in our country a regime of laws that said that people could maybe get married, but not if they married "the wrong kind of person" — so that people could not marry someone of "the wrong race." That was wrong and we changed it. Then there was a time in our country's history when women who got married became the legal property of their husband. Women actually lost rights by getting married. Well, that was wrong and we changed it. There was a time in our country when people who got married could not get out of their marriage, no matter how violent it had become, no matter how abusive, no matter how much it had failed. That was wrong and we changed it.

Many of those changes took decades of work and civil-rights fighting and litigation. The same people who are opposing gay people's freedom to marry today are making the same kinds of arguments that were made against the inclusion of these people and the equality that we sought to bring to the institution of marriage.

Even with the License Framed above the Bed

I mentioned that there was a time in our country's history when people were not allowed to marry someone of "the wrong race." It wasn't until 1948 in our country's history that the first court struck down that ban on interracial marriage. It took up until 1948 to get even one court to say this was wrong, and that was a four to three vote by the California Supreme Court.

What happened after that decision? It took nineteen years before the question got to the United States Supreme Court. That case came about when Richard and Mildred Loving got married. They were not able to get married in their home. They had to leave their home state of Virginia, go to Washington, get married, and come back. Now, when they came back, they were legally married. Their marriage certificate hung over their bed. But nevertheless, the police burst into their bedroom and arrested them for the crime of marrying the wrong person. They went to trial. They were criminally prosecuted and they were convicted. The judge in their case sentenced them to a year in prison, but then agreed to suspend the sentence on condition that they leave Virginia and go into exile for twenty-five years. Well, they did. They went and they got a lawyer and they came back and they sued.

The Virginia courts upheld their conviction for wrong marriage. One of the judges in that case said, and I'm going to paraphrase, "Almighty God created the races — red, brown, yellow, white — and he placed them on separate continents that they might not mix. But for man's interference with God's divine Law and the definition of what marriage is, they would be separate today." Kind of an interesting way to refer to slavery. He upheld their criminal conviction.

Well that case percolated up to the United States Supreme Court in the best-named case ever, *Loving v. Virginia.* In 1967, the

Supreme Court said, "No! This kind of restriction on the fundamental freedom of marriage cannot stand. Marriage is an important personal choice that belongs to the couple and may not be discriminated against."

Prejudice and Inertia

We're not saying that the state has no interest. What we're saying is that the state has to show a good enough reason for interfering with people's ability to commit to one another and take on the responsibilities and protections of marriage. What's happened here is that every court now that has looked at this since the Hawaii courts began the examination has found that the government has no good reason for this discrimination. It rests on prejudice and inertia and, in some cases, ignorance. When the government actually has to come into court in the cool, clear light of a courtroom and show a reason for discriminating, they don't have one. In those cases where the government has no good reason, then the discrimination should stop.

Whenever people don't have a good reason for denying gay people the freedom to marry, they try to change the subject to, what about polygamy? What about brothers and sisters marrying? What about people marrying their dogs? Those are the same things that they said when interracial couples sought the freedom to marry. They said, "If we allow this, the next thing you know you're going to have people bringing their harems and camping at our gates." There are literally court cases that say that.

But these are just diversions. These are attempts to change the subject. The question is, what is the reason for this discrimination against these people? If the government doesn't have one, that discrimination ought to stop. The next case will be the next case. Marriage cannot depend solely on whom it excludes. Marriage ought to be about who is included, why are they included, what are the reasons, and maximizing people's ability to make those choices consistent with actual reasons, not just discrimination and prejudice.

Law Courts, Food Courts

It wasn't the legislatures in this country that ended race discrimination in marriage. It was the courts. If it were not for the courts, we would not have had *Brown v. Board of Education*. We would not have had *Loving v. Virginia*. We would not have had the decisions ending legal disenfranchisement and legal subordination of women. Courts play a tremendously important role in our constitutional system, protecting religious minorities, protecting racial minorities, protecting women, and, we hope, protecting lesbians and gay men.

Now, on the other hand, that doesn't mean that it's only up to the courts. To me what's important is not just what people are saying in the law courts, but what people are saying in the food courts. We need to get out there and talk with non-gay people and show them that there is no good reason for this discrimination and help them get used to the idea.

One of my personal mantras as I've been running around the country working to advance our freedom to marry has been that there's no marriage without engagement. We have to engage non-gay people in a discussion about something that most of them have never really had to think about before, the idea of gay people getting married. I realize that that is a new idea for many people.

It's our job, and by that I mean gay people and fair-minded non-gay people who care about equality. It's our job to engage people on something that they really haven't had to think about before — how the denial of marriage harms real, live gay families. What I find is that as we talk with people, and as people hear more, like the courts did about how there's no good reason for this discrimination, they're moving in the direction of supporting gay people's equality and ability to make this decision for themselves.

It's More Than Just Sex

I think we've moved pretty far in our society from the medieval image, where marriage belongs not to the couple but to the community. Where the whole community follows the couple into the bedroom to watch them "consummate," which means that the man takes possession of the woman as a property matter, and then they hang out the sheet as evidence.

In medieval times and in other periods in history marriage was about a lot of different things that we don't think about it as being today. Even more than reproduction it was actually, in most places, about property and about dynastic unions — uniting families for the purposes of collecting their property and keeping it together instead of dividing it. Then there were issues of primogeniture and passing the property on through the male line and so on, depending on the culture.

All of that is clearly not what Americans think about as marriage being today. Our constitution respects the freedom of the individual and of the ability of each of us to make our life plan, rather than making us the tool of our kin and clan, or of the state, or of the property interests. In our society today, marriage is best understood as a commitment between two people, hopefully to love, to take on legal responsibilities toward one another, to receive and to deserve protections and benefits from the society and from the government which they have paid for as taxpayers. If they are raising kids, to do so in a structure that we hope will bring the most to those kids.

That's what marriage is for in our constitutional life. It's so important a decision for those couples that when a group of Americans came before the United States Supreme Court in 1987 saying that the government wasn't allowing them to marry, the Supreme Court said, "You cannot withhold the choice of marriage even from those Americans." Those Americans were prisoners. The Court said the freedom to marry with all the attributes of commitment and responsibility and access to protections and benefits is so important that it cannot be denied even to convicted murderers.

If it can't be denied to convicted murderers, how can it be that in all fifty states today, no matter how committed their relationships, no matter how much they love one another, no matter how much they need the protections and benefits for their loved ones, gay people are the only Americans who are not allowed to say "I do" and take on that civil, legal responsibility?

I don't think that's what most people, gay or non-gay, think of marriage as being about in our society. We believe that intimacy and affection and sex belong to the couple, not to the community. It's not for the community to police. You know what's more, anyone who's ever been married will tell you that marriage is about a lot more than just sex.

So what we're talking about here is the intimacy, the affection, the commitment that belong to the couple, as well as the legal respect, the legal support, and the legal responsibilities that people undertake when they get married. We're saying gay people should have no more and no less, play by the same rules, enter the structure, have those responsibilities and protections as they choose, to protect their families, our loved ones.

We Don't Like This Kind of Person, So . . .

Obviously the state is entitled to have reasonable age limits, and people can argue a little bit about what those are. Some states allow fourteen year olds to marry, other states set it a little higher. Half the states, in fact, allow first cousins to marry. But in all those cases, what is clear is that they have to show a reason for doing it. They can't just off the top of their head say, "We don't like this kind of person, so we're not going to allow you to marry," or, "We don't like whom you're marrying, so we're not going to allow you to marry."

We believe that the choice of marriage is so important that it belongs to the couple. Although the state may impose reasonable restrictions, such as protecting minors and so on, that's very different from jumping into the lives of adults and saying, "We don't like who you're marrying so we're going to discriminate against you and stigmatize your marriage."

Let's also remember that when people get married that doesn't necessarily mean that the state approves of whom they marry. I think all of us have the experience of watching a friend get married and saying, "Why is she marrying him?" Or "What do they see in each other?" But does that mean that the government should be stepping in and policing that marriage? We believe people should be making these choices for themselves. When a deadbeat dad gets married, or when a prisoner gets married — both of whom have been found by the courts to have the fundamental right to marry — that doesn't mean the state is saying, "We love your relationship." What it means is that the state, in our country, is saying, people make these decisions, not the government.

Enough Marriage Licenses

It has only been seven years that the vast majority of Americans have even had to think about the words *gay* and *marriage* in the same sentence. In just that seven years, we're seeing 30 to 40 percent already supporting this, while two-thirds of the public believe this is going to happen. Which means that the momentum is with us, despite the onslaught of right-wing attacks, despite the fact that politicians have ducked for cover and most of them have refused to lead.

Voters of a certain age, the younger voters, are more likely to support it. Kids today understand, why are we even interfering with this? A generation from now, people are going to look back on this and say, "I can't believe that society used to discriminate on the basis of sex, just like it used to discriminate on the basis of race, when it came to two people in love."

The force of history is clearly with us. As long as we reach out in good faith and patience to fair-minded, non-gay people and talk about this, most people are going to realize the sky will not fall when people are treated equally. There's enough marriage for everyone to share. It's not like gay people are going to come in and use up all the licenses and then there won't be any licenses left for non-gay people. We can all share in this and build together, protecting our families and working on the things that really matter, instead of the things that divide us.

David Frum

David Frum is an author and journalist who resides in Washington, D.C. He argues that permitting same-sex marriages would change the definition of marriage itself.

Modern Marriage, Modern Trouble

I think the bare numbers don't even begin to describe how troubled the institution of marriage is. You can't gauge the trouble by looking at any one statistic, the divorce rate or the out-of-wedlock birth rate. You have to put them all together. What you see when you put them all together is that the custom, the convention, of raising children in stable father-mother relationships, which used to be the fate of the overwhelming majority of society's children, is now actually becoming the situation of a minority of society's children.

Most children will spend a piece of their childhood in something other than a marriage. For at least part of the period until they are eighteen, they will be in a stepfamily, they will be in a single-parent household, or they will be brought up by a cohabiting couple. That experience of being born to a father and a mother, growing up with a father and a mother, and reaching adulthood with a father and a mother is an experience that fewer than half of the children born in the year 2000 will have. Not so long ago, 75 percent or more of American children could look forward to reaching the age of adulthood with both the father and the mother. In the past, for those children who didn't, the main reason was because one parent or another died.

Make Your Choice, Honor Your Choice

So this is a new thing. How did it come about? Marriage in American society reflected two great American principles. One was you're free to make your own choices. This is not like Europe. We don't have arranged marriages. We never have. You make your own choices, but, once made, you must honor your choice. When marriage was a stable institution, it was entirely up to you to go in, but once in it was not so easy to get out. That principle was defended not so much by law as by custom. The American norm was, our laws favor divorce but our customs discourage it.

That norm began to break down in the late 1960s because we began to believe two things about people. We began to have much less respect for the active individual choice, and we also began to be much less insistent that once a choice was made that it had to be honored. So we changed our rules. In contemporary American society, you can often be married without intending to get married. That is, you live with a woman without marriage and have a child by her. The state will come along and say you have some of the obligations but not others of marriage. At the same time, you can actually undertake a formal marriage, and it's terrifically easy to dissolve. We have quasi-marriages that aren't really marriages. We have cohabitation, where people aren't legally married but are living as if they are. We have couplings in which people are sort of legally married, but are not living as if they are and are creating babies by purchase rather than by conception. We've got a whole jumble of arrangements, but all of them are based on the rejection of the principle of "free choice, but stick by your choice."

Why Did Culture Change?

Different eras have different ideas about what people are like and what they need. A hundred years ago we believed you should be left alone to make your own decisions because that's freedom but the consequences of your decisions must be borne by you because that way we encourage people to make good decisions. A hundred years ago, people would say, "Look, you make a contract, you make a business deal, even if it turns out badly, you have to stick with it." That's how we encourage people to make better deals.

Now, we don't look at it that way. What we say instead is we are prepared to accept the negative impacts of protecting people from their choices because we can't bear to see those consequences fall on people. We have much less respect for people as free agents. We see human beings as sort of pitiful creatures of their circumstances, of their race, of their background, of their language.

You can see this in area after area of life. A hundred years ago if you wanted to live near a river that flooded because you could buy land more cheaply there, you got the benefit of the cheaper land, but if there was a flood that was very much your problem. Today, we don't look at it that way. Today, we say, "Well, even if you did get a better deal, if there's a flood that's going to be all of our problem." The result is many more people live in places that get floods.

That principle is true in marriage. A hundred years ago if a man and woman lived together outside of marriage and the woman got pregnant and had a baby, the society would say to her, "You have no claim on that man. You didn't marry him. You want him to act like a father? He can if he wants to, but we won't make him for you. Your failure to insist on marriage before making the baby is going to land on your hand. You're going to suffer the consequences of that." We're not prepared to do that today. We're not as robust in that way. So we say, "Okay, well, we will protect you from the consequences." By protecting people from the negative consequences of a bad choice, you encourage the bad choice. The result is that many more babies are born outside of marriage because we allow people who don't get married and have children to have many, even most, of the benefits of marriage. The government will come along and collect some money from the child's father on your behalf.

From the point of view of many women, that's the best of all possible worlds. You get involved with some loser, you have a baby by him, you don't really want him around, but you would like him to contribute to the support of the child. The modern state says, "Fine. We will do that deal." It's no wonder that that has tended to crowd out marriage in the poor sections of society.

If Marriage Is So Good, Why Bar Anyone?

We've done two things. One, we have made marriage a much easier institution to get out of. Two, we have transferred many of the benefits of marriage to people who aren't married, thus making marriage relatively less attractive. A marriage is a big step and a lot of people find it frightening. So if you say, "Look, if you cohabit you can get half or two-thirds of the benefits of marriage without any of the scary implications that loom so large to a twenty-one year old," you're going to find you have a lot more cohabitors.

As for gays, you're simply bandying empty compliments. It is not the laws that make gay marriage impossible; it's the nature of things. When you say the law, despite the nature of things, will create a status and call it gay marriage, what you're doing is you're taking a kind of cohabitation and equating it with marriage. That tends to undermine marriage.

Gay marriage has a lot of implications for the raising of children that are very, very troubling, and it will spill back into real marriage. For example, one of the things I think that we should be very much determined to do is to protect children from being turned into commodities. This is, I think, the real, the most fundamental, of all issues involved with marriage. It's not just that by overthrowing marriage we have made adult life less pleasant and agreeable and safe and secure, although that's true. What you tend to do when you weaken marriage is to sever child rearing from marriage, and that turns children into commodities. That's what sperm banks are.

When a woman goes to a sperm bank, there are two contracts that have to be signed. One is a contract between the father and the sperm bank, where the father says, "I hereby renounce my child in exchange for a fee." The other is a contract between the mother and the sperm bank, in which she says, "As part of the deed and sale, I hereby release this man from any obligations." Here's what you've done. The father, for money, is being relieved of his fatherly responsibilities, and the mother, also for money, is cutting him out of his fatherly responsibilities. Both are asking the government to enforce those contracts.

You can put every sperm bank in America out of business tomorrow if the government said it was just not going to enforce those contracts. If later on the father wants access to his child, he'll be able to have it like any other father. If later on the mother wants child support from the father, she'll be able to get it. The sperm banks only work so long as the government agrees to enforce a contract for the sale of children. I think that's an outrage.

Now this is where the gay marriage becomes so problematic. If you were to create this status among gays and call it marriage, what you would be signing on to is a vast program of treating children as articles, commodities of sale.

Blurry on the Way Out

You are missing something. It comes down to the part about sticking by the choice. Traditional marriage said you are free and you're not free. The choice is not that you and your wife can work out any deal you like and every marriage will have a completely unique legal code. The choice was, "Here is this institution. You may enter it or not, and here are its rules. The man must support the wife. The man must contribute to the upkeep of his children. The woman in turn has certain obligations. Now you, man and woman, you are free to make your choice about entering this institution, but once in it you are bound by it." That was the old way.

The new way is to say, whatever you want, whatever you want. You want to come in on terms where the man doesn't have to support the children? Fine. You want to come in on the terms in which some third party is brought in to substitute for the father in some ways and not in others? Fine. It is no longer clear cut. It is, rather, a blurry set of individual arrangements.

The rise of cohabitation is linked to the rise of divorce, because when it's blurry on the way in, it's going to be blurry on the way out. The reason that we used to make the lines so clear is because we believed it was so important to the successful raising of children to have a bedrock — a reliable, unbudgeable contract arrangement between the man and the woman.

I read recently about a case in Vancouver of two men and two women; they cross-fertilized each other. That is, Man A fertilized Woman C, and Man B fertilized Woman D. Then, while the two men lived together and the two women lived together, they then treated themselves as a four-person family and raised the two children, who were produced with four parents. Well, if you have four parents, you have no parents. It is not true with parents, the more the better. One of the problems with it taking a village to raise a child is if the whole village is raising the kid, the kid doesn't have his own room. That's sort of the implication. Every room is yours; no room is really yours.

You have four parents; you have zero parents. That is what we are signing up for.

What we are doing by creating this institution to be called "gay marriage" is smashing marriage and replacing it with a whole new set of arrangements that apply to everybody, not just homosexuals, everybody, in which marriage is a unique contract between any two or more adults who want to enter into it and set by any rules. It makes marriage impermanent, and it turns children into commodities.

Vermont already made it possible, even before the gay-marriage decision, to have gay adoption. So they are already encouraging the raising of children in non–mother-father households. Adoption is so difficult even under the best of circumstances, and now they're saying we're going to promote not the best of circumstances, but the worst of circumstances. This strikes me as recklessness with children to an almost unimaginable extent.

What is going to happen with the Civil Union Law is it's going to strike a chain of litigation that is going to consume the country over the next twenty years. Ultimately, the Vermont decision is going to go or marriage in the rest of America is going to go. As things are going now, it looks like marriage will lose. It looks like the Vermont decision is going to be the norm, and marriage throughout the United States is going to vanish as a distinct legal status, even though it may remain in the name and people may still have weddings. It's already in the process of vanishing. In Europe it has vanished, and in Canada, it's nearly gone.

It's Not a Sign of Health

To say that marriage is alive and well because so many people want to get married reminds me of the Mark Twain joke that "quitting smoking is easy, I've done it hundreds of times." The fact that people get married four and five times, the fact that men want to marry men and women want to marry women, the fact that there's going to be demand for polygamy and brothers marrying sisters — this is not a sign of marriage's health. It's a sign, rather, that we have so lost sight of what marriage *is* that we are unable to come up with the most minimal definition of the difference between marriage and nonmarriage.

Fewer than half of American children are going to grow up inside of marriage. If you look at the poor half of American society, you will see that marriage is already a minority form. Even leaving aside the question of divorce, whether people get married at all is becoming a minority form. So, no, marriage is not a well institution, it's a very sick institution, and it's even sicker in all the other countries in the West, which I think gives us a glimpse of America's future.

A Middle Ground?

No, there is no middle ground on this question. You're either having marriage as we've understood it as an institution, which people enter of their own free will but are then bound by their choice, or you are having a variety of cohabitations, some of which may begin with or have in the middle a visit to a priest. But the fact that some of these cohabitations are blessed by some kind of church official does not alter the truth that you have a regime of sequential cohabitations, based on the needs of adults, in which we permit children to be bought and sold.

So it's either going to be one way or the other way. I'm afraid, very much afraid, that at the moment the way we are going is toward a society of temporary, serial cohabitations in which children are treated like commodities for purchase and sale.

Leslie and Rich

Leslie and Rich have no regrets about their decision to marry and say that friends who used to feel sorry for them now envy them.

Just a Piece of Paper?

Leslie: I think being married is really great. To have the support of somebody else that you know is always going to be there is great. It's funny at this point because we're realizing that you don't need friends like you did before. I mean, friends are still very important, but we have each other and that's such a great thing to have.

And more so when we see most of our friends aren't married yet. We have a lot of single male friends who are hitting their thirties about now, and they're ready to settle down. But they're having a really hard time finding somebody, and I feel really bad for them. It's funny, because five years ago they felt bad for us. We had these little kids and we couldn't do everything that they could do and we couldn't go out every night. Now, it's kind of transitioned. It's really interesting to see because you can tell that they really wish that they were, maybe not in our exact position, but close to that. I wouldn't want to change it. I'm completely happy.

Rich: For the most part, marriage is probably the one largest decision you'll make in your life. To have had that over basically before starting college, it was probably a huge stress reliever. Not that we knew we were going to get married and not that we could guarantee it, but we thought we were going to get married. It was just inevitable.

What about the pregnant couples who say they aren't going to get married until they can afford a big wedding? That hits a nerve. We chose to get married and that differs in the way you feel. You make a commitment and the commitment is made and it's there. As long as you know it's true and all of that kind of stuff, marriage is sort of superfluous as far as actually signing the piece of paper. That's our joke, actually signing on the dotted line. You know it's now official.

Leslie: Yes, I think we're kind of torn about that. I am anyway. Part of me is like, it is a commitment, and actually getting married — regardless of if you're in front of the justice of the peace or in front of God or whoever — you . . . I think you're still making that commitment. I think it's almost too easy when you don't make that commitment just to say, "Okay, this isn't working, so I'm not going to try to make it work and we're going to leave each other." It's almost like signing on the dotted line makes it more that you have to make it work.

As far as having kids, I'm kind of torn about that, too. I do think the best possible situation is to have two parents who love each other. I think kids need that. What I really notice is when he's traveling the effect on the kids is huge, absolutely huge. That makes me think even more that they need a dad and they need a mom. I think as far as mothers go I can do all the sports stuff with them, but they still need their dad. I mean, I need him, because when I'm having a bad day he's there to pick up the slack for me, and when he's having a bad day, I'm there.

Rich: Whatever it takes, I guess, to bind you. If it means you have to sign on the dotted line or if it's just an agreed-upon commitment. It's too easy to back out of things now, but by the same token people jump in too early. We knew each other five years. I don't know how other people feel, so it's tough to say, but we knew. I mean it just clicked, everything was there. If people feel that click, then I guess then they have every right to do whatever they want. But it just seems like that click can vanish too easily, and people just kind of say, "Okay, now we're getting a divorce," or "Now I'm just walking out," or "Now I'm leaving."

Leslie: Instead of trying to work through it. I mean, that's the big thing.

Rich: If signing on a piece of paper makes them, forces them, to rethink it and work through it longer, then I guess that's good. If they don't want to work through it, it doesn't matter what paper you sign or who you got married in front of.

Bishop Arthur M. Brazier

Bishop Brazier gives examples of ways his church is working hard to build and sustain marriages.

What Is Your Church Doing?

Our church is doing a lot of things to address the problems that exist today. Number one, we have a marriage-counseling program. I personally spend a tremendous amount of time in marriage counseling. But I also have relationships with psychiatrists and psychologists outside of the church structure because as a pastor I can give spiritual counseling, spiritual advice and prayer, but there are some situations where I do not have the skill or the psychological background to deal with some of these problems. So rather than giving them my best advice, I have relationships with psychiatrists and psychologists where these members can get good, strong, financial, psychological, and psychiatric counseling at no cost. It's a part of our system that if I send them there the church bears the cost of that counseling session or sessions.

Apart from that we have members on staff who do conflict resolution. A lot of marriages that are in trouble really do not need a psychologist. They do need someone who's skilled in helping them to resolve conflict. Some people think that the word *conflict* is always negative and it's going to end up in arguments of every kind, but conflict really means that there's a difference of opinion. If there's not difference of opinion there's not conflict. Some people just do not know how to handle it. So some skillful leading and skillful guidance in how to best approach the resolution of a conflict in a marriage where there is a difference of opinion can be done without a lot of psychological counseling. Sometimes you have to have it, but most of the times you do not.

We have all kinds of seminars and workshops with people who are not having problems with marriage. Not everyone we deal with in our church is trying to resolve some kind of conflict. We're trying to keep conflict from arising, so we have marriage retreats. We have celebrations of marriage. In fact, in a few weeks I'm going to preside over a second wedding of people who've been married for many, many years. We're then going to do their nuptials all over again. So there's a lot of ways that we're working to try to maintain healthy family relationships and not just have a program to deal with problems that have already occurred.

One of the things we try to do here is to recognize and reach out to men and indicate to them that they have a special place in the eyes of the Lord as being the head of their families. They are to be the head of their families. That does not mean that they are to be dictators but that there is a responsibility that they as men have. They should be the heads of their family not just in going out and making a living, but they also should be the heads of their family in relationship to their walk with the Lord and how that family relates to Jesus Christ. We try to reach out for men, letting them know that there are other men who are concerned about them. Men will respond to men more so than they will respond to women. We have a lot of men in our church who reach out to men to get them to understand their relationship to the Lord as being the head of their families.

I think that as a church we are doing our very best to keep marriages together. We're having problems, and I don't want to give the impression that we're not. We're having more problems today than we had thirty years go, because while as the Scriptures tell us, "We are not of the world, we are in the world," twenty-five to fifty years ago there was some support that the church got from the larger society. The larger society frowned on divorce, and the church benefited from that. But the breakdown of the marriage in the larger society, that concept of the freewheeling life, has seeped into the church. Many church members now are opting to follow the kind of lifestyle that, "If I'm not happy, I should get a divorce so that I can fulfill my desires and my ambitions in life." The larger society's moral values are breaking down, and there are repercussions in the church because people who are in the church come from the larger society.

When a Marriage Is Falling Apart?

The very first thing I would want to say to you if you were having marital problems would be, how do you see your wanting to get out of this marriage as it relates to your Christian commitment to Christ? What does that mean to the vow that you made when you stood in the church at the altar before God and all the witnesses and said that you were in this marriage for better or for worse, for richer for poorer, in sickness and in health? How does that relate to you? Many people have forgotten that they even said that. Some of them say that they have to say that in order to get married, but it doesn't mean anything, and that's one of the problems. I want to bring that back: You made a vow freely. No one forced you into this marriage. It wasn't a shotgun wedding. No one said you got to do this. You did it on your own. You said you loved her, you said you loved him. Now what has happened since the time you made that vow?

Then I try to get at the problems. Some of these things are minor, and, as I said, it's the new generation. "How is it affecting me?" There's a lack of willingness to compromise, a lack of willingness to talk things through. Sometimes I say, "Have you listened to what your wife says?" "Yes, but I don't agree with her." Well, that's not the point. The point is that's what she says, that's what she sees, that's what's real to her, whether you agree with it or not. That's what you've got to deal with. Or vice versa. She says, "I don't believe that's true." It doesn't make any difference. Maybe you're not doing what he says, but that's the way he sees it. So you've got to begin to stop talking past one another and start talking to one another. I see people who are listening, but not listening. They're picking up what you're saying, but they are forming their own opinion and their arguments, so when you get through, they start talking; they have really not digested what the other person was saying at all. They're talking past each other. I try to get people to talk *to* one another rather than talking past one another. You have to try to go back and find out, where did all of this animosity and hostility and neglect begin?

Why Marry?

We're not animals, we're human beings, and in a civilized society you have to have some kind of structure that has some permanence to it if we're going to bring children into the world. If we're going to have a society without marriage, what does that mean? Does that mean that we come together, that we live together and we enjoy each other sexually or otherwise, and children are brought into this world? But then one decides that the grass looks greener on the other side of the fence. Can they just pack up and take up and just haul off with no ramifications? What about the children?

I think a society without marriage is a society that is doomed to total destruction. Almost any society, civilized or uncivilized, has some form of family structure. So marriage, I believe, is the very backbone of our society today. That is why society is suffering, because of the way in which we view marriage so lightly. Children are coming into the world and families are breaking up. Kids are beginning to realize and understand that they have no really permanent place in the family. They do not know what is going to happen to their mother or their father from day to day. The incessant arguments that are going on in the home create the kind of insecurity for children.

The hostility that has developed between men and women is certainly not helping society. We've had this battle of the sexes for so long, but as someone said in a humorous way, the battle of the sexes will never be won because there is too much fraternization with the enemy.

Diane Sollee

Diane Sollee is the founder and director of the Coalition for Marriage,
Family, and Couples Education (www.smartmarriages.com), and
believes that good marriage depends on communication skills, not
good luck. By e-mail, she probably talks to more people about
marriage and divorce than anyone in the world.

One Step Forward, Two Steps Back

In America, the most romantic country on earth, 90 percent of us get
married at least once. When we marry, we really think that's what we
want. We think the ideal is to have a few children and stay with this
person for the rest of our lives. That's what we want to do.

Now, we've got this problem that we don't know how to make marriage work. We've been told marriage is not that important, and there
are all kinds of things contributing to the breakdown of marriage or the
nonformation of marriage.

A lot of people think marriage is such an embarrassment. You
make this big vow, this big pledge, and then it doesn't work. So I'll
avoid that, I'll avoid divorce. I just won't get married. I'll just live with
this person for the rest of my life. It doesn't make them less romantic
or less idealistic about wanting to be with an enduring partner, an enduring love, an enduring relationship; you know, totter off into old
age with the same person and be there with your children, your
grandchildren, and your great-grandchildren. We have the ideal all
over the world. And, I think, the problems are the same all over the
world.

The main problem is that we're operating on a lot of mythology.
We used to stay married because it involved property and our liveli-

hood. Now we have all this freedom. We're at the new millennium and we're coming off of thirty years of incredible revolution.

So, we got all of our rights and now we're looking around, and what do we have? I think women feel that if we've got women's rights but we can't keep our marriages together we've taken one step forward and two steps back. We're back to single parents with one income trying to collect money from a guy who's married to someone else now, and we're trying to support our children and hold our families together. So all of our rights really are wonderful. It's great that they're there and we don't want to undo any of the rights. But now that we've got this luxury, it's time to try to figure out how we live with all of those rights and still keep our marriages and our relationships together.

We Finally Found Out How Good Marriages Work

The reason I formed the Coalition for Marriage, Family, and Couples Education is because I was working in the field of mental health, and marital therapy really wasn't getting the job done. A lot of reporters would say, you've increased the numbers of marital therapists and the divorce rate hasn't stopped. We still have a 50 percent divorce rate. We've had a 50 percent divorce rate for thirty years. So what is going on?

I realized because of the job I had that there was all of this new information around. As we were going through our revolutions we used new, wonderful gizmos, new video cameras and computers, to study marriage. For the first time, instead of looking at just the marriages that failed, we looked at marriages that succeeded.

The population we used to look at was the people who would come to the marital therapist or the divorce court, and they'd say they were divorcing over irreconcilable differences. They would say they weren't compatible and they fought all the time. So that's what we thought caused divorce. We thought it was just a matter of finding someone you were compatible with.

Also in that same thirty years, we had a lot of misinformation coming down from the experts. People were sitting there folding the millionth sock and feeling unappreciated, and they'd turn on the tube and the experts would say, marriage doesn't really matter. What we care the most about in life are our children, and the experts said the marriage makes no difference. As long as you keep a good relationship with the kids, it doesn't really matter if you're married or not married. "Well, I'm not going to fold any more of his socks. I'm out of here. I'll go find happiness, if it doesn't matter for my kids." The experts also said that marriage benefited men a little bit, but women really did better single. Women were better off single than married

Then we got all our cameras and our computers and all this wonderful stuff that became available in the last thirty years and we started looking at the marriages that stayed together, that stayed happy and sexy and in love and enduring. We found out remarkable things. We found out how good marriages work. We're also found in the new research that marriage makes a huge difference for men and women and children — probably the family dog and the houseplants and the grandparents and the village, too. I mean, marriage really matters.

We've got new information about what a good marriage looks like. We couldn't give people a road map before. One of the sad things about marriage is that we've got all kinds of road maps for how courtship should go. We know what the first date should be like. We have pictures in our mind. We know what it looks like to be courting. We know how to play the coy games and the sexual dance. We know about flowers, romantic dinners, and dancing. We anticipate when he's going to propose, walking down the aisle on our father's arm, and our mother crying. But when that curtain closes and the wedding is over, we don't have good pictures for what to anticipate after the wedding. What does a second-year marriage look like? What does a marriage look like when you bring the first baby home? We have some pictures of Pampers and child care. But we don't have good pictures of what marriage looks like at year two, year four, year fourteen, or year forty. We don't know what to do to keep it going and keep it happy. We don't know reasons to keep it going. We don't know what to anticipate.

But now we can tell people how to make a good marriage, what are the common pitfalls, and how you'll know if you're on track.

We All Have Irreconcilable Differences

We've got so many myths in our heads about marriage, all of this romantic misinformation. The most dramatic thing the research found makes a joke of how we think about divorce. The number one reason given for divorce in this country is irreconcilable differences. The research finds that every couple — every happily, sexily married couple — has approximately *ten* irreconcilable differences — big differences, like Mary Matalin/James Carville level differences. They learn how to manage and have a good marriage in spite of their ten irreconcilable differences. The couples that do that have the skill to wall off their differences and keep them from contaminating the reasons that they married.

The research finds that the couples that go the distance, that stay happily married, disagree — get this — disagree the same amount and about the same things as the couples that divorce. There are only so many things a couple can disagree about. It's kids, it's a house, it's money, it's in-laws, it's friends, it's sex, or it's housework. That's what couples disagree about. Those are the things — money, sex, kids, friends, in-laws, and time. If you leave those ten disagreements in your current marriage and you move on to a new marriage, you're just going to get ten new areas of disagreement. The saddest thing of all is that the top ones will be your children from your previous marriages. Those will be your main, most rancorous areas of disagreement in those next marriages.

A lot of people don't know that second marriages and third marriages have a higher divorce rate than first marriages, because we're harkening back to this idea that it's about finding the right partner, the right person: How will we know they're the right person? We won't disagree. That's all faulty logic. It's all based on faulty premises.

What's the difference between the ones that make it and the ones that don't make it? The researchers have discovered with their great gizmos and laboratories that we all disagree about the same amount and about the same things, but we do it differently. One of the myths about marriage is that somehow we're going to interview this person during the dating process and there shouldn't be differences. We must think somehow that the wedding ceremony is a lobotomy or something, and that everyone's going to stay the same from this point on. But we promise to stay together for life; we don't promise not to change.

Disagreement is normal in a marriage. You're going to disagree, everyday, all day long, because in marriage your partner has a vote and input on everything: what time you're going to go to bed, what kind of bed you're going to sleep in, what time you're going to get up. You know, your work, your sex, what you're going to eat, how you're going to raise your kids, your religion, and how many times you can call your mother. I mean everything.

So we need to tell people how to handle this, and the research has shown us how to do it. The first thing is to get another myth about marriage out of our head. It's the crazy message that you get married and you become one person. That contaminates that whole differentiation. At the altar, the couple doesn't become one person. They become a couple married for life. You're still going to have your own brain. I'm going to have my own brain. There's no lobotomy. There's no merger. The couples that make it realize that and they respect that. They value that you're thinking about all these little and big problems with all of your history and all of your wisdom and all of your intellectual capacity. When a disagreement comes up, they don't panic. When you panic, adrenaline rushes in and you have no way really to function and to deal with the issues.

The great hope is that we've found out which behaviors exist in the marriages that make it and which ones don't so we can say to a new couple at the altar, "if you want this thing to work well and work happily and sexily you need to learn how to do more of these behaviors or those behaviors." Now, the really good news is that they are real easy behaviors to teach. We know how to teach them. We can teach them in weekend programs.

Men Like It

For the past thirty years, we've therapized marriage. We've operated on the premise that if your marriage is in trouble there must be a mental illness problem or a mental health problem. We get you to a therapist, we get you a diagnosis, and we get a treatment plan. The idea was that someone is diagnosed with a character disorder. The outcome usually was a divorce. Instead, if we think of it as a skill-based relationship, we realize that a lot of these couples that go the distance have all kinds of character issues. They all had childhoods. They've all got histories. They've all got certain ways of interacting. A lot of them can be happily married. So we look at what they're doing differently and then we teach it, and we teach it as we would teach in a health class or a driving class. It's like driver's education. Men like it because it's not all this therapy stuff. It's not hit a pillow and cry and show your feelings and get your feelings out about your mother or father or whatever. It's none of that. You don't even talk about your problems. We know what your problems are if you're married. We know what your issues are. We know the five things you fight about. We show you the behaviors, and you go home and you practice them in the privacy of your own marriage. You make your own marriage more skillful and healthier.

If we were doing this on television for the nation and we only had an hour or two, we would teach the most important skill set. The most important skill set is how to handle disagreement, since all couples fight. By the way, the number one predictor of divorce is when couples avoid fighting, either because they don't want to disagree or think it will lead to divorce. That's the number one predictor of divorce. When we look at a couple, if they habitually avoid conflict, they're going to go down pretty soon. If you can't disagree, you can't talk about anything. If you can't talk about what to do, when to do it, and how to do it, because you might disagree, you just shut down.

The Skill Sets

The first skill set is to welcome disagreement as part of the healthy marriage. Welcome that there are two brains involved, wonderfully involved. One of you is not off having an affair already. You just care about this relationship and this is where you do your fighting. You're going to disagree here.

The skills about how to handle disagreement sound almost too simple, unless you're in a class with your own beloved doing the most romantic thing you can possibly do — learning how to handle disagreement. It is to discuss issues in a prescribed way, so that we agree when we're going to discuss them. We agree that we're going to use the skills we've learned in the class. We're going to understand each other's position. That's the most important thing — that I'm going to fully and completely understand your position.

The way you know you've done it right is you can go away and come back in three days and completely represent your partner's position on the issue. You often don't need to resolve the issue. That's why we've got ten irreconcilable differences in all marriages. But you do need to understand each other's position. Often that solves the tension in the marriage. We have different opinions about this issue. This one is mine. This one is yours. Got it? Got it.

Then, there are other sets of skills, like the ones about change. As I said, couples get married, they don't stay the way they were at the altar. They're going to change. They're going to read books, they're going to get promoted, they're going to have experiences, and they're going to change. In a good marriage, you understand that instead of saying, "Oh, I'm changing. I've got to go find a new partner." You figure out how to explain to your partner that you're changing. You build in little skills and rituals about how to update your wishes, hopes, and dreams.

There is this whole idea that marriage is so boring. You're married to the same person for fifty years. There's an idea that no one gets to do that unless someone has a bad accident on the honeymoon and they're brain-dead for all those years. Instead, every morning you should wake up, you open your eyes, look over there, and wonder who he is today. That's how we should think about it. A marriage is a very lively thing because you're both constantly changing.

There's another skill set that teaches expressive skills. I grew up in Minnesota and there were a lot of Swedish farmers around. There was the saying that there was the Swedish farmer who loved his wife so much he almost told her. This is to help Swedish farmers and all those other people actually say what they're feeling. Oftentimes a guy in the early part of the relationship will say, "Oh, I love you." And she'll say, "Why? Why do you love me?" Then the guy goes mute and he can't think. Then he quits saying it if he's going to have to say why every time. He's just not going to say it. That's not what he was in the mood for when he said, "I love you." He didn't want to talk about why. He was in the mood for other things. So, he quits that noxious question.

Instead, you teach the couple that it's good to express appreciations for each other. You want to have that built into your relationship. You're on a walk or you're on a long car trip or you're falling asleep or whatever and you say, "Honey, I need appreciations." He knows what that means, and he can say three or four things that he appreciates about you and vice versa. It's wonderful in a marriage because we think our partner isn't noticing but we find out that they are.

Why Not Just Skip It and Avoid the Egg?

People should have more confidence. A lot of our younger people now and older people too have gotten this new idea that marriage is what causes divorce. I'll skip marriage; I won't have to deal with divorce. I won't have egg on my face and have to go through divorce court. So we'll just skip that. We won't look stupid. We won't ever get divorced because we won't get married.

So they decide to cohabit. Well, that's fine too. I'm not against that, although I would like it to be an enduring cohabitation that they can count on. Cohabitation doesn't give the benefits of marriage because it's not really enduring. People can't really invest in it. The good thing about marriage is you can invest in it. You can decide not to spend money going to Aruba and decide to spend money on a new refrigerator instead because you think you're going to be there for thirty years with the refrigerator. In cohabitation, you're not quite sure. So you tend to go to Aruba instead. You're not more likely to stay home with the kids, because you think you better keep your workplace resume going and keep your credentials up. You're not willing to stay home and invest. But whatever the situation, whether it's a cohabitation, whether it's a marriage, whether it's dating, everyone can use these skills.

Whoops, It's Marriage

There is a brand new awareness about marriage and it started in the mid 1990s. We became able to talk about marriage finally because it suddenly became okay to talk about fatherhood. Before it was like marriage didn't much matter. You know kids were going to be okay as long as you had good one-on-one relationships with them. Then people started noticing a lot of the things that were going wrong — such as delinquency, school failure, teen pregnancy — and they started linking that to fathers. Once that was done, people said, "Wait a minute. If fathers are important, what's the best way to link fathers to their kids? Whoops, it's marriage."

It's still not really okay to talk about marriage, because of the fear that we will marginalize the people who are divorced or never married. But we realize now that if you're married you have someone who can stay home and watch the kids while the other person goes to the board meeting or to the city council or the PTA. You've got more resources. So in 1996 we passed the welfare to work bill. It's the first time the legislators said we should spend money to increase marriageability. Get people off of dependency, get them educated, and get them in work programs. What was revolutionary was the support for marriage in two-parent families.

So, then everyone's looking around saying, what do we do to support marriages in two-parent families? The only things the experts have been focusing on are rolling back divorce laws, mandating premarital counseling — even though research shows that premarital counseling as we practice it doesn't work — and increasing access to marital therapy, although the research shows that doesn't really work.

Premarital counseling has been like a big pep rally — a big pep rally before a football game, but the football team has no skills. Now we've figured out that the premarital counseling, unless it teaches skills, isn't going to go anywhere.

Now we definitely have all the legislators in all the states, who've realized that divorce really costs a lot of money. Taxpayers pay for divorce and family breakdown, and we need to find a way to help couples. It isn't like some moral crusade or marriage movement. I don't like to think of it that way. It isn't that the legislators are saying you should get married or you should stay married even if you're unhappy. What they're banking on is that every survey we've ever taken in this country of any age group — *Seventeen* magazine, old folks home, in-between — people say their number one goal is to have a happy marriage and family. That's the number one goal. So the legislators are banking on that. That's what people want. They don't say, "I want to get married, have a few kids, and get divorced."

People want this. If we could find a way to help them do it, then that's what the marriage movement is about. I call it a marriage renaissance, because I'm so confident that if we can get people the new information, the new research-based, optimistic information, they can do what they want to do. I'm not for telling anybody to do it. I'm saying if you want to do it, if you want to have a happy marriage — an enduring, satisfying, sexy, long-lasting marriage — here's the tool kit, boys and girls and men and women.

It's Not Politics, It's Not Religion

I say we're all having the same problem. Feminists can't keep their marriages together and neither can the right-wing Christian conservatives. No one is able to keep their marriages together. Baptists have the highest divorce rate of all, and that's for a lot of other reasons than just that they're Baptist.

I think the idea is to bring everybody together and have everyone take this information. You can take these skill-based courses, and you can make them so perfectly secular that you can teach them in gay and lesbian classes or right-wing Christian classes. You can add whatever you want to add, but the main part is to have the skill set. It can be Catholic premarital education, Baptist premarital education, Jewish premarital education, atheist premarital education, or feminist, or humanist, or whatever you want. But just get those skills.

Marline Pearson

Marline Pearson says we must elevate the discussion about the need for sustainable relationships.

What Should We Do?

For starters, I think the focus needs to be on the next generation. I think that young people really are hungry for help. I'm enthused about some of the prevention education I've incorporated into a class I teach called "Marriage and Family." I have to say that in twenty-three years of teaching, I have probably never felt of more use. Young men really like it. It's not therapy. It's not touchy-feely. It's really straightforward. Women like it.

I also feel that these kinds of prevention tools and prevention education would be useful in terms of larger social policy, family support and family strengthening efforts. I have a lot of young students who are in cohabitating or dating relationships and they're going to have a baby or already have a baby. I call these fragile relationships. The support that we offer fragile couples or fragile families is usually parenting help, health care, or job-related help. Yet we don't do anything to help them stabilize or improve their couple relationship. I'm very hopeful here. I think that this is a real tool that can be used. I sometimes call it the missing piece of prevention.

The state of Wisconsin has a new marriage initiative, and I would love to see relationship education as a part of the package of family support measures. Right now we do nothing to help couples, whether they're married or not, and yet their relationship is probably the key support structure for the family.

There's an information deficit in the area of relationship education. While I don't want to pretend it's the magic solution, we really do know a lot more than we used to know. There are basic things about communication, handling conflict, dealing with the things that push your buttons, building good relationships, plus the patterns that build and the patterns that destroy relationships. I'd like to see this given stronger billing or at least equal billing with sex education. We seem to have decoupled sexuality from relationships. The kids may know a lot about contraceptives. They may know a lot about sexually transmitted diseases. They may know a lot about risks. But they don't know a lot about relationships. They don't know a lot about building good relationships.

Everyone should have a Relationship 101 course, and not just in high school. I would like to see relationship workshops and programs available through colleges, HMO's, wellness programs, health clubs, work programs, and even lunchtime programs. I'd like to see marriage and family classes and relationship classes for life. I find that young people are hungry for help.

When you think about what's out there in the popular culture, I mean, any magazine you pick up is form over substance, it's flash, it's ten hot moves to get your guy. Young people are really, really hungry for help, and yet what's out there so superficial.

Relationship Education Alone Won't Do the Trick

As I said, I think we ought to be offering relationship programs that have substance, but I don't think relationship education alone will do the trick. I think ultimately we need to elevate the discussion about the need for sustainable relationships. I think we need to confront the crisis we have. I ask myself, is there a place beyond which our web of intimate connections has become so fragile and so transient that we just cease to be a civilized people? I think we've really got to elevate this discussion about the need for stable relationships, sustainable relationships.

We really need to talk about what stable relationships mean and what marriage means. Here I think the silence of the elders is absolutely tragic. And when I say elders, I'm not talking about eighty year olds. I'm talking about my generation. I'm the baby boom. I think we have either been silent in terms of talking to younger people or we've just been very negatively cynical. We're the generation that went through the sexual revolution and the divorce revolution and the feminist revolution. There are lots of gains. There are lots of things we learned. We do a real disservice just to pass on our disappointments, our losses, or just to be cynical. I think we really have to ask ourselves, what do we want for our children? What are our dreams?

I have two daughters. I have an eight year old and an eleven year old. If I'm really honest, what do I wish for them? I really want them to get a good education. I want them to have a good career. But I also want them to find good love. I want them to have great marriages. I want them to have love and meaningful work in their lives. Again, I think too much of our talk with young people has been about failure, failed relationships, disappointments, and risks. That's all very important. I'm not saying we shouldn't do that. But I think we also have to talk about our dreams and what we'd like for our children.

Beyond Politics

I'm of the opinion that in some ways, right now, we're in the best of times and the worst of times. In some families, things have never been better. You have men and women who are in egalitarian relationships. They're both responsible and involved in breadwinning. They're both involved with the children. The men are really hooked in emotionally to their wives and to their children. On the other hand, we have this other reality which has become darker and darker. Men are increasingly disengaged from the family. Women are stressed, totally stressed, going it alone. That was never my vision of feminism, a world of separatism where men are so separate from the family and women are going it alone.

I'd really like to see us get beyond conservative and liberal and understand the need to attend to the crisis of our basic relationships in marriage and family. On one hand, I think the liberals have kind of missed the boat in thinking that the problems of family can be fixed by the village and outside forces. In all good will, I think liberals hope that by providing supports to strengthen the family that'll just translate into more stable families. I think that's naive. I don't think that will happen. Creating and maintaining a marriage has some of its own dynamics. The transmission belt is broken. Young people need a kind of a wisdom or guidance. A lot of young people don't have models. There're trying to recreate things as they go. There are no road maps. I guess what I want liberals to understand is that there are two kinds of poverty. Attending to the material poverty is not going to necessarily solve the poverty of connections. On the other hand, it's been to easy for conservatives to think all that matters are family values, and if you just take a covenant vow and have good family values, everything will be okay. That lets them off the hook in terms of supporting the real kinds of material resources that families desperately need, such as jobs and health care.

I'd like to change the motto from "It takes a village to raise a child" to "It takes a village and a family to raise a child." Those are the two things that we need to attend to. We really need to face the crisis of connections, and we also need to deal with the material problems.

Orlando Patterson

As we saw earlier, Orlando Patterson maintains that culture can be changed. But in a world where many children are being raised by working single parents, he argues that it will take increased governmental involvement and greater effort by schools to improve the problems caused by marital and family breakdown.

Who Is Bringing Up the Kids?

I'm concerned that with the poor and especially with the African-American poor, the question is, "How do you change that?" Clearly, we have to start thinking about the child-rearing function. The state has got to expand the resources and not just daycare programs. The state has got to expand education programs, which means more than just learning arithmetic and writing and social studies. It also means learning how to become a competent adult, learning the kind of values that guarantee success in the broadest society. We're not doing that.

The welfare reform laws, which I supported, went only halfway. They insisted mothers work. We know that this has positive effects on children. Seeing your mother as someone who is a competent adult and someone who works is good. Seeing your parent, the only parent you have, as someone who is completely dependent and who never goes to work is not good. So that's one of the reasons why I, for one, and many others, strongly supported that reform. The tragedy is that it didn't go far enough. If you insist mothers work and mothers are the only parent, the question then is, "Who is bringing up the kids?" What we've done is to create a real nightmare situation for a whole generation of poor kids. For poor working people — and most poor people are working — the problem is, who is bringing up the kids? Nobody is.

We're creating a situation where in another ten to fifteen years we may have a whole generation of kids who are just wild. Talk about wilding. It's the law of the jungle. It's the law of the streets. They will be brought up by the streets. When does a mother who's working two jobs and is dog-tired have the time to bring up her kids? Middle-class people can hire nannies. They can send their kids to expensive daycare centers while they work. Both mommy and daddy work, but mommy and daddy have enough money to make sure that the kid is being socialized, going to a good school, and so on.

There are two sets of problems here. There's a problem of how we want to bring up children to be competent in a complex, postindustrial society. There is also the more basic problem of how we're going to bring up children to prevent them from becoming criminals. Both of those involve radical engagement with the child-rearing process and a recognition of the fact that we can no longer simply ask the nuclear family to do it.

The nuclear family will be with us for a long time, although alternative patterns of child rearing are emerging (single mothers with their friends or alone, gay families, and so on). Whatever family form you're talking about, the demands of our society are such that we need to find a way of allowing one of them to stay home and do the child-rearing function. That still happens in Japan, although even there that is changing.

If we're not doing that because our economy demands that both parents work, then we have to do the logical thing and ask, "Who's going to bring up these kids? Who's going to take up the slack from the fact that the major agent of socialization now has to work?" It has to come from the public sector. That's what other countries have done. That's what happens in Western Europe, and that doesn't mean socialism. That does mean having a more rational approach to public policy.

Mass Psychotherapy?

When I speak about the need to change attitudes and behaviors and recognize cultural problems, I'm not envisioning mass psychotherapy for African Americans, which is what some people seem to think when you mention a cultural problem. There are many different ways of approaching the problem of attitudes and behaviors. Look at the attitudes which we call racism or notions of racial superiority, or the cultural attitudes, which were behind Jim Crow; to change that system we didn't insist that all whites go through psychotherapy. No. There are ways of changing a culture through legal changes, through the social-economic signals you send, and most important of all through the educational system. Take Germany: It was a totally Nazified country in 1945, due not just to the Nazis but also to a long tradition building up from the nineteenth century. You had the massive program of educational change — de-Nazification — which lead to tremendous changes in the attitudes of the younger generations of Germans, who are in many ways the least racist of Europeans now.

It Has to Be the School

It's remarkable what you can do with an educational system if you're prepared to. What I'm suggesting is that we have to really start thinking about radical changes in our educational system: how we can begin to shape the attitudes of our kids, re-shape those attitudes, and not only among the poor, but among the middle classes, too. We have a real problem right now in the way in which another educational system has shaped our attitudes, that educational system being television. It has been a powerful shaper of values, making it even more important that we have accounting measures. It has to be the school.

This is the one area in which the differences between conservatives and, shall we say, nonconservatives can be highlighted most. Most Americans are reluctant to think in terms of the school as an area which shapes values and attitudes. We've had this problem in the past. In the nineteenth century, there was strong resistance to the expansion of the educational role of the family to the school. It was felt to be an invasion on our sacred right of a family. I'm afraid we've come to another point where we have to expand that role even more in the sense that the values, the attitudes of the poor people, they need help in shaping them. We have a postindustrial society in which the task of socialization and child rearing is becoming more and more complex and lengthier and lengthier.

One of the things which will lead into greater inequality is the fact that middle-class people have the resources to spend more and more on the training of their children, not by themselves but by professionals. They are sending their kids out of the home to train, and doing it for longer and longer periods of time. College has become just an extension, in many ways, of high school. So, we have this situation where one side of the population has indeed moved ahead and made the revolution in terms of seeing the need for training. From the age of two or three, you have little upper-middle-class kids being coached as to how best to get into the ideal kindergarten, where they have to take exams. The parents aren't doing that. These schools are training them. We have one part of the population using professionals to train their kids, while we're saying to the other part, "Oh, the family is sacred. You must do all of that." But we're not even giving them the resources to do that. We tell them, "You better go to work and you better each work two jobs." You won't have the time to do it. So this is an absurdity. This is a tragedy we have right here. It's a tragedy not only for African Americans, but also for all poor Americans, even middle-class Americans. But in the case of African Americans, it's most acute.

We have to think about doing the parallel to what the upper-middle-class people are doing. We need to send kids to kindergartens which are whole day affairs, starting the schooling system much earlier, and making school hours much longer. We also need to think of the teacher not just as someone who's imparting formal knowledge, but as someone who is imparting informal knowledge. That's going to cost a lot of money.

My emphasis on culture does not lead in the direction of Dan Quayle's, which is to say that because it's cultural, government has nothing to do with it. Indeed it's just the opposite because we recognize the problem of culture and because we recognize that parents have less and less proportionally to do with the outcome — the outcome being a grown, competent adult. That's precisely why a government has to do more and more in order to help those without the resources to train their children, to train them to become competent adults.

Teaching More Than the Three R's

Clearly the fact that women now work is going to make a difference in the nature of human relations. Their growing independence will mean that the rate of divorce is going to be greater. That's something we just have to live with. However, while Americans in general have high rates of divorce, they also have high rates of remarriage. So we're still sold on marriage and that's good.

I think one of the things schools will have to do much more of is to teach relationships. Teaching child rearing involves some of the most important skills in life. We don't teach them. It's far more important learning how to interact with other human beings, especially male-female relationships and how to be a parent, than how to be a nuclear physicist or mathematician. Yet we never think of teaching it. I'm suggesting that the schools of the future will have to think about relationships and parenting and how you teach that.

Precisely because our world is changing so fast, we can't rely on transmitted practices. By the time these practices are transmitted to the world, they have changed. You need a school system which is alert to these changes — changes in human relationships, changes in parenting relationships, and so on. I'm thinking of a much broader educational system, and a different kind of teacher, not just someone who's teaching the three R's. Unfortunately, people are emphasizing just the opposite. People are saying "let's get back just to the three R's." We're going to have to spend much more money to get the kind of teacher and the kind of school I'm thinking of.

Does it scare me to put this responsibility in the hands of government? It doesn't scare me to put the responsibility of teaching in the hands of teachers. Why not? We put the responsibility of running our army in the hands of the government. I think it depends on how it's done. It also depends on whether people still have a choice in how teachers are trained. As long as we have a democratic process, we'll have a control. This is a great thing about democracy. We'll have input in how this is done.

The Street Teaches

We already have a problem. We have two kinds of problems here. We have the problem of what we're going to do with the future generation. We have the problem of what may be a lost generation. A large number of kids have been abandoned by their fathers, and because their mothers are apt to spend more and more time away from them, they're being brought up on the streets.

We've been patting ourselves on the back with respect to the declining crime rate. I don't know if there's a criminologist in this country, maybe one or two but very few, who are not worried about what's down the line. We cannot continue solving our crime problem by building more and more prisons. At this rate, there are more people in prisons than in schools. We cannot solve our problem by abandoning rehabilitation and insisting that the government have nothing to do with what produces criminal behavior. This attitude is so counterproductive. The best way to guarantee that you're going to have criminals is to remove the child-rearing function, not socialize people. They're going to end up on the streets being brought up by the worst possible element. The second best way to guarantee that people become criminals is to take nonviolent people and lock them up with violent people. You're absolutely 100 percent certain that when their prison sentence is over in six years that you will have hardened criminals. That's what we're doing right now. I dread to think what's going to happen in another fifteen years. Sooner or later we're going to run out of funds, and there's going to be a taxpayer revolt against building more and more prisons and putting more and more policemen on the street.

I dread to think about the future, because in another ten or fifteen years, if things continue at the present rate, we either will have a huge criminal population, which we are creating right now, or the rate of criminal victimization will increase. It will increase both as a result of the criminals that we are creating by throwing nonviolent people into prison with violent ones and throwing away the key and as a result of our failure to socialize kids properly.

I dread to think of the future because I think of a world in which people who can afford it live locked away in gated communities or very expensive apartments in the cities in which all hell is going to break loose. For others, they are living in more unprotected urban areas.

William J. Doherty

According to William J. Doherty, there is a need for a new attitude toward marriage and more community support for marriage.

Intentional Marriages/Auto-Pilot Marriages

One of the many things facing modern couples is very, very busy lifestyles. We've had a historical increase in the percentage of wives working outside the home. We have an invasion of media in the home, people watching TV. We have children increasingly being very busy. In fact, I'm using the term "the hyperactive family" as a way to think about the incredible busyness of many families.

One of the things that happens to couples, particularly after they have children, is that they do less and less together as a couple. I talk about an "intentional marriage," one where people are mindful and planful, among other things, about the time they spend together. Most people fall in love by having what I call "rituals" together: they go to dinner, they go skiing, they go for walks, they find time together as a couple to do things they enjoy, to be in conversation, to be romantic. That's how they fall in love. After they get married they settle in, and, particularly after they have children, they frequently do not do the very things that got them to fall in love. I worked with a couple one time that was just a gorgeous couple. I asked them how they met. They met on a dance floor, a country western dance floor. This was in Oklahoma and they were really good. In fact, they were so good people used to just swarm a circle around them and watch them dance. I asked them when was the last time they'd danced. Twelve years ago when they got married. They had not danced since. The very thing that brought them together was what they stopped doing.

When I talk about having an intentional marriage, I distinguish it from what I call the automatic-pilot marriage. When you get married, you start concentrating on other things. In an intentional marriage, people decide how to spend their time together, finding ways to be a couple. In an automatic-pilot marriage, you just figure you got married, you spent your $12,000 to $18,000 on the wedding, you have your place to live, you have your jobs and your kids, and the marriage will take care of itself because, after all, we love each other. That's not the way it works. The average drift of marriage is toward less feeling of closeness over time. That doesn't mean people are not committed, that they don't love each other, but they're gradually drifting apart because of jobs and kids and television and all that. An intentional couple says, "How are we going to paddle here? What are we going to do for ourselves?"

Let me give you my two main examples that I give to couples when I work with them. One is to find fifteen minutes a day, if you have kids, to talk together, to have a cup of coffee together — sometime other than when one of you is collapsing with tiredness — to talk about your day and visit with each other. Not to talk about how you're going to pay the bills, and not to talk about anything that you're angry about, but just to visit. Also, to have a date every other week. You know, get a baby-sitter and go out as a couple, go to something that would be pleasant, and make sure you have some time to talk. Those are examples of being intentional and mindful about nurturing a marriage.

Community Support for Marriage

The thing that I am working on now is what we're calling the Minnesota Marriage Initiative. It is trying to create more community support for marriage. Family life and marriage, in particular, are too isolated nowadays. We need a lot more community support for marriage. I just had this thought the other day as I was driving. I thought about the number of people who have helped me as a parent to raise my children. There's a long list of them: grandparents, family members, and teachers going back to preschool. There is a pretty long list. All of these people's faces were coming to me as I thought about the people who have helped me as a parent. Then I asked myself how many people helped me grow my marriage and sustain my marriage for twenty-eight years. I had more trouble. I had more trouble thinking of who directly has done that. Indirectly, yes, I mean people who love me and love my wife and are related to us. I thought that maybe I'm not being very imaginative, so I asked my wife the same question. She had the same reaction.

The number of people who have helped us as parents to raise our children is long and deep. But not the number of people who directly ever asked us how our marriage is going; what they could do for us as a couple; offered to watch the kids so we could do something as a couple; asked, when was the last time you got away as a couple? How is it going for you now that you have kids? Are you finding some time together? Those are examples of questions, and offers of help, that we don't generally have of in our society.

So couples are expected to grow their marriage on their own in an increasingly busy and fragmenting world. That's something I think we need to change. I don't have the exact answer of how to do it. But I believe it is as important or more important than communication-skills training and all of the other professional services for people who are in trouble. All of that's important and I work in those areas, but there's something about the isolation that leads people to think that they are uniquely suffering from certain problems. Also, to know that other people care about your marriage and are willing — not to be intruding on your life — but willing to be helpful is a direction we have to go.

Some faith communities are doing this in terms of what they call marriage mentor programs. Couples who are married ten or fifteen years, who are screened for having pretty good marriages, and who get some training are assigned to a willing, engaged couple to go through the marriage process. They meet with them a few times a year to talk, to share what they've learned, and to be a mentor for their marriage. So that's an example where you have somebody who is concerned about your relationship — again, not in an intrusive way — but that somebody cares and is supportive. I think we have to do a whole lot more of that.

We've Got to Do Something

Sociologists have spent a century describing the decline in marriage but tend to be fatalistic about whether anything can be done about it. I believe we have a responsibility to do something about the decline of marriage, to try. And I think we can. We have massive efforts when we see that children are suffering. We started the Head Start program, for example. Rather than just say, "Well, there's a trend toward kids growing up in families that have difficulty educating them, and that's a product of this capitalist society and the social stratification in our system," no, we say, "There are some kids in trouble and we've got to do something."

In my state of Minnesota, a legislator twenty-five years go said, "We have to be doing more for parents and young children." We now have a program where 40 percent of all children under age four are involved in early childhood family education and their parents are involved. We have 250,000 families involved as a way to try to make a difference for parents and young children.

There is no reason that we should be fatalistic about the decline in marriage, especially at a time when we know that people still aspire to it. Ninety percent or more of Americans aspire to a lifelong, successful marriage. And many gay and lesbian people want to have a recognized marriage the same way. So what we have is a society that still values this as a major life goal. We cannot take a historical, deterministic argument that marriage has been in decline for centuries and there's nothing we can do. We simply have to experiment in various ways to turn this around. I have gotten more radicalized about this since my children have moved into the marrying age.

We will be abandoning that next generation and not doing our responsibility if we don't do our best to find a way for them to achieve what they want out of marriage. It's got to be a modern marriage. It's got to be based on equality between men and women, but we simply have to try to prepare this next generation better than we were prepared.

I think we need to create a marriage ethic that would say that it's irresponsible to get married without preparing for it like it would be irresponsible to get a driver's license without getting behind the wheel and learning. And it's irresponsible not to get marital therapy if your marriage is in trouble. The analogy I use there is, "We know it's irresponsible to let a relative die without having a doctor called. Why should we have a marriage die without an all-out effort to see if professional help will save it?"

If we don't do anything, I think the outlook is poor. It's poor. Many of those in the generation in their twenties have come from families of divorce. We know that their likelihood of divorce is 15 percent higher because they come from families of divorce. They are more frightened about it, and some of their attitudes going into marriage are a bit more tentative.

I was talking with a military counselor, actually a clergy person, who says that she runs into young people now who say, "I'm not so sure he's the right guy, but we can always get a divorce if it doesn't work out." So we have more people going in with those sorts of attitudes. What we know from the research is that those very attitudes lower the quality of the marriage and make you more likely to break up. I understand that young people are more tentative now. My answer is that we have to do something for this next generation or they are going to have an even worse time than my generation did.

Controversial Covenant Marriage

One of the things we talk about is what we call a covenant marriage option for couples considering marriage. The standard marriage in the no-fault marriage system is one that does not require preparation. It does not require that you seek help if your marriage is in trouble, and the marriage can be terminated unilaterally by either party by simply saying, "I want out." They don't even have to give a reason. The covenant marriage option involves people freely choosing to have a marriage where the standards are higher and legally enforceable. Their standards are that they would get twelve hours of premarital education, and if their marriage gets into trouble they would get twelve hours of marital therapy. Thirdly, and this is the controversial one, there would be a two-year separation period, a two-year cooling off period, before they could dissolve the marriage, except in the cases of adultery, abuse, abandonment, unilateral abandonment, or felony conviction. If those are present they can move immediately to dissolve a marriage.

The third one is the one that creates the controversy. Nobody that I have talked to is against premarital education and marital therapy. But some of the concerns about covenant marriage are that it would trap people for the two-year period, when their marriage is basically a lost cause. My response to that is it gives people the opportunity to seek help and to slow things down. They can get a legal separation, they can get child support, and other kinds of things. There are many people who, if they pause and reflect and cannot move immediately to the divorce process, can turn this around. There is a way in which many people now get on a divorce treadmill: They've had a hard time and somebody wants out. That person doesn't want to get help, because they're sure or they're in love with somebody else. Once they see the lawyer and they start the process, they're on a sort of treadmill.

So I believe that it can be a responsible choice that people make in advance to say, "We will not go in that direction, and we will have a two-year period of reflection in seeking help before we end this." But this flies in the face of the American sentiment that, "I don't want my options limited. I want to be able to do what I want to do, when I want to." A lot of people oppose it because it's a voluntary restricting of one's options in the future, and they don't think that the state should even allow people to do that.

There's research going on now that shows it's women who are more interested in this choice than men, and they convince the men to do it. We also know that low-income women are more favorable toward this than upper-income women.

Think of it this way: this goes against the thirty-year history of making marriage easier to get out of. Even though it's voluntary, it puts a speed bump in the pathway of divorce and this goes against the grain of a lot of folks.

An Option to Raise the Bar

Marriage has never been just a private institution. It's a publicly recognized institution. The law books are thick on marriage. Every society that's ever been studied, premodern and modern, has regulated marriage as a foundation of the society. Part of the myth of marriage is that it's just a private relationship, and that it's just a piece of paper. That is a huge myth. When you get married you have in-laws. When you're dating or you're cohabiting you don't have in-laws. Anybody who has been married knows that having in-laws is a big thing. You are responsible for each other financially. We have obligations to each other. If I get sick and disabled, it's not only that she has obligations to me, her family has obligations to me.

A marriage is a web of public, communal relationships that we somehow in the last thirty years have gotten out of our consciousness. We think of it as just these two people in love and they form this marriage. It is inherently a public relationship as well as a private one. In getting rid of the fault-based system for divorce, in which people are hiring detectives and that sort of stuff, we have unwittingly debased marriage. In creating our current marriage system, the bar is very low indeed.

What covenant marriage does is to say, "We will voluntarily hold ourselves to a higher standard." Why would any rational person do that? It's a form of marital insurance. It means that if you fall for somebody later on you can't just walk and marry that person. You've got to work with me on this. You can't marry your honey for two years. She's probably on to somebody else at that point. So it is a public relationship, a communal relationship. I want to give people an option to raise the bar.

Peter

Peter is married and he and his wife have a four-year-old son. They each gave up successful medical careers to run a business together and have managed to blend romance with everyday work in their candy store.

Our Marriage

I've been married a while to a wonderful lady; a Polish lady named Tina. She works here with me. I was a doctor and she was a nurse. She decided to give it up to help me in my mother's candy store and to raise our son. We adopted a little baby boy, George. He's four years old.

I think marriage is a compromise. The compromise is that you have to do a lot of listening and a lot of talking together and you have to understand each other. If you're going to be happily married, you have to have a common goal. It may be to retire together, may be to open ten stores or to educate our son. Marriage is a big, big sacrifice, and it's worth every minute of it if you share the challenge.

I think the best thing is that we have a lot of honesty going with each other. You have to be honest with your wife and you have to know your limitations. Marriage is a big sacrifice. I'm not an authority on it by any means.

Romance is good, too. There's nothing wrong with going dancing at night, or getting a baby-sitter and stopping for a couple of drinks and holding hands underneath the table, or sending some flowers. I think that's important.

It's important that I'm sixty and she still likes me. Maybe in a little different way than she did when I weighed 180 pounds instead of 240, you know what I mean? It's a little different love. Maybe I limp when I'm tired and maybe she'll hold my hand.

I think it's sort of important, sharing a life with someone. I think that it's the greater part of it. I think it's the greater part of sharing it. If you don't hold hands and neck a little bit, you missed out. That's all I have to say.

William Julius Wilson

William Julius Wilson argues that we must create stable jobs for men if we want to improve relations between men and women.

The Importance of Jobs

From a public policy perspective, if we really want to address these problems of marital strain and destruction in the African-American community, I think we're wasting our time by just focusing on trying to instill values in people and having special programs that are designed to encourage people to develop better relationships. That's okay if you want to do that. But if that's done in isolation, if that's not combined with some effort to open up opportunities for people to reduce the strains that are associated with economic opportunities, then I think these programs are going to fail.

You get some people that dispute that issue, saying that jobs are not that important. Many of these people have not done the direct research that I've done. We found very little relationship between joblessness and marriage after a child has been born out of wedlock for those ages thirty-three and over. But we did find very strong relationships for those between ages eighteen and thirty-three. The men who were employed were eight times more likely to marry the mother of their children born out of wedlock than a jobless male. I think that's a very strong relationship.

I have every reason to believe that if we could strengthen employment in the African-American community and provide greater economic security, it would reduce some of the strains and tension and would be reflected in more stable relationships. There may not be a significant increase in marriage, because we're running up against strong currents in the broader society, where marriage is no longer an institution that is considered to be strong and viable and stable; but, nonetheless, I would expect to see some improvements.

What Should We Do?

If you want to strengthen marriage or the marital institution, you have got to talk about comprehensive family supports. I mentioned, for example, how important it is to improve employment opportunities in these neighborhoods. I have just been reviewing the data on the impact of the tight labor market in the African-American community. We have the lowest black unemployment rate right now since the Bureau of Labor Statistics began collecting unemployment data in 1972. Black males, ages sixteen to twenty-four, with high school education, many of them with prison records, are working more, have higher incomes, and are committing fewer crimes than in earlier years. It would be great if we could set up policies to sustain full employment, create jobs, and provide training education, so that people can move into new jobs that are being created in this new economy.

The period from 1947 to 1973 was a very remarkable period in our history. It was a period in which a rising tide did indeed lift all boats, so much so that the poor became less poor not only in relative terms but also in absolute terms as well. After 1973, that all changed and the poorest in terms of family income fell further and further behind and a widening gap developed.

In that period from 1947 to 1973, not only did you have macroeconomic policy that highlighted full employment and was reinforced by higher productivity growth, you also had basic protections for workers and families such as adequate minimum wage, basic support for families on the job, fringe benefits, health benefits, paid vacation leave. Those supports began to erode after 1970. A lot of people were not covered by health insurance and didn't have some of the basic fringe benefits that workers took for granted in the earlier periods. It's showing up in greater and greater inequality. Not only did you have problems of economic growth, but also you had a lack of support for workers.

Now, recently, the economy has improved and there is reason to be optimistic that we could duplicate that period from 1947 and 1973. But we also have to recognize that even if the economy helps out workers, we still don't have the basic supports in place that we had back then. So there will still be a lot of financial strain on families.

We have made some efforts in recent years to address some of these problems, like expanding the earned-income tax credit, which is a wage subsidy for the working poor. We also passed a Family Medical Leave Act, where if a man or woman has to take some time off to deal with a sick relative or a child, they can take time off and not lose their job. But they don't get any wages. In Europe, they have a family leave act that pays people when they take time off. They don't lose their wages. That's how you strengthen families and reduce strain.

What I would like to talk about are factors that create strains in families and how we can reduce them. We can reduce them by having adequate health insurance for families and by having the kinds of programs that help them when they have special circumstances like a pregnancy and child care.

I am not saying that we have to do this primarily through the government sector. But through some sort of partnership between government and private agencies we can strengthen basic family and social supports. To the extent that we can strengthen our equalizing institutions that would reduce the strains on families so that they can benefit more from economic growth, it will be played out in healthier marital relations.

It's Men, Too

Right now, the policies to deal with the problems of low-income families seem to focus primarily on the needs and problems of low-income women; welfare reform, for example. Most single parents are women, so we're trying to ease their transition from welfare to work. We talk about doing a transition period for them, providing training and education with the welfare surplus that's developed. The states are using the surplus for stronger child-care programs, and transportation programs for the women to get to work, and job readiness programs.

But what about the men? They have been forgotten in this process — isolated. There are no comparable programs that provide similar services to men. I think it's unfortunate. In the long run, if one of your goals is to improve relationships between men and women, you certainly are not going to do it by only focusing on social services that are earmarked to low-income women. They should be available to low-income men as well.

The Black Church's Changing Role

The black church is increasingly getting involved in addressing social problems in the African-American community, particularly poor African-American neighborhoods. They've been addressing problems like gang violence and trying to work with the alienated youth and trying to encourage students to stay in school. Could they play a role and have they been playing a role as far as trying to help strengthen relations between men and women and ultimately marriages? Not to my knowledge. They haven't done much of that. But what is happening is that programs are developing where the state is funneling money through faith-base institutions that can effectively reach a lot of people with social services.

I think it would be a good idea to funnel money through churches to provide some basic services, including services like child care and so on. I've been impressed with what they've been doing thus far in dealing with some of the social problems in the communities.

Too Much Emphasis on Marriage

As far as I'm concerned, it does not necessarily have to be a stable, two-parent family. I would settle for a stable relationship between the mother and father outside of marriage as long they maintain good relations with their kids. I would expect that is much more likely to happen if you can remove or eliminate some of these problems that we've been talking about. I think there is too much emphasis on marriage and not enough emphasis on providing the conditions that improve the relations between mothers and fathers.

Think, for example, about Sweden. Sweden has a single-parent rate that's as high as the one in the United States, yet you don't associate poverty in Sweden with single parenthood. The poverty rate for single-parent families is comparable to the poverty rate of married-couple families. That's because they have stronger, more comprehensive family supports. That's what I'd like to see us progress on. I think that the children in Swedish families are better off because of that, despite the fact that the rate of single-parent families is comparable to that in the United States.

Not Another Generation of Jobless Adults

The society has to commit itself to a comprehensive program to address the problem of inequality. These cannot be programs that don't have a long-term basis. We must not only have short-term programs, but long-term programs as well, including, for example, comprehensive educational reform. I'm really concerned about not producing another generation of jobless adults. I am very, very concerned about the digital divide. We should have a long-term program to ensure that people in disadvantaged communities, particularly disadvantaged minority communities, have access to information technology. If we don't, we're in danger of producing a large generation of permanent economic proletarians.

What I am saying is that we should have a broad vision that not only looks at short-term programs but long-term programs that are designed to enhance the social mobility of a population that I called the truly disadvantaged. I would certainly focus on education, I would focus on the problems associated with the digital divide, and I would just be concerned about insuring that a lot of the young people growing up have a future.

My Changing Thoughts

Yes, my views have undergone some change because, I think, I've become a little bit more sophisticated in understanding the role of the environment and its impact on not only family relations but other relations and networks of various kinds. When I talk about a more sophisticated understanding of the environment, I'm talking about appreciating a relationship between structure and culture. That environment also includes cultural aspects of behavior that interact with the social structure.

Before, I used to place much more emphasis on the social structure or aspects like job discrimination, lack of opportunities, or poor education. Now I look at the extent to which the structural factors over time affect adaptations, which are played out in cultural behavior including worldviews, habits, skills, and styles. I think it's important to capture these things.

Right now, I'm pessimistic about the future. I am pessimistic because of the digital divide, and although there is some attention being given to that by civil rights leaders the society is still slow to react. I don't see any major programs in place.

I'm somewhat pessimistic, but not pessimistic enough that I throw up my hands in despair. I still feel that it's not too late to do something. That's one of the reasons I am involved in public policy, because I am trying to urge people to move in directions that I think are important.

I think that the mood of the country has changed somewhat. Some of this is associated with the lessening of tensions that come with an improved economy. People are more willing to talk about the need to improve conditions for families. They have basic family supports to talk about, health insurance and these kinds of things. I think there is much more attention given to family inequality today than there was in the first half of the 1990s.

We still have a long way to go, but I think that the gradual shift is encouraging. For that reason, I think that we should try to build on a shift in the public's mood as well as the shift in the orientation of certain politicians.

Nissa

Nissa says that just in the last three months she's started to believe in marriage again.

Mom Said I Didn't Have to Be Miserable

That was the whole reason that I got divorced. I would probably still be with him, just because I was so tolerant and confused and lost, but my mom called me and she said, "I want you to come see me. I want to get to know you. Just come out to Florida for two weeks."

Of course, my husband said, "Your mom's a psycho-bitch. You're not going out there. She's just going mess with your head. She's going to break your heart again." He had strings on me. There was a little war.

My mom said, "Please come see me. Everything's different now." So I went and saw her. I had a chip on my shoulder. I expected to control her, because I was always the mother. Excuse me; she put her foot down and said, "things are different now." In the two weeks that I was there, I learned so much about what I was doing and why I was doing it, why I was married. I had run away from a bad environment into another terrible situation, but it was better than the one I was in.

I realized that I didn't have to be miserable. My mom brought that to my attention. So I went home, packed up my stuff, and I filed for divorce. It was one of the little, cheap, ghetto divorces on the corner. I just got out of there.

Advice

What advice would I give an eighteen-year-old thinking about marriage? Wait 'til you're at least twenty-five. If you're in love with him, just wait. Go through school, date, and then decide. I actually have had younger girls not exactly ask me for advice on marriage, but relationships. You know, "I'm in love with this guy, completely in love with him, but I want to move to California and go to school for four years and he doesn't want me to go." Well, there's your answer. He doesn't want what's best for you. He wants what's best for him. If it's like that right now, it's always going to be that way. It's always going to be about him. It has to be fifty-fifty.

What about Sex?

The Big Black Book: God says don't have premarital sex. I don't know how he says it, but I just believe that when you have premarital sex there's a possibility of getting pregnant, and when you're neighbors or you're living in separate apartments you're not really ready to take care of a kid together. You know what I'm saying?

So . . . it creates a problem if you do get pregnant. So I think sex is for married people. And I'm working on that right now.

How am I working on it? Well, I did wait until I was married the first time, and I haven't been promiscuous, and I feel like he's my soul mate, so I don't feel . . . . God, it's so complex.

Basically, I'm breaking my morals. So I'm working on that. I've been talking to God a lot lately.

I'm quitting. I'm quitting premarital sex. But the scary part is I don't know if I ever want to get married again so that would make me, like, frustrated. So I don't know. Ask me in two weeks.

What Do You Think about Marriage Today?

Just in the last three months I've started to believe in marriage again. After my divorces and my parents and everything else, I thought marriage was a pain in the ass. Not that it's a bad thing, or that it's the wrong thing. It's just a pain in the ass, and I don't need any more pain. I have recently been getting more in touch with God and reading the Bible. Some people live by Buddhism or whatever. I live by the Bible. I got away from it, and I still do, especially when I'm drinking tequila. I don't really hear God when I'm drunk. But I believe that when two people really love each other, and it's fair, it's fifty-fifty relationship, then marriage is a gift and can be a beautiful thing. I just think that people settle for second best. They settle down with the wrong person, and it's screwed up.

It takes two solid people to have a solid relationship. My mom taught me that. She said, "You're always trying to fix things, and you're meeting these men that you are trying to fix. They want to change you. Meet someone that's already fixed and don't give yourself to them until you've given yourself to yourself. Marry yourself first. If you're a whole person and they're a whole person, it won't be a co-dependent relationship."

I would get married to have a house full of kids and do all the fun things that I did with my brothers and my mom that we didn't get to do with my dad. I would get married to have a family and to live the promise that God promises all of us.

What Is a Good Marriage?

Lots of kissing. Lots of sex. Honesty. Being yourself. Open, honest. We would both contribute financially and mentally and in every way to each other and the kids. He'd change the diapers; I'd change the diapers. Just being able to be free and be together at the same time.

John Witte Jr.

Of course marriage is just a piece of paper, says John Witte, but it's a piece of paper that's worth a lot.

Just a Piece of Paper?

Marriage, of course, is just a piece of paper, and it turns essentially on that certificate. But a lottery ticket is also just a piece of paper, and when it has a winning number on it that piece of paper is worth a lot. A little document that you sign, which is a mortgage contract that has thirty years of obligations that you have to discharge before you can own your home outright, is also just a piece of paper. It's what the paper signifies.

What that piece of paper represents in America law today is a bundle of rights, responsibilities, privileges, and immunities that these two parties, this couple, have vis-à-vis each other and vis-à-vis the community. And the children that come from your union receive as a matter of course, by reason of being your children, constitutional rights of privacy, of due process, and of equal protection. They fall on you uniquely because of who you are in a marital unit. Evidence laws have a variety of exemptions in place that preclude parties from compulsory testimony against their children or against their spouse, especially in criminal cases. Zoning, property, taxation, social security, and a variety of other laws are in place to turn upon the marital status of the party.

What you're buying into with that piece of parchment is a bundle of rights, a bundle of responsibilities, that are quite unique to the institution.